COMMUNION
OF RADICALS

COMMUNION OF RADICALS

The Literary Christian Left in Twentieth-Century America

JONATHAN McGREGOR

Louisiana State University Press
Baton Rouge

Published by Louisiana State University Press
lsupress.org

Designer: Laura Roubique Gleason
Typeface: Adobe Jenson Pro

Cover and title page images: Book, tools, and other objects featured in the *Catholic Worker*
newspaper.

Library of Congress Cataloging-in-Publication Data are available at the Library of Congress.

ISBN 978-0-8071-7582-8 (cloth) — ISBN 978-0-8071-7650-4 (pdf) — ISBN 978-0-8071-7651-1
(epub)

CONTENTS

6

New England's "Permanent of Rebellion": Catholic Socialism
in the American Grain ◆ 172

CONCLUSION

Weird Christian Socialism: The Literary Christian Left between Liberalism
and Antiliberalism ◆ 197

ACKNOWLEDGMENTS

It's a great pleasure to thank so many of the people and institutions who supported me in writing this book. At Washington University in St. Louis, where I was inducted into the practices of literary scholarship, Bill Maxwell was a patient and encouraging mentor, and he remains a model scholar, an enviable writer, and a good friend to have in your corner. Abram Van Engen has given hospitality, kindness, and advocacy crucial to my development as a scholar and a person. I could never have completed *Communion of Radicals* without fair and stable employment, and in this, I have been extremely lucky. In the Department of English and Fine Arts at the US Air Force Academy, I benefited from a faculty Works-In-Progress workshop and from countless conversations with brilliant colleagues, chief among them Tom McGuire. Another chunk of the book was completed during my time with the Department of Humanities at Newberry College, to whom I am also grateful. In the home stretch of publication, I'm pleased to have the support of my new colleagues in the Writing and Reasoning Program in the Department of English at Southern Methodist University.

Thanks to the Department of Special Collections at the University of Mississippi Library, who facilitated the archival research that undergirds portions of chapters 4 and 5. A version of chapter 1 appeared previously in the *Journal of American Studies*, and a portion of chapter 3 appeared previously in *Religion and Literature*; I thank the journals and their editors for allowing me to use that material in the book.

I'm grateful to the team at LSU Press who championed and strengthened the book, especially editors James Long and Neal Novak, the anonymous reviewer whose comments did so much to help me improve the manuscript, and copyeditor Susan Murray, who brought polish and consistency to the final product. Needless to say, the faults and errors that remain are entirely my responsibility.

Among the many others who deserve my thanks, I want to be sure to mention Leigh Schmidt, Rafia Zafar, Long Le-Khac, Vince Sherry, Steven Miller, Lynda Weaver-Williams, John Whittier-Ferguson, Alan Wald, Eugene Mc-Carraher, Kenyon Gradert, Hannah Wakefield, Asher Gelzer-Govatos, Ray Horton, the American Religion and Literature Society, and David Rachels.

I'm grateful above all to my family—especially my parents, my wife, Jennifer, and my children, Maggie and Charlotte.

This book is dedicated to the memory of Kelly Renee Caldwell, whose genius illuminated it—and me—at so many points, from its first inklings to its major revisions. I am so grieved that she will not see it in its published form.

COMMUNION
OF RADICALS

INTRODUCTION

DEFINING A LITERARY CHRISTIAN LEFT
Four Traditions of Dissent

In 1912, the Boston-based architect and writer Ralph Adams Cram (1863–1942) beguiled the aging Henry Adams (1838–1918) into publishing *Mont-Saint-Michel and Chartres*, a study of medieval art, thought, and architecture. Though the book was originally printed privately in 1904, Cram secured a national release by Harper and Row through his influence with the American Institute of Architects. In his preface to the work, Cram attributes astonishing powers to Adams, making him out to be practically divine. By his power of incarnation, Cram declares, Adams "merg[es] himself in a long dead time . . . thinking and feeling with the men and women thereof" (vii). Having assumed the nature of the Middle Ages, Adams resurrects them, "breathing on the dead bones of antiquity that again they clothe themselves with flesh and vesture, call back their severed souls, and live again" (vii). The undead ages thus raised are neither ghosts nor zombies, beings with which Cram, a sometime writer of weird fiction, was presumably acquainted: "And it is not a thin simulacrum he raises by some doubtful alchemy; it is no phantasm of the past that shines dimly before us in these magical pages; it is the very time itself in which we are merged" (vii). Adams's powers of incarnation and resurrection guarantee the real presence of the Middle Ages in his book, a presence in which the reader may participate through the communion of reading. The Middle Ages are present not only to the reader's imagination but also to his senses, "before his very eyes" (vii)—an effect only heightened by the inclusion of photographs in the Harper and Row edition. For Cram, to read *Mont-Saint-Michel and Chartres* was to have a visual encounter with sacred history, with divine presence in the past. To read this book is to behold an icon, not of an individual saint but of a saintly society.

This quasi-visual experience was, for Cram, at once "vastly heartening and exhilarating" and profoundly depressing (vii). Adams's reconstruction of medieval life only made more apparent the disasters suffered by labor, art, and religion between the thirteenth century and the early twentieth century. Cram hoped that this encounter with the religious past would drive Adams's readers to criticize the industrial capitalist order and to imagine a better future:

> If [the reader's experience] gives new and not always flattering standards for the judgment of contemporary men and things, so does it establish new ideals, new goals for attainment. To live for a day in a world that built Chartres Cathedral, even if it makes the living in a world that creates the "Black Country" of England or an Iron City of America less a thing of joy and gladness than before, equally opens up the far prospect of another thirteenth century in the times that are to come and urges to ardent action toward its attainment. (vii–viii)

By contemplating Adams's icon, Cram's idealized reader gains "new . . . standards for . . . judgment" of American life under industrial capitalism, a life figured by the metonymy of the "Iron City." Contemplation and criticism, Cram believed, led to imitation. To bring forth "another thirteenth century in the times that are to come" means to build new forms of social life that aim at the virtues glimpsed in the old. When Cram looked at Chartres Cathedral, he did not see an oppressive aristocracy best left buried in the potter's field of history. Rather, he saw something close to what the radical essayist Randolph Bourne did: "the great democratic Gothic society of medieval Europe" (Bourne 216). In Cram's telling, medieval cathedrals become monuments to a possible future as much as a lost past. His preface to Adams serves as a guide to his own ambitions as a writer: to criticize modern American life and inspire social reconstruction by illuminating the virtues of medieval Europe.

This book argues that Cram helped to inaugurate a literary Christian Left—a tradition of writers who drew radical political visions from their deeply ingrained conservative faith commitments—in the modern United States. At the turn of the twentieth century, Christian Socialists such as Cram and Vida Dutton Scudder uncoupled the demand for social equality from the idea of progress by criticizing industrial capitalism with an eye on sacred history and proposing new ways of living modeled on medieval monasticism. Subsequent writers including W. H. Auden, Claude McKay, Dorothy Day, Robert Lowell, F. O. Matthiessen, and Walker Percy carried forward Cram and Scudder's rebellious traditionalism into the Great Depression and the civil rights struggle. This lineage constitutes a strain of Christian social conscience distinct from the more well-publicized versions of religious liberalism or the "Religious Right": writers in the line of Scudder, Day, Auden, and Percy were social radicals *because* they were theological conservatives, and they comprise a neglected religious genealogy of American literary radicalism.

By showing how Christian traditions nourished radical thinkers, *Communion of Radicals* challenges both secular Left historiographies that tie the spread of democracy to the demise of traditional religion and Religious Right ideologies that assume the equivalence of doctrinal orthodoxy and political conservatism. The Anglo-Catholic Socialist critic Vida Scudder exemplifies this paradoxical orientation when she contends that "a really conservative view of Christianity carries with it a critical, not to say revolutionary, attitude toward society. Those who cling most ardently to tradition are likely to shock and alienate the surface orthodoxies of their day" (*The Franciscan Adventure* 320). Unlike many of her progressive contemporaries who saw history as an unbroken drama of moral uplift, Scudder understood history in terms of significant repetitions. For her, arguments in the 1930s over Christianity's relationship to capitalism reiterated thirteenth-century debates on the ethics of private property spurred by Saint Francis of Assisi and his followers. But if sacred history repeated itself, it also offered models to emulate, and Scudder made herself a modern disciple of Saint Francis as a Socialist churchwoman.

In naming Scudder's writerly strain of religious dissent a "literary Christian Left," I aim to flag this book's participation in ongoing conversations at the intersections of literary and religious history with radical politics. The first of these conversations concerns the histories and present possibilities of progressive Christianity. With every election cycle, American journalists seem to rediscover the untapped potential of a "Christian Left" as a source of votes for the Democratic Party.[1] More astute observers point out that left-leaning Christians have been on the American scene for a long time; in recent decades, however, they have lacked the cash—and thus the influence and public profile—of the Religious Right (Bruenig). "Talk of an emerging 'religious left' is ahistoric," affirms the historian Laura Alexander. "American religion has always had its liberal strains." The religious Left today isn't emerging, Alexander argues, but rather evolving to respond to new challenges, particularly those posed by climate change and migration. But by treating "liberal" and "Left" as contiguous, if not synonymous, Alexander raises the question of definition: what makes a Christian Left *leftist?*

Too much emphasis on distinguishing leftist from liberal can have pernicious effects on our understanding of American radical history. Thinkers such as Richard Rorty and Doug Rossinow emphasize the continuity, in American thought and practice, between these two distinct traditions of envisioning freedom.[2] On this understanding, the legacy of Cold War liberal anti-Communism distorts our memory of the long history of Left-liberal cooperation, overshadowing their collaboration with mutual suspicion (Rorty 40–46; Rossinow 1–3). The literary history I recount here often reflects that legacy of cobelligerence, as writers on the Christian left worked together with Social Gospel liberals to push for social reforms. But leftist Christians also criticized their liberal coreligionists, just as they did fundamentalists and other religious conservatives. While Left-liberal collaboration is crucial, this disagreement is also important.

Reading the literary Christian Left shows that some cleavage between Left and liberal predates the Cold War and even the first Red Scare of 1919, and these fissures can disclose profound theological disagreements. When Scudder wrote to the progressive Baptist Walter Rauschenbusch in 1918 to thank him for an inscribed copy of his book *A Theology for the Social Gospel* (1917), she championed, against Rauschenbusch's polemics, the radical usefulness of mysticism and sacramentality, challenging in the process his shallow, anti-Catholic historiography: "I hate your way of assuming that vital Christianity stopped about 200 a.d. and began again with the Reformation."[3] This is friendly correction offered to an ally, but it stands in for a wholly different historical sensibility on Scudder's part, ultimately reflecting her understanding of social justice as the communal outworking of a sacramental economy and not the heroic achievement of inspired, suffering prophets.[4] Where liberal religious reformers like Rauschenbusch generally prized spiritually inspired individual moral efforts to take the rough edges off of American capitalism, Christian leftists like Scudder sought an end to capitalism (whether by force or by evolution was a point of debate), and its replacement by a cooperative commonwealth, through communal action made effective by divine grace.

A *Christian radicalism* like Scudder's, in contradistinction to *religious liberalism*, comprises simultaneous commitment to doctrinal, historic theology and fundamental, structural social change. Theologically, the writers in this study stood to the right of the Social Gospel movement and the midcentury consensus of mainline Protestantism; politically, they stood to the left of the Progressive movement, the New Deal coalition, and the mainstream of Cold War liberalism. These values make for an uncomfortable fit with the contemporary center-left, neoliberal Democratic Party, whose spokespersons often credit their religions, in terms somewhat reminiscent of Rauschenbusch, for spiritual inspiration. *Communion of Radicals* reveals the Christian Left not merely as a Democratic voting-bloc-in-waiting, but as a transformative resource, offering a usable literary past as equipment for reimagining American politics and religion.

Van Wyck Brooks famously argued that "to discover, invent a usable past ... is what a vital criticism always does" (339). While I'd want to modify that claim to allow for other purposes of "vital criticism," this book shares Brooks's aim—even if he might be surprised by some of the literary forebears I find useful. Rorty makes a similar point to Brooks about national history when he argues that forming a historical "image of America" is crucial for the American Left's "process of deciding what to do next, what we will try to become" (11). Throughout this study, I show how the literary Christian Left fashioned images from sacred history—what I refer to as "social icons"—with the pragmatic intent of shaping the future of their ecclesial communities (and sometimes the nation as well). In turn, I offer a history of their efforts as my attempt at a useful image of the recent cultural past—an image both discovered in the historical materials I investigate and shaped by my own investments in Christian faith and social equality.

In so doing, I also hope to add a new chapter to the history of the literary Left, one uniquely focused on the contributions of religious writers to twentieth-century struggles for social justice.[5] For many writers on the left, art and activism are bound up with the pursuit of spiritual meaning, even, perhaps especially, when that pursuit takes the form of rebellion against inherited religious traditions. (Here the work of Jewish leftist writers such as Mike Gold comes to mind.) But the writers in this book take up a kind of rebellion-in-reverse. Their works reflect experiences of conversion, reversion, or reinterpretation in which they find themselves compelled not to reject but to embrace religious tradition in a completely changed way—embodying the distinction Auden, who reverted to Anglo-Catholicism in 1940, called "believing again" as opposed to "believing still" (Auden, *Forewords and Afterwords* 87).[6] When Peter Maurin (1877–1949) left behind a comfortable life teaching French to take up a Franciscan ethic of voluntary poverty as itinerant poet and labor agitator and eventual cofounder of the Catholic Worker movement, the cradle Catholic didn't leave his faith behind. Instead, he encountered that faith anew, and changed his life as its meaning changed for him.[7] Likewise, James McBride Dabbs (1896–1970), living on his ancestral plantation in South Carolina, became convinced through mourning the death of his wife that his bankrupt moderation on questions of racial justice had theological roots. Despite his longtime service as a lay elder in the Presbyterian church, he had come to believe more deeply in Unamuno's "tragic sense of life" than in the Christian gospel.[8] Dabbs's devotion to antiracist activism, which he maintained for more than three decades until his death, led him deeper into the Presbyterian heritage that told him God's providence brings good out of evil: a new vocation out of the loss of a beloved spouse, and a future of liberation out of a history of slavery.

The thick theological and ecclesiastical commitments shared by Auden, Maurin, Dabbs, and other writers on the literary Christian left put them in an uncertain relationship to many of their comrades in an era when the international workers' movement was led by an officially atheistic Communist Party. In his magisterial trilogy on the twentieth-century literary Left, Alan Wald uses "Left" to mean anybody "more radical than New Deal liberalism" (*Exiles* 13). His narrative rightly centers "pro-Communist" writers—whether formally Communist Party members, dissenting Communists such as Trotskyists, or of some other radical tendency—in an effort to correct the Cold War–enforced erasure of those writers' contributions to American literature (*American Night* 13, 225). While some Christian writers who were more radical than New Dealers, such as Matthiessen and John Brooks Wheelwright (1897–1940), were pro-Communist or Trotskyist in Wald's pragmatic sense, much of the literary Christian Left was ambivalent toward Communism or dissident Leninism, or even anti-Communist. Indeed, this was integral to the Christian Left's attraction for an anti-Communist Socialist like late-career Claude McKay (1889–1948). The histories of the pro-Communist, Trotskyist, and Christian wings of the literary Left complement one another as they overlap and diverge.

Laying out the story of the literary Christian Left alongside Wald's narrative can help to advance an aim we share: detangling the leftist ambition for equality from the discrediting "stain" of some American leftists' historical collaboration with and apologies for Soviet authoritarianism (Wald, *American*

Night 223). Christian leftists had good reason to be anti-Stalinist, and anti-Communist, before Khrushchev's revelations in 1956, before the political exigencies of the early Cold War, and before the brutalities of the 1930s—and most of them were. Members of the literary Christian Left were not united by practical pro-Communism (or anti-Communism); they disagreed on what stance to take toward the party. And while Christian leftists such as Scudder developed their social theories in conversation with Marx and Marxism, their fundamental, uniting convictions stemmed from other, theological sources.

The core affirmation of the literary Christian Left is that *human equality* and *human community* are achievements won by the life, death, and resurrection of Jesus Christ—the one who unites all humanity to God in his Incarnation. Equality and community, on this understanding, are not mere utopian dreams with no purchase on present reality; they are not foregone conclusions, our sure eventual destiny; nor are they possible accomplishments of human effort apart from divine grace. Equality and community are realities both inaugurated by Christ and still coming as he is to come, and they must be made tangible in the present life and work of his followers, who constitute Christ's Body: that is, the Church. It is this Body, and not the nation-state, a generic universal humanity, or a politically self-conscious proletariat, who is agent of the revolution envisioned by the Christian Left at its most distinctive.

But commitment to the Church leaves the literary Christian Left with its own discrediting stain to absolve, much like Wald's pro-Communist cadre. The organizations that bear the name of "Church" have been and so often still are the enemies of equality and community. From a Christian leftist perspective, if Christ unites all humanity to God in himself, then the violence the churches have perpetrated in sanctioning and carrying out slavery, racism, war, colonization, and oppression of women and sexual minorities is particularly grisly because it constitutes a kind of self-mutilation. While not abandoning the institutional churches, literary Christian leftists called them to repent of this destruction, reminding the bearers of ecclesiastical power that Christ is found among the outcast and homeless, who are his poor, who are indeed Christ himself, as the Catholic Worker cofounder Dorothy Day (1897–1980), who lived among the poor long enough to lose all sense of bohemian romance, put it.[9] The literary Christian Left cannot escape the censure often leveled against leftists of all stripes. Instead, they must tack between what Walker Percy (1916–1990) called "the failure and the hope" of a true community of equals promised in the Body of Christ.[10]

If the commitment to equality and community puts these writers on the left, rooting such values in the person and work of Christ is what marks them as specifically *Christian* leftists. A theological rationale from *creation*—humans are all made by God, in God's image, of one blood, are all God's children, etc.—translates readily into other religious idioms or into a secular grammar of universal human nature or human rights. Witness the opening of the Declaration of Independence: affirming "that all men are created equal and endowed by their Creator with certain unalienable rights" requires no further specification of the nature of the Creator, and no concept of sin or salvation. Christian leftists' reasoning from *redemption*, on the other hand, resists such translation, because it is more deeply embedded in a host of interrelated theological concepts. For example, twentieth-century Catholic radicals such as Day, McKay, and Percy expressed their belief in human equality by affirming that, in Day's words, "we are all members or potential members of the mystical Body of Christ" (Day, "Catholic Worker Celebrates" 1). This redemptive ideal of equality correlates to a redefinition of sin and salvation. The unequal distribution of resources, wealth, and privilege is both result and manifestation of sin, which humans cannot overcome apart from divine grace. Receiving grace means incorporation into the (mystical) Body of Christ, which implies not just the restoration of equality, but the achievement of a true, functional, and diverse community of "members" in harmonious cooperation. And this vision of the Body of Christ is not only the province of Roman Catholics. The Baptist writer Wendell Berry (1934–) insists on the same language of "membership" to describe his fictional community of Port William.[11] His fellow Baptist Will Campbell (1924–2013) found a similar Pauline emphasis when he contended that racial reconciliation is the practical outworking of the truth that "God was in Christ reconciling the world to Himself" (2 Cor. 5:19 NASB).[12] Such particularist religious convictions ran against the grain of the religious pluralism emerging concurrently in the United States during the period, a tension to which I return repeatedly but especially in chapter 3.

Because this Body of Christ extends through time, literary Christian leftists also held a remarkably positive view of the past, relative to many other radical and progressive intellectuals. Tradition, which G. K. Chesterton (1874–1936) famously called "the democracy of the dead" and Scudder named "the witness of other minds," fueled imagination and action for democracies of the living among writers on the Christian left (Scudder, *On Journey* 234). I divide my narrative account according to four particularly salient ecclesiastical and regional traditions: Anglo-Catholic Socialism, Roman Catholic personalism, Southern Agrarianism, and a rebellious strain of New England regionalism combining aspects of the other three.[13] Each of these streams comprises a dissenting intellectual tradition; each of them also offers a dissenting conception of tradition as one of its most important intellectual contributions. Devotion to sacred history fuels opposition to capitalist modernity for all four streams, bringing them together across theological, regional, and temperamental differences into a single current. This orientation to the past—a traditioned radicalism[14]—is the literary Christian Left's most enduring contribution to cultural history. The shape of such a traditioned radicalism is lent definition by some of my most surprising discoveries in this study: that apparently conservative values such as commitment to theological orthodoxy, reverence for the medieval religious past, agrarian devotion to the land, and the practice of elaborate sacramental worship drove and were driven by many writers' passions for social equality.

Imaginative writing and reading are what enable Christian radicals to commune with the past and with each other, empowering their work for the common good in the present. Their literary practice of communion, together with their Christic ideals of equality and community, lend force to the symbolic vocabulary of Eucharistic, sacramental meals I trace throughout the book. Perhaps the most striking example of this imagery is Auden's poem "The Garrison" (1969), which I unfold briefly here, giving a more expansive reading in chapter 2. The "savoury mess" at the center of this poem serves as a metaphor for sacred history's nourishment of radical social imagination:

> It's possible for the breathing
> still to break bread with the dead, whose brotherhood
> gives us confidence to wend the trivial
>   thrust of the Present,
> so self-righteous in its assumptions and so
> certain that none dare out-face it. (lines 9–14)

Communion with the dead lends "the breathing" courage to "out-face" the challenge of a "Present" both ethically "trivial" and imposing enough to warrant capitalization. That courage derives from the "paradigm," to invoke a word Auden uses later in the poem, of community left by the dead. The fructifying example of the past supplies the present task of imagining and practicing community. Auden limns this task in the poem's final lines:

> Let us leave rebellions to the choleric
> who enjoy them: to serve as a paradigm
> now of what a plausible Future might be
> is what we're here for. (lines 21–24)

Rejecting violent "rebellion," the gathering of "The Garrison" determine to live as a peaceful community of hope, feeding on the past with the knowledge that they will, in turn, be fed upon in the future. Yet their aversion to rebellion does not absolve the community of its present political task: namely, to model a more just future, rendering justice more believable in the present, a posture toward history that Paul Ricoeur terms "tragic optimism" (149). In his embrace of a radicalism without progress, Auden was a representative tragic optimist in the literary lineage I trace out here. Unlike Auden, however, some members of this lineage thought the pursuit of justice required precisely the "choleric" rebellion he rejected.

The deep imbrication of sexuality and religious practice with social imagination in "The Garrison" adumbrates a crucial critical theme of *Communion of Radicals*: its engagement with queer approaches to the problem of time and history. In "The Garrison," Auden speaks explicitly to Chester Kallman (1921–1975), his sometime lover and longtime companion and artistic collaborator:

> We, Chester,
> and the choir we sort with have been assigned to
> garrison stations.
> Whoever rules, our duty to the City
> is loyal opposition, never greening
> for the big money, never neighing after
> a public image. (lines 14–20)

This community, strengthened by feeding on the past and set against the powers of the City and its values of greed and ambition, is one that welcomes difference from sexual norms. It is Kallman, in fact, who sets out the "savoury mess" Auden likens to the Eucharist, the meal that makes communion possible between the breathing and the dead (line 4). Kallman is the priest of this sacrament, and the love that he and Auden shared—queer but by the time of the poem's composition chaste for more than twenty-five years—centers the community.

Auden shared the "anticipatory" approach to history evident in the poem with other "queer figures" who "looked to the past in the present in order to imagine the future" (Stein, "American Literary History" 863). Queer writers' characteristic approaches to history have been a major concern of queer studies over the past twenty years; more recently, scholars have taken particular notice of the convergence of queer historiographies with religious ways of relating to the past.[15] In chapters 1 and 2, I draw on theorizations of queer time and radical celibacy, as well as on histories of Christianity and homosexuality, to illuminate the mutual influence of sexuality and religion on Cram, Scudder, and Auden's unprogressive radicalisms. In chapter 6, I return to these themes in the life and work of the critic F. O. Matthiessen (1902–1950), finding in his relationship with the painter Russell Cheney (1881–1945) a vision of sacramental gay marriage influenced by Walt Whitman's poetic blessing of the body. In this way, I seek to expand the burgeoning conversation between religion-and-literature and queer studies to encompass self-consciously traditional forms of Christianity.[16] Just as sacred history inspired some writers' resistance to capitalism, similar commitments, often for the same writers, helped them to live a queerer form of life. In a similar manner, *Communion of Radicals* expands the purview of recent religion-and-literature scholarship on the "postsecular" orientation of twentieth-century American literature.[17]

Peter Coviello and Jared Hickman offer a persuasive definition of the postsecular as "an epistemological and methodological reorientation from which history might look different," that is, shot through with spirituality, whatever historical or geographical field one investigates (645–46). Count me in among the scholars who no longer expect to see religion inevitably waning as we look toward the present and future. However, I've noticed in my reading that many of these recent critical accounts—including defining treatments by John McClure, Joanna Brooks, and Amy Hungerford—envision postsecular religion as fragmented by the process of secularization. After the secular, religion persists in the form of "partial faiths," as McClure puts it. On the other hand, when scholars like Hungerford and Christopher Douglas consider more doctrinally robust forms of faith, they read twentieth-century American literature chiefly in light of the rise of the Religious Right.[18] In *Communion of Radicals*, I tell the story of American writers who claimed a full-orbed, traditional faith, but aligned themselves, in often troubled and never simple ways, with the political Left. I follow the philosopher Alasdair MacIntyre in conceiving of tradition as "an argument extended through time" about shared symbols and practices that puts the present in lively continuity with the past (12). By showing how this ongoing argument empowered radical social thought, I offer grounds for rethinking the assumptions underlying much postsecular criticism about what forms of religion are viable, interesting, and politically desirable in modern literature.

One surprisingly progressive way of reverencing the past I uncover in these pages is literary medievalism. In chapter 2, I argue that Auden's historical model for the community of "The Garrison" was the medieval monastery. Auden's medievalism is representative of many of the writers examined in this study, from Cram, Scudder, and Maurin, to McKay, Dabbs, and Day. In all of the ensuing chapters, I expand on many reasons for the predominance of medievalist imagery in their work. Nineteenth- and twentieth-century British and French medievalist intellectuals, including Chesterton, the art critic John Ruskin (1819–1900), poet Charles Péguy (1873–1914), and philosopher Jacques Maritain (1882–1973), exerted a strong influence on several of the figures whom I cover. Yet a more intrinsic appeal of the Middle Ages emerged from the simple fact that they preceded the full flowering of capitalist emergence. By appealing to this epoch, writers could recover social possibilities bypassed by the history of capitalist triumph.

Most important for my purposes, however, is what Bruce Holsinger calls "the sacramental sensibility motivating much medieval historiography" (5). This sensibility "finds in discrete past events and surviving relics the wondrous promise of an invisible totality it can only occasionally glimpse in the lived present" (5–6). Holsinger has shown how this sensibility made fragments of medieval cultural history into "productive sacraments of creative ingenuity" that allowed postmodern French theorists such as Bataille, Bourdieu, and Derrida to practice "interpretive and ideological resistance to the relentless inevitability of modernity" (5). Similarly, when Scudder, Cram, and Auden turned to the Middle Ages, they appropriated this sacramental historiography to subvert the presumptive inevitability of capitalist development. They were premodernist postmodernists avant la lettre.

This book discerns four streams of Christian radicalism, two of which I define ecclesiastically and two regionally, which coalesce into an underrecognized spiritual current powering the literary Left in the twentieth-century United States. Cram and Scudder's turn-of-the-twentieth-century Anglo-Catholic Socialism weds critical and imaginative modes of writing, undermining the materialism of industrial capitalism with a High Church spiritual Socialism.[19] Taking this tradition's literary contributions seriously leads me to offer a revisionary account of two of the century's most important poets, Auden and T. S. Eliot (1888–1965). Both men were converts to Anglo-Catholicism, and their religious turnings are often correlated by critics and biographers with conservative political retrenchment. I complicate the received understanding of the later Eliot's religious conservatism by demonstrating his commitment to a Catholic internationalism. Further, I argue that Auden's postwar writings on medieval monasticism reveal surprising continuity with, and even deepening of, the leftist commitments of his earlier work.

Next, I trace the stream of Roman Catholic personalism—an antifascist 1930s development of the French "social Catholicism" of the early twentieth century, emphasizing the centrality of the human person and the human scale in social organization. The itinerant philosopher Peter Maurin brought this philosophy from France to America and put it into literary and social practice together with the radical journalist Dorothy Day when they cofounded the Catholic Worker movement and newspaper of the same name in 1933 in New York City. Like the Anglo-Catholic Socialism of Scudder and Cram, Roman Catholic personalism drew on medieval sacred history to criticize capitalist, fascist, and Communist modernity. Unfolding the medievalist historiography of the Catholic Workers helps me to explain the movement's appeal to one of its most important and surprising literary collaborators: the Harlem Renaissance provocateur Claude McKay, who converted to Roman Catholicism in 1944. I argue that McKay's late poetry published in the *Catholic Worker* articulates a Black medievalism, a post-Communist idiom for his combined criticism of capitalism and racism.

Turning to regional categories for my definitions of the next two streams of Christian radicalism allows me to show how writers from different ecclesiastical communities collaborated to tackle social crises. In the next two chapters, I show how Protestant and Catholic southerners leveraged agrarian imagery and values to counter the region's characteristic economic and racial depredations. In this, I build on Paul V. Murphy's important work demonstrating the political fungibility of agrarianism—agrarians can be conservatives or liberals, reactionaries or radicals.[20] I recover the history of a left-wing agrarianism in the Socialist Fellowship of Southern Churchmen, founded in 1934, and its successor organization, the Committee of Southern Churchmen, established to carry forward the civil rights struggle in a Christian anarchist vein in 1965. This revised, ambivalent understanding of the political value of "the South and the Agrarian tradition" enables me to interpret the works of James Mc-Bride Dabbs, Walker Percy, and Wendell Berry as radical improvisations on their authors' inherited white southern traditions.

Finally, I return to the Boston of Cram and Scudder to consider how three of their literary successors—the poets John Brooks Wheelwright and Robert Lowell, as well as the critic F. O. Matthiessen—mined a rich vein of home-grown religious dissent. Where Cram and Scudder looked to England and the Continent for historical models of just community, Wheelwright and Mat-thiessen—heterodox High Church Protestants—and Lowell—at the time, a convert to Roman Catholicism—found theirs in New England's history of religious rebellion, from the Antinomian Controversy to Henry David Tho-reau's hermitage of civil disobedience on Walden Pond. I conclude by reading the meditations on Thoreau in Lowell's Pulitzer Prize–winning *Lord Weary's Castle* (1946) and Matthiessen's field-defining *American Renaissance* (1941) as pleas for a nonviolent Catholic Socialism in the American grain.

If the traditioned radicalism I discover in Scudder, Day, McKay, Percy, Low-ell, and Matthiessen seems occluded from our present vantage on American literary history, events in the ensuing decades offer some explanation for this obscurity. The Red Scare and rising homophobia of the early 1950s pushed queer Christian Leftism deeper underground. These forces may have led the aging Scudder to destroy most of her correspondence; they undoubtedly con-tributed to Matthiessen's suicide.[21] A distorted popular memory of the civil rights movement blunts the radical edge of its Christian activists.[22] The rise of the Religious Right in the 1970s and 1980s fused strong articulations of faith to regressive small-government politics in the public view. But occasion-ally, wild flashes of the Christian leftist current can still be glimpsed through these historical mists.

Jackson Lears claims that "all scholarship is—or ought to be—a kind of in-tellectual biography" (xx). This is true in the present case at least. After finish-ing college in the spring of 2010, I was lucky to secure a spot in a graduate pro-gram, despite departmental belt-tightening that shrunk the incoming cohort from the size of more prosperous years. As spring turned into summer and fall, I watched many of my equally qualified friends' searches for jobs or graduate schools languish. This hiatus in our personal progress narratives seemed to resonate with the system-wide shivers of the Great Recession.

When I visited St. Louis that March as a prospective graduate student, I discovered a clue that helped me set my intellectual course in response to this plight. After a late night sounding the depths of Kierkegaard and other, shallower subjects, I woke early on Saturday morning. My host, a second-year grad student, said vaguely that he had to take care of a couple things before we headed to the airport. When he asked if I wanted to join him, I agreed—groggily, and a bit warily. We drove from his apartment to the loading dock of a nearby grocery store in his housemate's car, a minivan in such bad repair that I had to sit on the middle bench and hold the sliding door closed at speed. We took on a load of no longer shelf-worthy but entirely edible food and delivered it to what I thought was a women's shelter.

This quote was painted on the wall of the dining room:

> We know Christ in the breaking of the bread,
> and we know each other in the breaking of the bread,
> and we are not alone any more.
> —Dorothy Day[23]

I only half-recognized the name. I learned later that we had delivered the food to Karen House, a Catholic Worker community north of downtown St. Louis. Day's words lingered with me that morning as my host took me to a protest downtown, then to breakfast at an anarchist bakery-slash-bookstore. And her words remained with me long after that. I carried them like live coals in the horn of my memory, until I knew that I could build a fire.

Studying the works and lives of Day and the other Christian radicals in this book has often felt, to me, like breaking bread with them across the years. I have tried to get some of that feeling into the writing of this book. The result, I hope, is that *Communion of Radicals* invites, but does not impose, a reading experience befitting its subjects: an experience of communion that discloses a vision of community.[24] This sort of reading experience does not necessarily depend on a shared religious profession. This book is intended for anyone looking to conceive social justice without relying on dubious progressive schemes of historical advance, as well as readers interested in a more complicated story of how faith and politics intersect than those proffered by religious conservatives or secular liberals. It's also written for people like me on that St. Louis Saturday morning: pilgrims in search of literary waymarks who want to deepen thick commitments to their religious traditions while embracing a politics that truly reckons with injustice.

In addition to a fuller understanding of twentieth-century American literature, what *Communion of Radicals* might offer such readers is hope. Political hope, as defined by the cultural critic and historian Christopher Lasch, fuels the struggle for justice in those who do not, or cannot, believe in progress: "Hope does not demand a belief in progress. It demands a belief in justice: a conviction that the wicked will suffer, that wrongs will be made right, that the underlying order of things is not flouted with impunity. Hope implies a deep-seated trust in life that appears absurd to those who lack it. It rests on confidence not so much in the future as in the past" (Lasch 80–81). By breaking bread with the twentieth-century literary Christian Left, I hope my readers might gain the confidence to bend "the trivial thrust of the Present" a little more toward justice.

I

A QUEER ORTHODOXY

Monasticism and Sexuality in U.S.
Anglo-Catholic Socialism

In Boston, in the spring of 1890, Vida Dutton Scudder (1861–1954) and Ralph Adams Cram (1863–1942) helped to launch a new experiment in Christian community: the Episcopal Church of the Carpenter. Boston's Puritan founder John Winthrop dreamed of a City on a Hill in which the affective and material ties of charity connected rich and poor. But that imagined city lay in ruins amid a Gilded Age culture that worshiped wealth and individual ambition. Scudder, a literary critic and professor at Wellesley, and Cram, an architect and bohemian *littérateur,* joined with other religious radicals at the Church of the Carpenter to preach the good news of Christian Socialism as the antidote to the gospel of greed. Their congregation embraced "all sorts and conditions of men," from wealthy philanthropists to hardscrabble labor leaders (Yeames 42).[1] It embodied the possibility of a new religious-social order—one that went beyond Winthrop's vision by aiming to ameliorate social inequality through moral suasion.

At the Church of the Carpenter, ancient liturgy fueled anticapitalist dissent. Scudder soon joined the "Brotherhood of the Carpenter" attached to the congregation, which proselytized on behalf of Christian Socialism, investigated the labor practices of local businesses, and helped the unemployed find work. Of their meetings, she recalled, "Not only did we worship together, singing with special zeal the Magnificat, but we had wonderful suppers, true agape, when the altar at the back of the little room was curtained off and we feasted on ham and pickles and the hope of an imminent revolution" (*On Journey* 165).[2] The Magnificat—a song attributed to the Virgin Mary in the Gospel of Luke and a staple of the Anglican Order for Evening Prayer—evokes a revolutionary God, dedicated to the overthrow of the rich and powerful and to the welfare of the poor and needy:

> He hath put down the mighty from their seat:
> and hath exalted the humble and meek.
> He hath filled the hungry with good things:
> and the rich he hath sent empty away. (Protestant Episcopal Church 22)

Though it attracted more than three hundred people to its inaugural service and enlisted more than a hundred members in the Brotherhood, the Church of the Carpenter sustained fewer than twenty regular communicants. After six years, it folded. But the spirit of the congregation—the idea of a worshiping community bound in and through ritual to seek the good society—lived on for the next five decades in Scudder's and Cram's writings on medieval monasticism.

Monasticism furnished Cram and Scudder with icons that enabled them to read the social future in the sacred past. Jackson Lears has noted that for Anglo-Catholic intellectuals at the turn of the twentieth century, "monasticism as a disciplined, ascetic way of life offered an eloquent witness against the emerging culture of comfort and convenience" (201). Instead of the bourgeois values of wealth, personal fulfillment, and family, Cram and Scudder modeled their vocations on the monastic vows of poverty, obedience, and celibacy. In their social thought, these vows became less counsels of perfection than principles of social reconstruction. Cram and Scudder took the vow of poverty as an injunction to oppose the exploitative system of industrial capitalism. They took the vow of obedience as a mandate to affirm what Cram called "definite, dogmatic, and sacramental religion" (*Gold, Frankincense, and Myrrh* 21).[3] And they took the vow of celibacy as an invitation to imagine, and to practice, communal forms of love bent toward social renewal that challenged and often exceeded the norms of reproductive heterosexuality.

At the end of the nineteenth and into the first decades of the twentieth century, as same-sex desires were increasingly medicalized and pathologized, Christian religious practices held open an important cultural space for queer writers. Because of historical Christianity's ethical prohibitions on homosexual acts, however, this space was strictly qualified. It was located primarily in traditions of celibacy that gave religious sanction to life aims not comprehended by successful reproduction and child-rearing in a heterosexual family.

Yet queer Christian writers such as Cram and Scudder exploited what they could of these celibate traditions, conceiving for themselves forms of life in which, by their own testimony, they experienced celibacy as the socialization, rather than the repression, of sexual desire. On the evidence of her autobiographical novel *A Listener in Babel* (1903), Scudder indeed felt this socialized desire as something like her true orientation: "Not ... the presence of one exclusively beloved, but the presence of all men, had ever been, so she believed, the substance of her unconscious desires," as "the craving for joy of a whole race sorrowing and dispossessed throbbed ... in her heart" (4). Just as their devotion to sacred history fueled Cram and Scudder's opposition to capitalism, it also nourished their queer existence.

By tracing the imbrication of sexuality, religion, and politics in Cram and Scudder's writings on monasticism, I seek to expand a burgeoning conversation between religion-and-literature and queer studies to compass self-consciously traditional forms of Christianity, American Anglo-Catholicism in particular. Recent efforts to join "a history of sexuality to a history of religion" in the study of American culture have illuminated the "nonsecular sexualities" lived out in post-Protestant religious formations such as spiritualism and Mormonism (McGarry 157–58).[4] I draw nearer to Elizabeth Freeman's discovery of approaches to "bodies, desires, fantasies, and affinities ... that contest the regime of modern sexuality" in "Catholic liturgical practice" ("Sacra/Mentality" 737). Freeman's analysis carefully separates Catholic liturgy from the Catholic theological tradition, finding in the work of the maverick modernist Djuna Barnes "remainders" of a liturgical understanding of the body and of desire (737).[5] I argue that Scudder and Cram reveal a different, and deeply counterintuitive, configuration of religion and sexuality in late nineteenth- and early twentieth-century U.S. literature. These two writers strove to hold liturgy and doctrine together, and they committed themselves to lay intellectual leadership of a Christian community premised on recovering deep continuities of practice *and* belief with the ancient and medieval church—namely, the Anglo-Catholic movement within the Protestant Episcopal Church in the United States. Paradoxically, Scudder and Cram aimed to unite deviance from sexual norms with loyalty to normative religious tradition. In short, they sought a queer orthodoxy, and they found precedent for it in monasticism.

Conceiving of monasticism as a religious community structured by passionate same-sex attachment, common worship, and common ownership,

Cram and Scudder melded nonnormative sexuality, religious practice, and anticapitalist radicalism. Cram emphasized the need for a radical break from mainstream U.S. culture, drawing on Benedictine monastic tradition to propose "Walled Towns"—beautifully built, self-contained, alternative societies. These Benedictine convictions took shape among the monks of the Caldey Island monastery where he visited and worked. Scudder took her cues from Saint Francis of Assisi and stressed presence with the poor and suffering, rather than retreat; she opposed monastic withdrawal almost as vigorously as she rejected capitalism. Scudder imitated Francis alongside her companion, the writer Florence Converse (1871–1967) and their sisters in the Society of the Companions of the Holy Cross, an Anglican women's order devoted to social justice and intercessory prayer. However salient their differences, Cram and Scudder each pursued a radical *ressourcement* of Christian tradition made possible, in part, by the extranormative forms of love they cultivated. As Scudder put it in 1931: "A really conservative view of Christianity carries with it a critical, not to say revolutionary, attitude toward society. Those who cling most ardently to tradition are likely to shock and alienate the surface orthodoxies of their day" (*Franciscan Adventure* 320).

When they each converted into the Anglo-Catholic tendency within Anglican Christianity after encountering European Catholic art on Continental tours in the 1880s, Cram and Scudder traded their familial connections to New England Protestantism for a spiritual kinship to the Middle Ages.[6] But as Anglo-Catholics, rather than Roman Catholics, Cram and Scudder laid claim to pre-Reformation Christian tradition without the social penalty of membership in what most New England Protestant elites still considered an immigrant church. Their preference for Anglo-Catholicism over Roman Catholicism was not merely a matter of prejudice or convenience, however. By their Anglicanism, Cram and Scudder declared their loyalty to the English Christian Socialist tradition of the churchman F. D. Maurice (1805–1872) and art critic John Ruskin (1819–1900), among others. A conversion to Rome, by contrast, was more likely to seem a conservative move before Pope Leo XIII's encyclical *Rerum novarum* (1891) spoke up for workers' rights.[7] If Anglo-Catholicism offered Cram and Scudder a partial exit from Protestantism and a portal into the Middle Ages, it also gave them the opportunity to identify with the radical heritage evident at the Church of the Carpenter.

Anglo-Catholicism doesn't map neatly onto the liberal-fundamentalist divide that cleaves Protestant-focused accounts of late nineteenth- and early twentieth-century U.S. religious history. Neither wholeheartedly embracing progress with pluralistic religious liberals nor implicitly endorsing the status quo with Protestant fundamentalists, Cram and Scudder turned to Christian sacred history for spiritual nourishment and political guidance. Turn-of-the-twentieth-century religious liberals like William James (1842–1910) affirmed a multiform sacred outside all dogma. His *Varieties of Religious Experience* (1902) was a key text for religious liberals, a compendium that testified to the common mystical root of all religions and to religion's essentially solitary character (Schmidt 14, 98–99). James's famous definition of religion is both individualistic and pluralistic: *"the feelings, acts, and experiences of individual men in their solitude, so far as they apprehend themselves to stand in relation to whatever they may consider the divine"* (31, emphasis in original). Like James, Scudder also investigated the varieties of religion. Daughter of a missionary to India, Scudder affirmed that "every definition of 'God' that I have ever met is helpful to me," and she closed her autobiography with a quotation from the Bhagavad Gita rather than the Gospels (*On Journey* 363, 434). But Scudder explicitly rejected James's individualist and pluralistic definition of religion as she encountered it in the writings of Alfred North Whitehead. She defined her own religion in organic, communal terms: "I remained an orthodox Christian because I knew that faith was an adventure; and also that it was a growth springing straight from life. . . . I am called a revolutionist, but I am also very much of an authoritarian—that is, I am humble enough to find tremendous force in testimony. Religion, says Whitehead, is what one does with his solitariness. I think this only partially true; my own approach is social, and the witness of other minds has great weight with me" (*On Journey* 234). Both James and Scudder sought a more catholic sense of the sacred. But while James moved beyond the strictures of any faith tradition in particular, Scudder's explorations drew her more deeply into Christian liturgy, history, and dogma.

Cram and Scudder gave fresh articulations to basic Christian tenets such as the Trinity and the Incarnation, recalling in some ways the project of Protestant fundamentalists. But in their hands, these Christian doctrines rebuked the dogmas of industrial capitalism. Cram argued that the enfleshment of God in the Incarnation ennobled matter and invalidated the crass materialism enabling the exploitation of both natural resources and human bodies (*Gold, Frankincense and Myrrh* 84–85). Scudder reasoned that the doctrine of vicarious atonement demanded a "class-sacrifice" of the haves on behalf of the have-nots (*Social Teachings* 148–51). The evangelical Protestant apologists of *The Fundamentals* (1910–15), on the other hand, considered Socialism tantamount to heresy (vol. 2:92; vol. 3:96). Like their liberal opponents, fundamentalists labored to show how smoothly religion could fit with modern ways of being and knowing—and, implicitly, of making a living. But Cram and Scudder each recovered Christian tradition to point up, in different ways, the incompatibility of modern capitalist life and Christian faith.

Anglo-Catholicism also set Cram and Scudder apart from their contemporaries who sought to ground radical social thought in Christian belief. Progressive Christians at the turn of the twentieth century—such as the Baptist theologian Walter Rauschenbusch, whose writings, including *Christianity and the Social Crisis* (1907), were the leading intellectual documents of the Social Gospel movement—followed a Jamesian trajectory away from liturgy and dogma, reading a slimmed-down Scriptural canon composed of the Gospels and the Prophets and urging social service as Christian moral duty. Although Scudder shared many of Rauschenbusch's aims, she pushed him and her other progressive Christian colleagues to develop a more elaborated theology and a more radical politics (Hinson-Hasty 24, 30–33; Corcoran 56–57). She further believed a more radical politics *followed from* a more full-orbed theology. For Scudder, Jesus's injunctions on behalf of the poor in the Sermon on the Mount might be interpreted as a call for private charity, but the doctrine of the Trinity calls for outright Socialism (*On Journey* 371). For his part, Cram decried revolution, although he did so in the name of the "spirit of real communism"—less egalitarian in reality than he makes it sound—that he glimpsed in medieval Christianity (*The Great Thousand Years* 31).

Scudder and Cram kept faith with the social idealism of their New England Protestant heritage even as they embraced Catholic forms of worship and belief. In 1884, Scudder was one of the first two American women to study at Oxford. There, Scudder, daughter of a Congregationalist missionary, picked up Anglo-Catholic theology from the second-generation disciples of the Oxford movement and anticapitalist dissidence from Ruskin's final public lectures. She subsequently volunteered with the Salvation Army and, on her return to the United States, pioneered New York's Rivington Street settlement house weeks before Jane Addams's storied Hull House opened in Chicago (Scudder, *On Journey* 78–85, 135). But it was at the Church of the Carpenter that Scudder first integrated her Anglican with her Socialist convictions, and she remained attached to the congregation throughout its tenure (Markwell 170–72). At the time of its demise, however, she was already moving leftward—and backward. By 1912, she strove to reconcile "conservative Christian and revolutionary socialist" as an Anglo-Catholic churchwoman and a member of the Socialist Party (Scudder, *Socialism and Character* vii).

In between were years of personal crisis. Scudder's labors in women's education, settlement work, and Christian Socialism made not so much as a dent in the hide of the industrial capitalist behemoth. When Wellesley accepted Rockefeller money over her protests in 1900, she felt betrayed. Under these pressures, Scudder suffered a neurasthenic breakdown in 1901 (Scudder, *On Journey* 180–83; Lears, *No Place of Grace* 212–13). When she had partially recovered, she made pilgrimage to Italy and found guides for her writing and life in Saint Francis of Assisi and Saint Catherine of Siena. Scudder drew "prophetic hints for socialists" from Francis's radicalized monasticism (Scudder, *Socialism and Character* 286–87). Francis and Catherine also helped her to resolve her personal crisis. Before her breakdown, Scudder had lamented the ineffectual and "purely inward torture, which only in rare moments can they believe to hold in itself some expiatory grace," suffered by the "sensitive souls" of privileged reformers "helplessly aware" of the great gulf fixed between them and the working masses (*Social Ideals* 178–79). In the stigmata with which both Francis and Catherine were afflicted, Scudder glimpsed a suffering no longer merely inward but palpable and salvific (Scudder, *St. Catherine* 13–14). Scudder shared, as they had shared, in the "sacrificial passion" of Christ's sufferings by publicly uniting with workers in the Socialist Party (Scudder, *Socialism and Character* 365).[8]

It was before the tomb of Saint Francis in Assisi that, in 1886, Ralph Adams Cram first felt compelled to pray. A year later, the lapsed Unitarian was converted during a midnight Mass in Rome (Shand-Tucci, *Boston Bohemia* 60–75). While Scudder studied at Oxford, Cram was touring the Continent to learn about architecture. Seeking an aesthetic education in Italy's churches, he was beguiled by the lure of the holy. Cram returned to the United States an Anglo-Catholic like Scudder and soon joined with her in Christian Socialist agitation at the Church of the Carpenter. But Cram marked his departure from the community with *The Decadent* (1893), a novella of intellectual debate pitting his apocalyptic vision of social renewal against Christian Socialist gradualism. The protagonist, Aurelian Blake, explains his loss of confidence to his Socialist mentor: "You taught me that we lived in another Renaissance; I know it now to be another decadence" (Cram, *The Decadent* 31).

At the country estate he calls his "monastery," surrounded by male companions, opium, and art, Blake awaits capitalism's collapse and guards "the seeds of the new life" to come (24–25). Even in this explicitly anti-Socialist text, the idea that animated the Church of the Carpenter—that a religious community could serve as the womb of a new world to come after capitalism—persists in transfigured form as a decadent monastery.

Cram had rejected by 1893 what Scudder abandoned only after her breakdown: the optimistic philosophy of social progress. Reflecting back on the "assumption of progress" drawn from "evolutionary thought" that was endemic to "the later nineteenth century," Scudder admitted in 1923 that "change is one thing, progress quite another" and "we can no longer lay the flattering unction to our souls that change inevitably or even naturally means advance; it is just as likely to mean decay" (Scudder, *Social Ideals* 320). As an alternative to the historiography of linear progress, Cram offers a wave model of history that he would go on to elaborate in later works: "Ah, that 'law of evolution'—I knew you would quote it to me sooner or later. You hug the pleasant and cheerful theory to your hearts, and twist history to fit its fancied laws. You cannot see that the law of evolution works by a system of waves advancing and retreating; yet as you say the tide goes forward always. Civilisations have risen and fallen in the past as ours has risen and is falling now. Does not history repeat itself?" (*The Decadent* 33). The assumption of linear progress leads ironically to "a vain repetition of history," whereas the sober recognition of history's repetitive structure can secure true progress, since evolution comes in waves (29). Industrial capitalism's new decadence is but vain repetition, despite its veneer of productivity; Aurelian Blake's new monasticism is productive, despite its appearance of dissipation. This distinction between vain and productive repetition is grounded in Cram's Anglo-Catholic understanding of the sacramental nature of time. The productive daily repetition of the liturgy connects worshipers to the past and anticipates the eschatological future of the kingdom of God. Cram and Scudder, feeling abandoned by the historiography of religious progressives, turned instead to this liturgical temporality. They found wisdom in sacred history about a future whose outcome was, to them, no longer assured. This shared, deeply felt existential dislocation in time drove them to medieval monasticism in their quest to find new imagery for their social visions.

Cram and Scudder shared their "anticipatory" relationship to history with other "queer figures" of the period who "looked to the past in the present to imagine the future" (Stein, "American Literary History" 863).[9] Through teaching, writing, and personal devotion to medieval literature and religious figures, Scudder found her "real home" either in the "Middle Ages or in the Utopian future": "I know that in both the nineteenth and the twentieth century, I have often felt homesick enough" (*On Journey* 126). Her temporal homesickness is inextricable from her sexual subjectivity. Scudder's conviction that material progress in the industrial capitalist West had failed to provide a home for social idealists like herself was predicated upon the felt discrepancy of her vocation as celibate reformer with the heterosexual marriage plot: "Until I was thirty, I wanted desperately to fall in love [with a man]. . . . I was eager for the experience without which, all literature assured me, life missed its consummation. Once or twice I tried to compass it, but I couldn't" (212). Feeling askew of the dominant life-narrative consummated by heterosexual marriage, she also grew skeptical of narratives of social development that made her present moment the cutting edge of progress. Her desire found a home in the medieval celibate religious communities she researched, imagined, and imitated.[10] But when Scudder moved toward the Middle Ages, she was also moving dialectically toward "the Utopian future." Though Cram married in 1900, same-sex, celibate monastic communities that would bring nearer "the far prospect of another thirteenth century in the times that are to come" remained the center of his social imagination (Cram, Preface viii). Both writers believed the road to modern social renewal ran through an imaginative engagement with the medieval past. For Cram, however, utopia could only be approached through a disaster worthy of the Dark Ages.

RALPH ADAMS CRAM: THE WALLED TOWN AND THE DECADENT ABBEY

In Cram's monastic writings, an ineluctable sense of doom jars with a dogged intuition of hope. Monasticism signifies both negativity and utopia for Cram: the refusal of the social project of modern Western civilization and the creation of an alternative society (significantly, an alternative society of same-sex religious community). This doubled affect comes through clearly in Cram's midcareer essay "The Great Thousand Years" (1908), in which he explicitly prophesies a civilizational crisis that will catalyze the redemption of community in a new form of Benedictine monasticism: "When the abandoned insolence of man, mad in his pride of life, has dashed itself to the stars and, falling again, crumbles away in impotent deliquescence, then perhaps will come the new prophet, son of S. Benedict (though perhaps in a new habit and with an amended rule), who as in 500 and 1000 and 1500, will release the souls of men from their captivity, and strive again to make all things new in Christ" (*The Great Thousand Years* 35–36).[11] Cram relishes decay. His paradoxically energetic description of civilizational entropy culminates in the purple phrase "impotent deliquescence," which conjures the grotesque image of a liquefying phallus.[12] Despite the reproductive failure this implies, Cram's hope for a new "son of S. Benedict" persists. This conjunction of images—the failure of civilizational reproduction figured as sexual impotence, on the one hand, and the "son" arising from the chaste reproduction of monastic tradition, on the other—shows that the architect and social visionary's language of building is inextricable from the languages of sex, of desire and of reproduction. For Cram, the monastic way of making "all things new" runs athwart the presumptions of progress. His break with normative conceptions of social development also implies a break with normative conceptions of sexual development issuing in heterosexual marriage and child-rearing.

Cram published "The Great Thousand Years" through queer monastic connections. The essay, composed in 1908, first appeared in *Pax*, the quarterly magazine of the Anglican Benedictine monks of Caldey Island, Wales, in 1910. Founded in 1906, Caldey was perhaps the most colorful experiment in monastic community among later nineteenth- and early twentieth-century devotees of the Anglo-Catholic movement within the Church of England (Hilliard 185, 192). Cram spent time at the lavishly furnished and architecturally splendid monastery during his British travels, and he carved a figure of Saint Benedict, as well as the Cram coat-of-arms, for an altar at Caldey (Shand-Tucci, *An Architect's Four Quests* 28). Benjamin Aelred Carlyle, a charismatic and alluring figure "of dynamic personality, hypnotic eyes, and extraordinary imagination," led the Caldey monks (Hilliard 194). Carlyle encouraged physical displays of affection and recreational activities such as nude swimming and reading Baron Corvo's homoerotic stories. Such features led Cram's biographer Douglass Shand-Tucci to describe Caldey as an "all but explicitly homosexual monastery" (*An Architect's Four Quests* 24–33). Carlyle's religious name, Aelred, refers to Aelred of Rievaulx, a twelfth-century Cistercian abbot (the Cistercians are an offshoot of the Benedictines) whose writings, especially the treatise *Of Spiritual Friendship* (ca. 1164), sanctified passionate love between men even as they preached celibacy for monks (Boswell, *Christianity, Social Tolerance, and Homosexuality* 221–26).[13] When World War I led Cram to republish "The Great Thousand Years" as a small book in 1918 with a new afterword, he dedicated the work to Carlyle, styled "Lord Abbot of Caldey."

The Caldey community helps us, in particular, to understand how monasticism functions in Cram's writings as a social organism that runs on desire. At the same time, monastic life redirects desire through embodied practices of ritual and recreation into religio-social renewal ("making all things new in Christ") without merely sublimating that desire into religion or politics. The celibate structure of desire produced remains susceptible of productive understanding as sexuality. It is tempting to read *through* the sensual celibacy of Carlyle's monks to see their activities either as a religious practice screening homosexual sex or as inauthentically sublimating sexual energies into religious practice. Benjamin Kahan rightly warns against the perils of such paranoid readings of celibacy and argues instead for a "depthless hermeneutic" that "leaves the knottedness of coding and difficulty intact, reading the blockage not as an impediment obstructing a flow elsewhere but an elegant formation in and of itself" (5). Under such a hermeneutic, Caldey emerges as a community in which monasticism sustained an atmosphere of Aelredian "spiritual friendship," intensely, often playfully sensualized through embodied practices. This incarnate friendship accepts the restraint of chastity, even as it also creates a communal love extending beyond the nuclear family and with the potential to transform social life. At the same time, the monastery also depends on sexual reproduction for its continued existence: new monks must come from somewhere. The communal love of Caldey was neither entirely sexually normative nor entirely nonnormative. A married man and father when he visited Caldey, Cram moonlighted as a monk, putting on for a time the abbey's celibate communal ethos of incarnate friendship and appropriating it for his social criticism.

The practices sanctioned by Carlyle at Caldey shouldn't be thought of as wholly aberrant to monastic tradition. The transformation of desire—and not its repression or manipulation—has long been a primary function of monastic discipline, as Talal Asad argues with respect to Aelred of Rievaulx's more famous Cistercian colleague and contemporary, Bernard of Clairvaux. Bernard's practice is particularly relevant because he was dealing with many men who took up a monastic vocation later in life, after military service in which they had had both sexual and violent experiences: "Monastic rites in the programme of Clairvaux are thus not to be seen as ways of repressing a socially dangerous psychic force . . . nor are they simply to be understood as inculcating new values" (Asad 174). Instead, "rites are at the center of the *transformation* of pre-existing ideas, feelings, and memories"—including sexual ideas, feelings, and memories (174, emphasis in original). Asad stresses that the transformation of desire always risks transgression because of "Bernard's deliberate decision to court danger in order to overcome it. The novice is thrust into ambiguity and contradiction, and his *fragmented* self made the precondition of a virtuous reformation. Such a decision was connected to the fact that with adult recruitment the danger of sensual desire could not be dealt with directly by simple rejection: the re-description of pleasurable memory was necessary" (175).

Such a redescription of desire did not deny the perceptions and pleasures of the body. In his *Mirror of Charity*, a work traditionally thought to be written at Bernard's request, Aelred of Rievaulx deems physical attraction good in itself: "We must not shun it as if it were evil, nor must we allow ourselves to be too much drawn to it. It is near to the inclination that leads to vice, and unless we are on our guard against the latter, we can be carried away by it. But as long as we find virtue among the attractions which appeal to us in anyone's outward appearance, and as long as we allow ourselves to be drawn by it moderately and sensibly, then we have nothing to fear" (119).

But Aelred's language of moderation belies the intensity of connection— portrayed with imagery of kissing and sleeping together—that he attributes to a virtuous friendship.

> Someone to whom one is deeply united by the bonds of love; someone in whom our weary spirit may find rest, and to whom we may pour out our souls . . . someone whose conversation is as sweet as a song in the tedium of our daily life. He must be someone whose soul will be to us a refuge to creep into when the world is altogether too much for us; someone to whom we can confide all our thoughts. His spirit will give us the comforting kiss that heals all the sickness of our preoccupied hearts. . . . And we will be so deeply bound to him in our hearts that even when he is far away, we shall find him together with us in spirit, together and alone. The world will fall asleep all round you, you will find, and your soul will rest, embraced in absolute peace. Your two hearts will

lie quiet together, united as if they were one, as the grace of the Holy Spirit flows over you both. (139, first ellipsis in original)

Cram's principal innovation in this tradition is to emphasize social reformation over personal holiness as the aim of transformed desire.

Cram's visits to Caldey thus afforded him intervals of heightened medievalism within his modern life. There, Cram could sustain his "allegiance . . . to the *medieval* church . . . that Aelred Carlyle was clearly dreaming about at Caldey" (Shand-Tucci, *An Architect's Four Quests* 33). But in his writings, Cram sought a more lasting synthesis of same-sex communal love with family life. *Walled Towns* (1919) imaginatively integrates his public life as prominent architect and paterfamilias with his semiprivate life as aspiring queer monastic by portraying a Benedictinism for what he calls "the human family" (36). The medieval walled town exemplified a quasi-monastic separatist community embracing "groups of natural families, father, mother and children" alongside single-sex monastic communities. The logic of this model, Cram emphasizes, is one of addition, not supersession: "for the monks, canons-regular and friars, of the old tradition and the old line, will be as necessary then as ever; instead it will be an amplification of the indestructible idea [of monasticism], fitted to, and developing from, the new conditions that confront society" (36). This logic of addition speaks both to the structure of Cram's concept of history and to his personal life insofar as marriage and children were, for him, an addition to, not a replacement for, same-sex relationships.

Walled Towns' middle chapters constitute a fierce polemic against a progressive ideology of history, "the nineteenth century superstition that life proceeds after an inevitable system of progressive evolution, so defiant of history," in favor of a history structured by intervals (20). Here, he systematically elaborates his theory of historical change in terms of five-hundred-year waves of civilizational rise and fall (fig. 1). These waves, similar but not precisely symmetrical, describe a temporality of simultaneous forward motion and backward resonance. Although time moves ever onward and historical circumstances always change, the similarities between different intervals allow the student of the past to gain historical wisdom. For Cram, that wisdom finds expression through creative imitation of heroic figures, especially saints like Benedict of Nursia. Rather than stranding monastic forms on the forgotten shores of the past, then, Cram's waves reactivate and add to those forms but

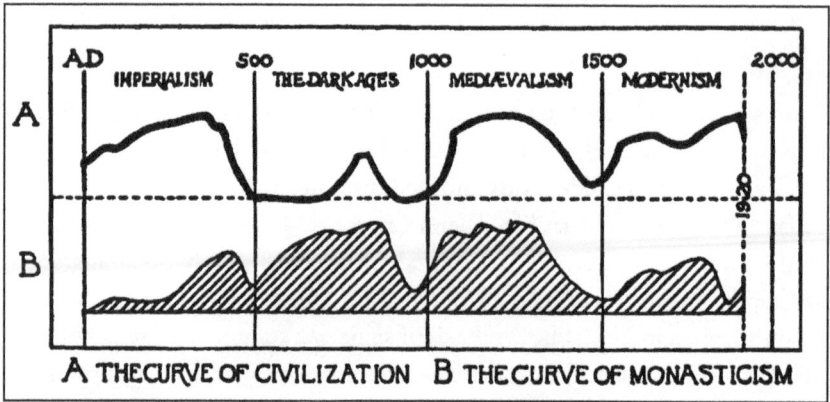

Fig. 1. Ralph Adams Cram's graph plotting the development of civilization against the development of monasticism in *Walled Towns* (1919), 33.

do not altogether replace them. Monasticism endures to "transmute itself into new forms"; the type calls forth new antitypes (*Gold, Frankincense, and Myrrh* 14). Refreshing the sixth-century vision of Saint Benedict just as he understood the tenth-century Cluniacs and the sixteenth-century Jesuits to have done, Cram proposes a twentieth-century monasticism (*The Great Thousand Years* 35).

Walled Towns figures that monasticism at its most utopian. The book ends with a sketch of a new Walled Town called "Beaulieu" and a rousing call to imitate its scheme of social redemption (59). It opens with a pair of tableaux in which Cram juxtaposes an ideal medieval walled town against a grimy modern industrial suburb, taking the latter scene verbatim from his novella *The Decadent* (1893). A scandalous work that betrayed the influence of European Decadent writers—especially Joris-Karl Huysmans and Oscar Wilde—notorious for depicting and/or practicing sex between men, Cram's book was originally published anonymously. His publisher, Fred Holland Day, in a letter, referred to Cram's writing *The Decadent* as "doing the Oscar" (qtd. in Shand-Tucci, *Boston Bohemia* 366). Compared with *Walled Towns*, *The Decadent*, written while Cram was a single man and a central figure in Boston's fin-de-siècle cultural Bohemia, is almost unremitting in its negativity.

A crucial text for a full understanding of Cram's monastic vision, the novella, subtitled *The Gospel of Inaction*, depicts same-sex communal desire on monastic lines bent toward social catastrophe rather than social transformation (Shand-Tucci, *Boston Bohemia* 35–46, 140ff). Malcolm McCann, a Socialist, finds his former protégé Aurelian Blake gone luxuriantly to seed at Blake's New England estate, called, in a reference to Dante, "Vita Nuova"—literally, "new life."[14] Inside Vita Nuova, dissolute young white men, attended by Black men and a Japanese woman, lie about on couches in an opium haze, surrounded by books, paintings, and sculptures representative of both Eastern and Western cultural splendor. While the men in the story focus their overt sexual attentions on Shiratsuyu, the Japanese woman, the novella erotically charges the relationships between Blake and his "brothers" through phallic imagery like this quivering, spurting snake:

> [A] dark figure with closed eyes, swaying softly as it leaned forward . . . while the curtains closed, fell with a long sweep gently toward the brazier,—not as men fall, but as a snake with its head lifted high might advance slidingly, and as it came, droop lower and lower until it rested prone on the uncrushed flowers. So Enderby, heavy with the suave sleep of haschish, came among the smokers and dropped motionless in the midst of the cushions. The movement set a tall glass quivering until it fell to one side, and the yellow wine sank slowly into the silky fur of a leopard skin. (12)

The scene at Vita Nuova seems calculated for maximum outrage to the Socialist McCann: exploitation along the lines of class, race, and sex, compounded by the accumulation of wealth and, worst of all, an atmosphere of amoral languor. But in its unproductiveness, inefficiency, and anachronism, Vita Nuova affronts the capitalist work ethic as much as the Socialist sense of justice. Blake explains to McCann that he no longer considers Socialist reform to "the system of the nineteenth century" radical enough (37). Rather than work to improve liberal capitalism, Blake preaches its passive destruction while preserving the beauties of the past against the present order's demise. So he takes the monastics for his model: "Even as in the monasteries of the sixth century the wise monks treasured the priceless records of a dead life until the night had passed and the white day of mediævalism dawned on the world, so suffer me to dream in my cloister through evil days; for the night has come when man may no longer work" (41). In its luxury and sensuality, though not in its languor (no vigorous nude swimming here), Vita Nuova prefigures the Caldey monastery that Cram would later frequent.

The book's elaborate frontispiece underscores its status as a social icon for the reader's contemplation (fig. 2). Designed by Bertram Goodhue (1869–1924), Cram's architectural partner and creative soulmate and "after some

Fig. 2. Bertram Grosvenor Goodhue's frontispiece to *The Decadent* (1893) by Ralph Adams Cram. Courtesy of Falvey Memorial Library, Villanova University.

fashion, lover," it depicts Shiratsuyu attending Blake and his companion Eveleth (Shand-Tucci, *Boston Bohemia* 140). Cram is the model for Blake in the foreground; Goodhue is the model for Eveleth in the left background (Shand-Tucci, *Boston Bohemia* 140).[15] Several elements of this image directly echo fifteenth-century Russian iconographer Andrei Rublev's famous representation of the Holy Trinity.[16] Three figures, dressed in flowing robes, occupy the three segments of both images. Depths are compressed in Goodhue's image as in Rublev's icon, drawing the three figures into strong lateral relationships. Two of the heads of Goodhue's figures—Shiratsuyu's and Eveleth's—tilt downward in deference, while Blake's head looks up and out, clear-eyed, emphasizing the strong Cram chin. The angles of the figures' heads in Rublev's icon, too, show deference to the figure of the Father, seated at the left. A few supercharged symbolic elements rest in the immediate foreground of the frontispiece, in front of Blake's hammock—an elaborately bound book, a single flower, and a hookah, the smoke of which caresses Blake's head and wraps around Shiratsuyu, drawing the pair together, before rising toward the ceiling. The book and the hookah are mentioned in the text: beautiful medieval volumes stock the Vita Nuova library, and *The Decadent* itself apes their appearance. A cross is just visible on the cover of the book pictured in the frontispiece; it stands for all the cultural riches of Catholic Europe. The hookah, like Shiratsuyu herself, whom its smoke embraces, represent an intoxicatingly lovely East. The flower isn't mentioned in the text, but Shand-Tucci tells us that a single carnation was a coded emblem of love between men in the period (*Boston Bohemia* 142).

Like Rublev's icon, Goodhue's frontispiece is an image of hospitality—at least, after a fashion. It offers us a gracious host and a comfortable guest to look upon. However, at the center of the image, vying for attention with Blake, is the servant Shiratsuyu. Goodhue's frontispiece treats her with more humanity than the text does. In the image she is grossly orientalized and objectified (though, to be sure, Blake is also objectified), but in the text she is reduced to the status of mere decoration. Blake and Eveleth are seated, whereas Shirayatsu stands to serve. Rather than Rublev's image of equality, of mutual recognition in table fellowship, Goodhue and Cram construct an image of hierarchy. The medium of communion is vaporous intoxicant rather than Abraham's sacrificial meal. Instead of beauty, we have aestheticism; instead of mutual rest, we have the leisure of some powered by the labor of others. Where Rublev's icon offers an opening welcome to the viewer, Goodhue's image excludes the viewer: Blake's transverse position cuts the spectator out of the circle. *The Decadent* is finally an anti-icon, an outrageous act of symbolic sabotage.

The quasi-monastic community of *The Decadent* incarnates a sort of being toward destruction dialectically opposed to the "being toward reform" evident in Cram's later Caldey-inspired monastic writings such as *The Great Thousand Years* and *Walled Towns*.[17] Unlike the exemplary community of *Walled Towns'* Beaulieu, Vita Nuova recapitulates—in heightened, grotesque form—the social ills of the nineteenth-century order it condemns. Instead of by faith, the members of Vita Nuova's community are bound together by despair. To the extent that Aurelian Blake's decadent abbey symbolically concentrates the exploitative forces that threaten the integrity of social order, *The Decadent* refuses the futurity of civilization—at least, in its industrial capitalist form. Even in *The Decadent*, however, Cram leavens his pessimism with hope. "Within my walls, which are the century-living pines," Blake declares, "is the world of the past and of the future, of the fifteenth century and of the twentieth century" (41). Out of the death of the capitalist order—and out of the premodern past—will come the new life promised in the name of Blake's estate. But in *The Decadent*, that new life will come only through wholesale spiritual revolution, not piecemeal political improvement—messianic rupture, not steady progress.

The Decadent's negativity highlights what is at stake in the queerness of Cram's Benedictinism, even when he articulates it in a utopian register—that is, its refusal to reproduce the sociopolitical status quo. For Cram, this status quo was defined by ever-increasing aspiration toward greater size and control; his most stinging epithet for modern Euro-American civilization was "imperial." "For five hundred years there has been unbroken, cumulative progress towards the imperial scale in all things, and the perfection of this system was achieved during the first decade of the twentieth century," he wrote in 1918, parodying Saint Paul's famous paean to Faith, Hope, and Charity: "Imperial States, Imperial Finance, Imperial Industry rose triumphant over society, and the greatest of these was Imperial Finance" (*The Great Thousand Years* 63). Benedictine monasticism modeled "*communal life conceived in the human scale*" rather than the Imperial (63). In this sense, Cram's monasticism, as a sort of antisocial sociality, could serve as a productive mediating figure for the debates between antisocial and social versions of queer theory—between those who, like Lee Edelman, emphasize queer negativity's "threat . . . to social order as such" and those who, like the late José Muñoz, insist that "queer aesthetics map future social relations" (Edelman 11; Muñoz 1).[18]

Cram's appropriation of Christian monastic tradition enabled him to imagine human-scale communities of incarnate friendship where desire, directed but not destroyed by the discipline of chastity, participates in the renewal of all things. Although his Walled Towns integrate nuclear families and same-sex monastic communities side by side in a larger whole, they also police the boundary between them. In Beaulieu, "each family must maintain a separate house," and "no multiple houses of any sort are permitted," though the town includes "several conventual establishments" (71–72). As in Cram's life, his writings leave the tension between normative and nonnormative forms of communal love unresolved. His thought is riven through by such paradoxes or contradictions. A handicraft renaissance and a guild system power the Walled Towns' industry—though citizens also own small factories in common. Under the leadership of prophet heroes, each Walled Town is religiously unanimous—though they're also voluntarily constituted. In a lecture on workers' housing delivered in 1918, Cram maintained that "to live decently and in an environment that has some elements of attractiveness if not actual beauty" was a "natural right" of every person, whether proletarian or bourgeois ("Scrapping the Slums" 761).[19] That Cram considered beauty, but not the franchise, a universal right is typical of his political outlook. Though his criticism of modern life may be powerful, Cram's vision ultimately appeals only to a privileged few.

VIDA DUTTON SCUDDER AND FLORENCE CONVERSE: WEDDED SISTERS OF SAINT FRANCIS

In the new conclusion to the 1923 edition of her book *Social Ideals in English Letters*, Scudder criticized Cram for seeing the Middle Ages "in rose-color, as the one epoch of true freedom" (339). At the time, she was a quarter century into her own medieval quest, and she had begun work on the two Franciscan books in which that quest would culminate. As her assessment of Cram reveals, Scudder was more discriminating in her approach to the Middle Ages and more ready than the architect to find aspects of "true freedom" in modernity. This qualified medievalism explains her devotion to Saint Francis, a figure whose elective poverty sums up so much that is beguilingly strange about medieval Christianity and whose rootlessness uncannily prefigures the modern condition.

Scudder's Franciscan writings implicitly criticize Cram's neomonasticism within the shared framework of medievalism. In her major statement of social theory, *Socialism and Character* (1912), Scudder allows that "monasticism held distinct prophetic hints for socialists," especially its architectural and agricultural practices that fostered vital common life and labor (286). But monasticism serves as a faulty signpost for Socialists in its reliance on "corporate segregation of elect individuals," whereas "the Franciscan movement, on the other hand, carries us out into the open" and away from the cloister; its "unworldliness and devotion [are] carried on spontaneously among normal men" (287). The early Franciscans abjured cloisters in favor of "the cloister of the whole wide world" because of their ethics of property, which Scudder considered the mendicant movement's greatest prophetic hint to modern radicals (Scudder, *The Franciscan Adventure* 313). While monastics disclaimed private possessions, they sometimes held great wealth in common with their orders. However, Saint Francis—and his more extreme followers, known as the Spiritual Franciscans—repudiated all property whatsoever. Scudder insisted on the value of the Spiritual Franciscan ethic not because she believed common ownership of property to be wrong; she was, after all, a Socialist. Rather, Scudder challenged the complacency of a modern monastic imagination content to pursue true community for a select few but indifferent to injustice beyond the boundaries of the cloister, or the Walled Town.[20]

Scudder dramatized her quarrel with monasticism in her novel *Brother John: A Tale of the First Franciscans* (1927), in which a young English lord abandons his wealth and privilege to become a friar. After joining with an extreme, apocalyptic faction among the Franciscans, who expect their practice of Francis's poverty to "inaugurate the coming age," John is disciplined by the Order's leadership, and he dies in prison (331). Early in the book, John visits his uncle, the subprior of a Benedictine monastery, who is appalled that his nephew has "joined a company of lazy vagabonds" (30). When John examines his surroundings, "the contrast between the noble Benedictine monastery and the mean little [Franciscan] house he had left at Exeter flashe[s] through his mind. To be frank, the monastery smelled clean" (30). His defiance flaring, John asks his uncle to consider which of their vocations is more Christ-like: "Your community is rich and strong. You are sheltered; I would follow One who was shelterless. You are fed; I would be one with all the hungry. You live secure in this fat and pleasant priory; my new brothers wander over the world, ignorant of security, sharing the common lot, begging their way or earning it by their labor" (33). Here we are equally distant from either pole of Cram's Benedictine dialectic—the decadent abbey Vita Nuova or the Walled Town Beaulieu. Brother John would condemn the former for its pleasant riches and the latter for its isolated strength.

Nevertheless, as with Cram's monasticism, Scudder's Franciscan mendicancy signifies both negativity and utopia. In *Brother John*, negativity takes the mystical name of "naughting," releasing the soul from all attachments to achieve union with God in Nothingness (*Brother John* 311–23). The elective poverty of John and his fellow friars is part and parcel of this spiritual practice of detachment. But in the narrative, "naughting" also looks like an attachment, a practice that anticipates utopia: when John and his brothers chant the litany of naughting, they cavort in fields, pick flowers, and dance hand in hand. Unlike Cram's built-to-last Walled Towns, Scudder's utopia is fleeting, carried in human relationships and constituted by gestures, as when John kisses the cord of a habit that once belonged to Francis and declares, "I am henceforth of your fellowship, my brothers" (27).[21] Such gestures open onto "the not-yet-here," always promised eschatological social possibilities that never fully arrive (Muñoz 90–91). Nor does utopia ever fully arrive in *Brother John*. Told in flashbacks from John's prison cell, the novel's form foregrounds defeat and refuses narrative progress (Markwell 233–34). For Scudder, however, a utopia deferred ensures the perpetual pilgrimage of the radical conscience. Indeed, she rejected cloistered partial utopias like Cram's Walled Towns because, like the fictional Brother John—and, ironically, like the early Cram—she hoped for an apocalyptic transformation of the social order rather than enclaves of religious community.

Scudder's Franciscan pilgrimage took her to the landscape of the saint's origins. In the summer of 1911, she wrote the preface to her book *Socialism and Character* (1912) while staying at the holy mountain of La Verna in Tuscany. It was while praying on the mountainside at La Verna that, in 1224, Saint Francis of Assisi received the stigmata, co-suffering the wounds of Christ in his own body (Robinson). Scudder traveled with her companion, Florence Converse; Converse's mother; a liberal-minded Italian baron; and the baron's Jewish American wife. The pilgrims skipped the easy tourist's route and followed the saint's rocky path up the mountain—until that path proved too much for their automobile and they were forced to renounce the comfort of motorized conveyance. A farmer donated a donkey to the group, and the elderly Mrs. Converse rode bareback while the rest climbed on foot. The next day, horses—styled in biblical idiom by Scudder as "four great white beasts"— towed the overwhelmed auto into La Verna (*On Journey* 315). The automobile shocked the friars; many had never seen such a machine before. Some called it sacrilege, others a miracle. The anecdote allegorizes one major argument of *Socialism and Character*: in order to reach holy heights, the forces of modernity needed help from premodern, even preternatural, powers.[22]

In the preface she composed at La Verna, Scudder navigated the difficult rhetorical challenge that *Socialism and Character* presented. Having recently left the comparatively comfortable precincts of Social Christianity to join the Socialist Party of America, Scudder penned the book as a double apologia, commending Socialism to her coreligionists and defending Christianity to her comrades. Alienated on the one hand from Socialists who considered religion the people's opiate and on the other from churchmen who thought Socialism a demonic force, Scudder nevertheless thrilled at her act of solidarity. She spoke of herself as a proselytizing "convert to socialism" and painted her political choice as a leap of faith: "We have known what it is distrustfully to content ourselves with 'near-socialism'; to take refuge in timid platitudes concerning brotherhood and democracy; to assuage inward unrest by philanthropic zeal and social service. For us, for many, none of these things suffice. In full allegiance to political socialism, in alliance with the international socialist party, we find a satisfaction which they were powerless to afford, and it is a satisfaction we should like to share" (*Socialism and Character* vi). "The cost" of her leap to Socialism, Scudder admitted, was "frankly speaking, not small," although she knew her adversities paled beside those of the working people on behalf of whom she agitated (vi). Because of her political views and activities, within the next year Scudder would resign from Denison House, the Boston settlement she had helped to found almost twenty-five years before, and endanger her job as professor of English at Wellesley College (Corcoran 7–8). When stigmatized for her new allegiance, Scudder looked to Saint Francis for encouragement. But Francis's ecstatic agony at La Verna was more than just an example to Scudder. She believed that she could share with the saint in the "sacrificial passion" of Christ's sufferings, along with "all who would spend themselves for the world's need and rescue it from its sins by the very anguish of their penitence, following the Captain of their salvation" (*Socialism and Character* 365). In her social struggle, Scudder understood herself to be sacramentally bound across time and space to Christ, to Saint Francis, and to her contemporary comrades.

Foremost among those comrades was Converse, a New Orleans–born poet, novelist, and assistant editor at the *Atlantic Monthly* (Corcoran 109). Converse had been Scudder's student at Wellesley; she joined the work at Denison House and the prayer of the Society of the Companions of the Holy Cross, and she went on to become, if anything, a more ardent Socialist than Scudder herself. From 1919, the two women shared a house in Wellesley together with their mothers and, occasionally, other housemates (Corcoran

108). Framed as an epistle dedicatory to Converse, her "Comrade and Companion," Scudder's preface to *Socialism and Character* publicly declared the love, Socialist conviction, and Christian faith that she shared with Converse. This document was the central token in a lifelong exchange of book dedications between the two women (Maglin 18–19).

Throughout their careers, Scudder and Converse exploited the dedication's paratextual function to publicize their love. As Gérard Genette puts it: "Dedicating a work is a public act that the reader is, as it were, called on to witness. A typically performative act . . . for in itself it constitutes the act it is supposed to describe" (134). As an act that "proclaims a relationship" between two people through the public performance of a witnessed utterance, a book dedication resembles nothing so much as a marriage (Genette 135).[23] Converse knew this well: her first novel, *Diana Victrix* (1897), ends with its two heroines who much resemble the author and Scudder, social activist Enid and author Sylvia, deciding to live together after having rejected marriage proposals from men. To seal their bond, Sylvia gives Enid a copy of her just-published novel. In the final line, Enid opens the book: "It was dedicated to her" (362).[24] Converse also dedicated her second novel, *The Burden of Christopher* (1900), to Scudder, who, in turn, dedicated *Socialism and Character* to her. A vow witnessed by her readers and sanctified by the presence of Saint Francis, Scudder's dedication cements their love to their Socialist radicalism and Franciscan devotion.

Yet this intense love was by Scudder's account chaste. And that chastity was not incidental but crucial to the sociability of their love, rendering their particular bond the nucleus of a wider structure of socially transformative desire. By Scudder's admission, Converse "entered the inmost region in my power to open" (*On Journey* 220).[25] But for her, the way to that "inmost region" was not through physical sex acts. Addressing her celibacy head-on, Scudder teases the reader of her autobiography with the "empty secret" of her sexuality.[26] "At this point the reader—if I have any—will immediately become less languid. He knows what to expect. He is now going—yes, you anticipate—he is going to hear about my Sex Life" (*On Journey* 210). Her revelation of her celibacy reads as strangely sexy. By delaying gratification through interruption, Scudder's syntax builds up her reader's arousal. That very delay seems to promise erotic fulfillment, but Scudder ends in perpetual deferral: "I am sorry to disappoint" (210). She insists, humorously, that her own reticence on the matter of sex stems from lack of interest rather than prudery: "I am not squeamish and I don't think I am a prig. . . . My imagination is immune from shock; but I do not see why one should pay so much attention to one type of experience in this marvelous, this varied, this exciting world" (211–12). Scudder's rhetoric of celibacy refuses to sublimate either her desire or her readers'. Instead, she recruits desire through her style before channeling it into the various and profound romance of activist friendship centered on, but not exclusive to, her relationship with Converse.

This poem is inscribed next to the preface on the flyleaf of Converse's personal copy of *Socialism and Character*:

> Lo, here is felowschipe;
> One fayth to holde
> One truth to speake,
> One wrong to wreke,
> One loving-cuppe to syppe,
> And to dippe
> In one disshe faithfullich
> As lambkins of one folde.
> Either for other to suffer alle thing.
> One song to sing
> In swete accord and maken melodye.
> Right so thou and I good-fellows be:
> Now God prosper thee and me.[27]

The poem places the love of these two women in the wider context of Christian worship—particularly, of those worship practices that function as rituals of union, a theme the poem drums home by repeating the word "one" seven times. The poem references two methods for receiving the blood of Christ in the Eucharist: "to syppe" the "loving-cuppe" or "to dippe / in one dish," via the intinction of the Host. The Eucharist is the quintessential rite of Christian union, forming worshipers into a body as they partake of the Body of Christ. Congregational singing "in swete accord" likewise performs congregational unity by actively joining voices; singing appeals to the sense of hearing alongside the senses of sight and taste activated in the Eucharist. A determination to fight the injustice that prevents unity ("one wrong to wreke," with "wreke" in the sense of avenge or make right) and a willingness to suffer for the good of others flow naturally from these embodied practices of unification.

These practices fold the love of the couple into the worshiping community. The "here" where "felowschipe" is found is at once the space of intimate friendship ("two lambkins") and the space of church community ("one folde")—particularly the women's community of the Society of the Companions of the Holy Cross. "Felowschipe," then, refers to a ritualized, sacramental love shared by the poem's "thou and I" as well as by other worshipers. It is a love at once exclusive and inclusive, private and social. Articulated through the imagery of embodied liturgical practices—especially the Eucharist—"Lo, here is felowschipe" expresses a communal love of incarnate friendship which admits varying degrees of closeness or intensity, but places the friends on the same level of authority.

If in many ways this "felowschipe" sounds like a marriage, it most directly resembles the medieval Christian institution of liturgically consecrated same-sex "wedded brotherhood" that historians such as John Boswell and Alan Bray have brought to scholarly attention over the past thirty years.[28] Boswell pioneered research into medieval Christian liturgies consecrating same-sex unions: "Passionate friendships, especially among paired saints and holy virgins, continued to exercise a fascination over the early Christians . . . and in time were transformed into official relationships of union, performed in churches and blessed by priests" (Boswell, *Same-Sex Unions* 280). While Boswell emphasizes the sexual potential of such relationships, Scudder's defense of chaste friendship leads me to align her with Bray, for whom friendship "has a facticity all its own, is a direct challenge to the foundations of much work on the history of sexuality" (Davidson). Scudder likewise argues that friendship plays no second fiddle to sex, and contemporary readers should take her claim to celibacy seriously even while recognizing the radical challenge to heteronormative scripts for womanhood that her vowed "felowschipe" to Converse poses. While it is unlikely that Scudder and Converse knew about the particular ceremonies for "wedded brotherhood" discovered by Boswell and others beginning in the 1980s, "Lo, here is felowschipe" intuits just such a historical possibility.

I read the poem's adoption of morphological and orthographic conventions of Middle English as a stylistic form of "temporal drag": at once "a crossing of time" akin to the transgression of gender boundaries and "a *productive* obstacle to progress, a usefully distorting pull backwards . . . a necessary pressure upon the present tense" (Freeman, "Packing History" 728–29). This temporal drag registers a longing for the intimate and social possibilities of sacred history—like the institution of wedded brotherhood—and the desire to make the future in accordance with those possibilities. Explicit ecclesiastical recognition of their attachment was not available to Scudder and Converse in the Episcopal Church in the early twentieth century. Instead, they solemnized their bond through the sacrament of publishing.

Though this shift from medieval spoken liturgy to modern printed literature seems to betoken a process of cultural secularization, in this case literature actually becomes a vehicle for returning repressed aspects of religious tradition—that is, the Christian tradition of liturgically consecrated same-sex unions—to cultural consciousness. Scudder and Converse reimagine the medieval tradition of wedded brotherhood, first of all by claiming the tradition for women, otherwise unprecedented in the male-dominated archive of medieval liturgy. By writing in the vernacular rather than in ecclesiastical language, they add a further ahistorical twist. "Lo, here is felowschipe" enacts the historical fantasy of a socially conscious medieval vernacular Christian worship service that consecrates the love of two women for one another. In this wedded sisterhood, the vision of the Church of the Carpenter returns in queer medieval form.

Scudder never wavered in her conviction that the broken-down automobile of industrialism could climb the holy mountain with a little help. Early in her career, she believed that the motor of social evolution alone could do the trick, but later she came to believe that the great white beasts of social revolution would have to drag it. For a brief period, she countenanced revolutionary violence as a regrettable political necessity, but her Franciscan studies helped her to imagine a nonviolent "Christian Revolution" to which she committed her labors from the late 1920s forward (*On Journey* 302–6, 328–29). Cram could only conceive of rebuilding the social order after catastrophe, not of transforming it. Scudder's Franciscanism reflects her—presumptuous, perhaps—desire to identify with the working poor as well as her radical demand for total social transformation. Cram had no interest in identifying with the poor, and he believed that liberal capitalism could only be transformed through withdrawal into voluntary separatist communities that would school the rest of the world in human flourishing. His Benedictinism was an elitist aesthetic project: craft a beautiful image of community to oppose the "Iron City" of industrial America (Cram, Preface vii). Scudder's Franciscanism was a populist ethical project: live simply in the secular world as a present sign of contradiction against that world's principalities and powers. Despite these differences, medieval sacred history provided both authors with a grammar of dissent from normative progress narratives of political-economic and sexual development.

Through literature, Cram and Scudder blur the traditional Christian distinction between secular and religious vocations—between the calling to live and work in the world of temporal concerns and the calling to live and work in communities devoted to prayer. This renegotiation of boundaries both resists and accommodates a process of secularization. By modeling worldly life on the religious, Cram and Scudder reclaim, at the level of social imagination, some of religion's lost turf. In another sense, their secular monasticisms testify to the loss, in modern Western culture, of a theological rationale for life peculiar to the world of temporal affairs. Still, their religious response to secularization differs crucially from recent critical accounts of the postsecular that envision religion as persistent but fragmented, hollowed out, or marginalized by secularization.[29] Narratives of splintered faith need to be supplemented by accounts of faith as the desire and pursuit of the whole. Such treatments will necessarily attend to traditional forms of religious belief. Full-orbed faith, like Cram's or Scudder's, may have political perils, but it also possesses extraordinary resources for radical social imagination.

The reckoning of literary history I offer in this book attempts to account for those resources and the twentieth-century American writers and social movements they sustained by examining the emergence of the Catholic Worker movement in the 1930s, the same decade in which Cram and Scudder published their final major works. Though the movement's Roman Catholic cofounders, Dorothy Day and Peter Maurin, were inspired more often by European thinkers than by their American Anglo-Catholic predecessors, Maurin quotes Cram in one of his long manifesto-like poems published in the *Catholic Worker* newspaper.[30] The Workers lived a common life in urban houses of hospitality and rural farm communes; some, including Day and Maurin, embraced celibacy. Much like Scudder, they looked especially to Francis of Assisi as a medieval monastic exemplar to guide their literary, religious, and political opposition to industrial capitalism. Many Catholic Worker communities and publications continue to thrive today. Scudder and Cram's queer orthodoxy finds further echoes in the American and Anglo-Catholic later career of the gay English emigrant poet (and friend and fellow traveler of Day and the

Catholic Workers) W. H. Auden—especially in his postwar writings that recover the idea of monasticism as a form of communal religious protest against
a corrupt but putatively Christian empire, discussed in the next chapter.

Cram and Scudder paved the way for these later writers when they crystallized their social criticisms and social hopes in medieval-inspired images of
same-sex communal love sustained by Christian belief and practice. The normative pressure of reproductive heterosexuality on the loves that each nurtured pushed them toward times and social forms in which they could imagine their affections would be welcome. They turned to the monastics in the
hope of inaugurating new forms of life imbued with the virtues, eclipsed in
capitalist modernity, that they glimpse in their contemplations of the past.
And they realized, in partial yet profound ways, these new-old forms of life
for themselves. If in some sense Cram wanted to turn back the clock on modernity, Scudder reminds us that hours marked by prayer are permeable to
the future as well as the past—to utopia as well as sacred history. Both in
their literary works and their lives, the histories of sexuality, social thought,
and religion that they discern come together in the unique formation of a
queer, Socialist, orthodox Christianity. In our current moment—a time of
legal milestones marking increased mainstream acceptance of the rights of
queer people, as well as virulent backlash to these advances, of renewed public
debate on Socialism, and of heightened attention to religion across academic
and intellectual discourses—that formation deserves this closer look.

The literary Christian Left I trace in this book has its roots in Anglo- and
Roman Catholic social theologies whose most important early reception point
in America was the circle of turn-of-the-twentieth-century Anglican/Episco-
pal Socialist intellectuals, of which Cram and Scudder were the literary lu-
minaries. Some of those who carried on this tradition were likewise Anglo-
Catholics, including two great transatlantic poets who doubled as penetrating
social essayists: Auden and T. S. Eliot. Situating these men in the traditioned
radicalism of Cram and Scudder, I'll argue, puts pressure on the narratives
of conservative religious decline that often attach to their careers. In the next
chapter, I give reasons why we should hear a radical call for full employment
in the midst of the Depression—"*A Church for all / and a job for each / Every
man to his work*"—in Eliot's 1934 pageant-play *The Rock* (act 1, lines 90–92).
Likewise, I argue we should see Auden's Christian conversion as a transformation of, rather than a total break with, the leftist politics of his early period.

2

CONSTANTINE'S "HISTORICAL MISTAKE"

Religion and the State in T. S. Eliot and W. H. Auden

T. S. Eliot (1888–1965), perhaps more than any other twentieth-century writer in English, has come to embody the political dangers of strong faith alluded to at the end of the previous chapter. And with good reason: though he repented of the anti-Semitism he expressed in the 1930s, his cultural criticism of the 1940s maintained a frank elitism as well as a Christian nationalism that looks particularly alarming today. In his influential 1953 book *The Conservative Mind*, Russell Kirk identified Eliot as one of the foremost figures of the twentieth-century intellectual Right (411–12). But just because Eliot's concatenation of literature, politics, and religion—classicism, royalism, and Anglo-Catholicism, respectively, as he put it soon after his conversion—is so well-known and influential, a literary history of the Christian Left, and especially of its Anglo-Catholic Socialist stream, needs to account for it.

In many ways, Eliot fits the mold of the radical artist-critic-convert exemplified by Vida Dutton Scudder and Ralph Adams Cram.[1] As an American drawn to Anglo-Catholic Christianity who sought to coordinate religious revival with societal reconstruction, all the while sussing out the functions of literature and criticism in those tasks, he stands in Cram and Scudder's tradition, whether he knew of these particular forebears or not. He would certainly have disapproved of Scudder's critical methods and literary craft, not to mention her political commitments.

Eliot was no Socialist; he believed the stratification of social classes produced positive social goods. He wanted class distinctions maintained and the classes' mutual obligations emphasized. At the same time Eliot was, like his precursors, a strident critic of international capitalism who sought a more virtuous society. Cram's example has already shown a certain porousness between Left and Right political alignments among early twentieth-century religious intellectuals committed to questioning the foundations of bourgeois society, and one can discover surprising resources for progressive social thought in illuminating conservative writers. I propose that reading Eliot as an inheritor of Anglo-Catholic Socialism can help us unearth what is useful in his Christian social criticism—the part of his corpus perhaps most maligned and least studied.

I find Eliot's social thought particularly useful in contrast to that of W. H. Auden (1907–1973). At the beginning of his career, Auden inherited many of Eliot's modernist poetic innovations in difficulty, irony, and dialectical variety; after his reversion to Anglo-Catholicism in 1940, he also picked up the elder poet's religious-social concerns. Auden's imaginative vocabulary and sexual identity render him a more obvious literary descendant of Cram and Scudder's queer monasticism than Eliot. But Auden too, like Eliot, often faces the charge of increasing political conservatism and poetic decline after his religious turning—a critical commonplace I call the "Two Audens Thesis." In Auden's case, however, this charge is less deserved than in Eliot's. For my purposes here, Eliot and Auden furnish a similar contrast to Cram and Scudder, a sort of generational echo of fundamental tensions in twentieth-century religious-social criticism.

In this chapter I highlight one of those fundamental tensions by showing what's at stake in Eliot's and Auden's respective stances on *Constantinianism*. Named for the first Roman emperor to convert to Christianity, Constantinianism is what theologians call "the complex of institutional changes and alliances that led Christians in the West to see churches and nation-states to be aligned within a God-given order within which Christians would exercise leadership" (Cartwright 629). Eliot's social thought embraces this coinherence of spiritual and temporal power. Beginning in 1930s by calling for literary "orthodoxy," Eliot's Constantinianism culminates at the beginning of World War II with his theory of a "Christian State." In his rather sparse poetic output of the 1930s, Eliot's Constantinian criticism finds its objective correlative in "Choruses from 'The Rock'" with the figure of Peter the Hermit, the itinerant preacher who fomented the First Crusade, mobilizing the killing power of the state for religious ends.

In this light, Auden appears almost a perfect theopolitical foil to Eliot. According to Alan Jacobs, Auden's opposition to the Constantinian project of Christian Empire that fuses spiritual and temporal power is the cornerstone of his political theology ("Auden's Theology" 174–77). Auden thought the adoption of Christianity by the Empire was a debacle for the faith—a kind of second Fall from grace, a great "historical mistake," to borrow a phrase from his poetic series "Horae Canonicae." In Auden's thinking, Constantine's conversion symbolizes the disastrous attempt for Christians to wield state power in any historical circumstance, not excepting the present.

Despite this fundamental divergence on Constantinianism, however, both Eliot and Auden rely on the idiom of medieval monasticism. If Eliot's Peter the Hermit is a religious critic whose moral pleas move the state to coercive intervention, Auden's hermits and monks condemn the commingling of religious authority with state power. In an important unpublished essay titled "The Fall of Rome," crucial to my analysis below, Auden contends, *pace* Eliot, that "the eremitic movement, and the monastic movement which succeeded it . . . [were] movements of protest not against Paganism but against worldly Christianity"—against, that is, the complacent, prosperous life made possible by the Constantinian collaboration of Church and Empire (225). Thus, for Auden, monasticism is the shape political resistance takes in a late-imperial context. As such, it provides him a durable model for responding to the political problems of "our whole world-wide technological civilisation" in the long late-imperial moment following World War II (227).

Like Cram and Scudder, Eliot and Auden envision the social vocation of the religious poet-critic in monastic terms: from literature's relatively independent vantage vis-à-vis the society from which it arises—set apart like a monastery from the City—the imaginative writer with critical vision issues prophetic warnings of injustice. Yet Eliot refuses to take the autonomy of literary culture for granted the way Auden does; in some ways, he's a better materialist critic than Auden despite the latter's leftist bona fides. Through imagery of city and suburb, the two writers work out competing versions of the critic's responsibility. Eliot's hermit-critic wanders out from the city to excoriate the vapid suburbs. In Auden's "suburb of dissent," on the other hand, a quasi-monastic community of critics sets up an alternative way of life to the capitalist city. While Auden's social imagination may seem at first blush more politically promising, Eliot's may teach the deeper lesson, because he begins by subjecting literary culture itself to rigorous social critique.

T. S. ELIOT: CONSTANTINIAN
CRITIQUE OF LITERARY CULTURE

In an April 1929 review of one of Eliot's essay collections, the critic Edmund Wilson (1895–1972), em-dash-ing and exclaiming, rams Eliot's book with an ironic "if only" clause: "T. S. Eliot's . . . is a world of seventeenth-century churchmen, who combine the most scrupulous conscience with the ability to write good prose—if it were only not so difficult nowadays for men who are capable of becoming good writers to accept the Apostolic Succession!" (440). The intent of such a sentence is to run fantasy aground on rough reality. The sailing image is Wilson's: "New York, in particular, just now, is like the great glass mountain of the *Arabian Nights,* against which the barques of young writers are continually coming to grief" (440). A reef of skyscrapers, New York becomes a synecdoche for the modern American reality Eliot ignores at his peril. By looking to Europe for cultural wisdom, Eliot stands athwart historical progress. "Europe itself is becoming more and more like America every day," Wilson concludes, and "it is up to American writers to try to make some sense of their American world—for their world is now everybody's world" (440).

It was in the preface to *For Lancelot Andrewes* (1928), the book under review, that Eliot infamously declared his allegiance to classicism in literature, royalism in politics, and Anglo-Catholicism in religion, with a pithiness he came later to regret. Wilson assures his readers that such a viewpoint has nothing to offer modern ills. Under Manhattan's glass mountain, he could see clearly what the London fog must have obscured for Eliot: the signal modern realities of democracy and religious pluralism undercut any moral authority to which a royalist and High Churchman pretended. Secular intellectuals, Wilson writes, are instead thrown back "for our new ideals on a study of contemporary reality and the power of our own imaginations"—as long as those imaginations are applied only to the aforementioned contemporary reality (441). Wilson lays out his judgments with the cool assurance of his cultural authority, slipping into the first-person plural at the end of his essay. This review set the tone for the puzzled, dismissive reception of Eliot's postconversion critical output. Eliot, however, was not alone in turning to religion at the end of the 1920s. The evidence for this shared turn is right in Wilson's essay. Beneath his ebullient confidence in the secular metropolis, Wilson indeed seems bothered by the encroachments of the City of God.

This is to say that the problem for Wilson, and his review's greater rai-son d'être, is just how many writers—some of them capable, even, of good prose—in fact found it in them to believe in the Apostolic Succession in the last days of the roaring decade. In Eliot, Wilson "recognizes a point of view which is by way of becoming fashionable among certain sorts of literary peo-ple," though usually with more "sentiment" and less "real and living belief" than Eliot evinces (437). The twentieth-century renaissance of Thomas Aquinas's philosophy, typified by the French Catholics Jacques Maritain and Etienne Gilson, troubles Wilson (438). He also derides the recent Catholic conver-sion of the poet, novelist, and filmmaker Jean Cocteau, which occurred under Maritain's counsel (439). Wilson's essay constructs a secular literary main-stream beset by a befuddling crosscurrent of newfound traditional Christian-ity. But Wilson is unsure whether to pay this resurgent religious tendency the compliment of refutation or to content himself with its easy dismissal.

Precisely six months after Wilson published his review of For Lancelot Andrewes, the stock market crashed. The onset of the Depression made the search for more sustainable forms of community, for alternatives to liberal capitalism, into a live issue of practical life, not a mere diversion for windy fabulists. "The future is as blank in the United States today as the situation is desperate," Wilson wrote in a January 1931 editorial for the New Republic (530). In the same article, even that most hard-headed and realistic of critics made clear that he had turned fantasist, calling in a frankly "utopian" fashion for "socialism" (529). The dire economic context, where the need for new social ideals was felt so acutely, lent fresh urgency to efforts to imagine new forms of art and life. Wilson's turn to a European-inflected utopian social imagina-tion makes the writers he condemned in his review of For Lancelot Andrewes look prescient by comparison. In this respect, the conservative Eliot, by look-ing to sacred history to shape the blank future Wilson described, was ahead of the curve.

Wilson rightly points out the difficulty posed by religious pluralism to the critic with definite religious convictions, and he warns against the naïve ro-manticizing of any past epoch as a golden age. But the greater failure of imag-ination in the essay is Wilson's, not Eliot's. Wilson reads Eliot's creedal pro-nouncement of classicism, royalism, and Anglo-Catholicism with the grim literal-mindedness of a six-day creationist, neglecting the aesthetic and meta-phorical dimension of Eliot's religious criticism. Eliot's seemingly stodgy dec-laration is actually a gesture of revolt, a mini-manifesto, a cry "launched in the anterior future . . . a hope, a claim, a pose, a desire" (Puchner 24). Eliot's preface attempts to bring into being a mode of social resistance that doesn't yet exist; it's not an uncomplicated call to return to the past. Wilson relies on a false opposition between imagination and tradition when he restricts imagination's diet to a meager ration of "contemporary reality." Why shouldn't imagination draw sustenance from the richer fare of historical fantasy when conceiving social relations otherwise? Tradition is imagination's contrary collaborator, not its sworn enemy, for traditions themselves are not given but must be constantly imagined anew.

For Eliot and other Christian intellectuals including Vida Scudder and, as discussed in chapter 4, John Crowe Ransom, one important discursive form that tradition-fueled social imagination took in the 1930s was advocating religious "orthodoxy."[2] This discourse of orthodoxy construes religion as historically and creedally specific, as the beliefs and practices of a particular community, that is, the Christian Church. Eliot found in this language a fit idiom for the social criticism of atomized modernity, a grammar for articulating an antiliberal politics. Orthodoxy, in this sense, was anti-Communist and antifascist as well as antiliberal; it emerged during the Depression years as a kind of political "fourth way." As a tool of political rhetoric, the discourse of orthodoxy allowed Christian critics to construe liberalism, fascism, and Communism as "heresies" against which their communitarian alternatives claimed theological superiority. In the 1930s, orthodoxy limned the radical middle pioneered by traditionalist Socialists Cram and Scudder. Yet the claim to be orthodox was also ironic; it named no actually regnant political or religious ideology but the idiosyncratic protest of a minority.

Eliot's invocation of orthodoxy implied at least three values which ran counter to the American Protestant heritage. First, orthodoxy accords theological authority to historical tradition, rather than direct individual interpretation of authoritative Scriptures. Orthodoxy likewise emphasized the visible church community and its public worship practices, drawing from the wells of Catholicism and Eastern Orthodoxy. The public and ecclesial character of orthodoxy set Christian critics of Eliot's ilk apart from the technocratic moralism of Protestant liberals, for whom the liberal (American) state had largely superseded the Christian church as the site of God's redemptive work in the world. The discourse of orthodoxy also distinguished critics like Eliot, Ransom, and Scudder from the private moralism of Protestant fundamentalists, who had little to say about social and economic structures and instead focused their preaching on personal vice and individual conversion. Finally, orthodoxy implies enforcement, the coercion of would-be heretics: an affront to the American ideal of separation of Church and State. This Constantinian commingling implicit in his idea of orthodoxy Eliot would later explicitly theorize as a Christian State.

When Eliot developed "orthodoxy" and its attendant concepts of "heresy" and "blasphemy" into a working vocabulary for the social criticism of literature in the 1930s, he was further developing his idea of "tradition" and of the critical binary of classicism vs. romanticism he relied on throughout the 1920s. The two main differences between Eliot's traditional-classical criticism and his orthodox criticism are the latter's explicit theological content and its recognition of literature's entanglement in wider social, political, economic, and religious histories and discourses. "Tradition" in 1919's "Tradition and the Individual Talent," for example, names an exclusively literary tradition, a procession of great poets. But the later criticism involves what Eliot called in 1939 "the operation of a social-religious-artistic complex" (*Christianity and Culture* 49). Across the Depression decade, dissatisfied with a merely literary criticism, Eliot demonstrated aesthetic judgment's entanglement with ethical and political judgment. Yet, acutely aware of "the danger of suggesting to outsiders that that the Faith is a political principle or a literary fashion," Eliot insisted that his particular judgments were not to be taken as the only possible positions for a Christian, though they were rooted in his Christian theology (*After Strange Gods* 28). Criticism, he believed, was a Christian duty, but committed coreligionists could legitimately disagree in their applications of theology to life and art. By the eve of World War II, Eliot had articulated the rudiments of a Christian social theory.

As the Eliot scholar Ronald Schuchard notes, later readers have tended to see Eliot's moral-religious criticism as, at worst, "sins against literature," at best, "a post-conversion indulgence" (52, 146). More damning are the criticisms by Marjorie Perloff and others that allege that this material shows Eliot at his most racially and religiously bigoted. And this is true. Eliot's religious and racial intolerance is not ancillary to his social theory. His remarks in *After Strange Gods* about the supposed undesirability of "free-thinking Jews" point up the deeper problem that religious pluralism, the variety of belief and unbelief in a democratic society, presents for orthodoxy as a discourse of social criticism—a problem made all the more acute for Eliot by his mixing of ecclesial and political power (20). Yet, as I will show, Eliot's nativism and elitism compete in these texts with an impulse toward an embracing catholicity.

In his Depression-era social criticism, Eliot worked the seams of conservatism and radicalism. *After Strange Gods*, originally the 1933 Page-Barbour Lectures at the University of Virginia, begins with an acknowledgment of the Twelve Southerners' *I'll Take My Stand* and indicates Eliot's intellectual comradeship with Ransom (15–16).[3] In his footnotes, Eliot likewise acknowledges G. K. Chesterton (1874–1936) as an ally (21). A British Catholic novelist and journalist, Chesterton developed "distributism" as a scheme of property redistribution and anti-usury economics in response to the teaching of papal social encyclicals like 1891's *Rerum novarum*. Eliot's "Catholicism and International Order" was originally delivered as a lecture to the Anglo-Catholic Summer School of Sociology at Oxford and later published in *Christendom: A Journal of Christian Sociology*, which also published essays by Vida Scudder. This school and journal were headed up by the Anglo-Catholic social thinker and sometime guild Socialist M. B. Reckitt (1888–1980) (Jarrett-Kerr). Eliot developed his social ideas within this varied matrix.

The stated aim of *After Strange Gods* is the moral criticism of contemporary literature, prosecuted in the name of orthodoxy. By "orthodoxy" here, Eliot doesn't exactly mean theological correctness. For him, orthodox writing is more but also somehow less than Christian—writing informed by the Christian tradition, communitarian rather than individualistic, that takes seriously the relationship between metaphysics and morals, the question of objective Good and Evil. But the lectures are incoherent at this crucial point of definition. In the first lecture, Eliot says that "tradition" must be supplemented by "orthodoxy" because while the former is a matter of feeling, the latter is a matter of intellect. Without the rational discipline of orthodoxy, tradition may become mere prejudice (29–30). In the second lecture, however, he seems to make orthodoxy the substratum of belief rather than belief itself: "We are not concerned with the authors' *beliefs*, but with orthodoxy of sensibility and the sense of tradition" (38, emphasis in original). This tendentious shift in definition that deemphasizes belief in favor of sensibility is part of an argument claiming James Joyce, Catholic apostate, for the side of orthodoxy against D. H. Lawrence as representative heretic. By "heresy" Eliot means "extreme individualism in views" and the fetishization of artistic originality as an end in itself (32). Eliot envisions "good" artistic innovation as a conscious dialogue with the past, whereas "bad" innovation glorifies the ego of the contemporary individual genius. The spiritual-artistic libertarianism that Eliot calls "heresy" was more favorably named "spirituality" or "religious experience" by Protestant and post-Protestant liberals.[4]

When Eliot designates an author orthodox or heretical, he insists that this is not a judgment of literary merit. "In my sense of the term," he declares, "perfect orthodoxy in the individual artist is not always necessary, or even desirable" (*After Strange Gods* 32). Orthodoxy by definition can only reside in an entire community, whereas every heresy contains a core of truth that a great artist may illuminate. The two terms give Eliot a way to talk about the mixed moral effects of an author's works in the wider culture—to determine whether, on balance, they promote conversation with the past and the community or the wanton expression of the individual personality.

In his third lecture, Eliot complicates the communitarian-individualistic binary of orthodoxy versus heresy by introducing a third term—"blasphemy." Here he takes up the theological recuperation of blasphemy begun in his 1930 essay "Baudelaire," originally the introduction to the English translation of Baudelaire's *Journaux intimes*. In the Baudelaire essay, Eliot argued, "genuine blasphemy, genuine in spirit and not purely verbal, is the product of partial belief, and is as impossible to the complete atheist as to the perfect Christian. It is a way of affirming belief" (*Selected Essays* 373). In *After Strange Gods*, he takes this a step further, figuring literature as a field of dire spiritual conflict where the Devil exercises his influence through the heretic, the liberal individualist. In this battle, the blasphemer is a reluctant partisan on the side of the orthodox:

> My point is that blasphemy is not a matter of good form but of right belief; no one can possibly blaspheme in any sense except that in which a parrot may be said to curse, unless he profoundly believes in that which he profanes. . . . Where blasphemy might once have been a sign of spiritual corruption, it might now be taken rather as a symptom that the soul is still alive, or even that it is recovering animation: for the perception of Good and Evil, whatever choice we may make—is the first requisite of spiritual life. (*After Strange Gods* 52–53)

While the orthodox upholds the claims of the community over the individual and the heretic makes the individual ego the sole locus of value, the blasphemer lives in paradox: blasphemy is the anguished cry of an individualized soul that nevertheless affirms the ethical and theological standards of the community. Schuchard probably overstates the case when he says that Baudelairean blasphemy "delimited the center of [Eliot's] moral theory," since Eliot's anatomy of the blasphemous speech-act locates that act structurally at the periphery of orthodoxy (131). Nevertheless, the positive prominence Eliot gives to blasphemy should warn us not to dismiss *After Strange Gods* as simple moralizing or crude theological reductionism. Rather, it's a rough and sometimes contradictory attempt to sketch out a communitarian ethical theory of literature.

With "Catholicism and International Order," the properly political stakes of Eliot's theory of orthodoxy become explicit. No longer merely completing "literary criticism . . . by criticism from a definite ethical and theological standpoint," as he put it in "Religion and Literature," Eliot consummates his ethical approach with an account of international politics (*Essays Ancient and Modern* 93). In "Catholicism and International Order," orthodoxy and heresy name political theologies rather than literary sensibilities—though the two are, of course, connected. Political heresy derives from the inappropriate application of spiritual truths in the temporal sphere:

> The ideas of authority, of hierarchy, of discipline and order . . . may lead us into some error of absolutism or impossible theocracy. Or the ideas of humanity, brotherhood, equality before God, may lead us to affirm that the Christian can only be a socialist. Heresy is always possible; and where there is one possible heresy, there are always at least two; and when two doctrines contradict each other, we do not always remember that both may be wrong. And heresy may extend, of course, into affairs of this world which people do not ordinarily judge according to such standards: we might expect to find it, for instance, in some forms of Fascism as well as in some forms of Socialism. (*Essays Ancient and Modern* 118–19)

Here Eliot associates fascism with what we might call the "authoritarian heresy" and Socialism with what we might call the "humanitarian heresy." Both are partial truths that become dangerous when made the whole of politics. For example, when humanitarianism becomes the whole of politics, it can turn into a kind of authoritarianism—the "genuine oppression of human beings in what is conceived by other human beings to be their interest" (119). The alternative to these heretical approaches is not simply liberal-democratic capitalism, however. Eliot offers a sarcastic assessment of globalized market society that would almost sound at home in the mouth of an antiglobalization protestor. "The conquest of space has made it easier for people to fight from greater distances. . . . [I]n America . . . you can get fresh vegetables and fruit at any time of the year, and none of it has any flavour" (125). Commerce and technology, which were supposed to unite the world in bonds of mutual advantage under liberalism, have failed to deliver on their promises.

In fact, Eliot is loath to offer a specific positive program for international order. He makes some approving remarks about John Maynard Keynes's economics and gestures toward a few movements with which he has sympathy: "the yearning towards regionalism," as in Southern Agrarianism; "some kind of credit-reform"; and Chesterton's "distributism" (127). This reservation about the proper response to the crisis of liberalism is not an oversight but a keynote of Eliot's argument. "The Catholic cannot commit himself utterly and absolutely to any one form of temporal order," he argues, because his or her ultimate loyalty is to "the Kingdom of God" (128). Not only can the Catholic not commit himself or herself wholly to secular projects of renewal; he or she also ought to be skeptical of the efficacy of those projects: "The Catholic should have high ideals—or rather, I should say *absolute* ideals—and moderate expectations: the heretic, whether he call himself fascist, or communist, or democrat or rationalist, always has low ideals and great expectations" (122). Joining with others in social betterment, Eliot's skeptical Catholic activist brings a theological reality principle to bear on the proceedings, a recognition of human sinfulness and limitation that discourages belief in immanent salvation through social organization. Nevertheless, Eliot's is not a counsel of despair. "There is a certain saving egotism," he writes, "which prevents us from despair so long as we believe that there is anything we can do which may possibly help to improve matters" (132). Eliot moves from tragedy to Ricoeurian tragic optimism by tempering his gloominess with slow hope.

That slow hope for social justice is the hope of orthodoxy, which Eliot invokes by name for the first time in the lecture's final sentence. Though living in a discredited political and economic order and beset on every side by heretical alternatives, there is another way, Eliot argues, for the Christian: "There must always be a middle way, though sometimes a devious way when natural obstacles have to be circumvented; and this middle way will, I think, be found to be the way of orthodoxy; a way of mediation, but never, in those matters which permanently matter, a way of compromise" (134–35). A middle way, a way of mediation but not of compromise—this sums up the alternative that the critical discourse of orthodoxy offered in the troubled decade of the 1930s. In his acknowledgment that orthodoxy must needs be sometimes "devious," Eliot echoes his approbation of literary blasphemy. *The Idea of a Christian Society*, delivered on the eve of war in 1939, puts the matter even more starkly: "If you will not have God (and He is a jealous God) you should pay your respects to Hitler or Stalin" (*Christianity and Culture* 50).

"Catholicism and International Order" is long on the criticism of political heresy and short on description of the orthodox alternative. That alternative is only gestured at and hinted toward. Its development waited for *The Idea of a Christian Society*, Eliot's most sustained work of constructive social theory. But even here, as the "idea" of his title suggests, Eliot contents himself with sketching a social icon, projecting a vision of religious community inspired by the British past but not beholden to any previous epoch in particular: "I shall confine myself to a slight outline of what I consider to be essential features of this society, bearing in mind that it can neither be mediaeval in form, nor be modelled on the seventeenth century or any previous age" (*Christianity and Culture* 20). In this, he departs from the unabashed medievalism of his predecessors Scudder and Cram.

Eliot proposes a society constituted by the Christian State, the Christian Community, and the Community of Christians. By the Christian State, Eliot means a national government that recognizes Christianity as its official religion and proclaims its intent to rule in accordance with Christian principles (*Christianity and Culture* 21). By the Christian Community, Eliot indicates the renewal of the parish system, where the mass of proximate believers are united by religious practices (23–25). By the Community of Christians, Eliot means an elite of religious intellectuals who guide the Christian Community (28–29).

In *The Idea of a Christian Society*, Eliot leaves behind the vocabulary of orthodoxy and heresy, for the most part, but the structure of his argument, which identifies the turn away from liberalism to a Christian social order as the only alternative to totalitarianism, places it firmly within the social-critical discourse of orthodoxy. Indeed, the terms "Christian" and "pagan" come to take the place of "orthodoxy" and "heresy" as Eliot's terms of analysis and evaluation: "I believe that the choice before us is between the formation of a new Christian culture and the acceptance of a pagan one" (*Christianity and Culture* 10). Eliot goes on to claim that "the fundamental objection to fascist doctrine . . . is that it is pagan" (15–16). This shift in diction represents an escalation of orthodoxy discourse, not a break with it. In 1933–34, at the time of *After Strange Gods*, Eliot saw the literary field as an in-house squabble between different literary styles still belonging to the same overall tradition; he even categorized his heretical writers by the sort of dysfunctional Protestant upbringing each had. But with World War II in the offing, Eliot came to view cultural politics in terms of a clash between altogether different religions.

To frame political conflict as religious conflict like this immediately raises the question of what would happen to non-Christians in Eliot's "Christian society." Eliot answers that they would be tolerated. At best, this may be construed as a condescending response to the problem of religious pluralism. But this is not Eliot's last word on the subject. When confronted with pluralism of various stripes, Eliot is forced to work through his simultaneous commitments to the values of particularity and universality, a conflict inscribed in the ambivalently nationalist and internationalist signifier—"Anglo-Catholic"—of the Christian tradition he embraced. Eliot's lament for the standardization of culture consequent with the spread of global markets can quickly take on an ugly nativist cast. But an embracing rhetoric of Catholic internationalism also leavens Eliot's social writings, as in this passage from "Catholicism and International Order": "Catholics should, in any questions of foreign relations, be able to feel a sympathy with foreign points of view which is much better worth having and more effective than diffuse good-will. I believe that there is a Catholic habit of thought and of feeling, which is a bond between Catholics of the most diverse races, nations, classes and cultures" (*Essays Ancient and Modern* 131). In *After Strange Gods*, Eliot acknowledged that the calcified, instinctive prejudice of tradition needs the theological discipline of orthodoxy to keep it flexible; more orthodoxy on this point may have made Eliot more liberal-minded. And even Eliot's internationalism is a *Christian* internationalism, as he goes on to say that he's been made cognizant of his Catholic sympathy with foreigners when talking with his nonreligious countrymen. In Eliot's vision, limits—the limits of creed, the boundaries of orthodoxy—simultaneously connect coreligionists across state borders and drive wedges between citizens of differing faiths.

During World War II, in a regular ecumenical gathering of antitotalitarian religious intellectuals known as "The Moot," Eliot pressed the claims of catholicity further than he had before.[5] In a paper delivered in 1944, ten years after *After Strange Gods*, Eliot prescribed the following sentimental education for "clerics" like himself and the members of his audience: "The cleric himself should be partly, though not altogether, emancipated from the class into which he is born; an out-caste. He should, to some extent, be able to look upon, and mix with, all classes as an outsider; just as he should, to some extent, get out of his own country. These are counsels of perfection, to which none of us attain. He should also have a supra-national community of interest with clerics of other nations; so as to work against nationalism and racialism (provincialism) as he does against class" (qtd. in Kojecky 243–44). Equipped with such sympathies, the "clerical elite" as envisioned by Eliot is a force for social change, while social class "is an influence for stability" (qtd. in Kojecky 241). By this point, Eliot's vision of the good society required both the persistence of class structure and clerical incitements to change, played off one another in a balance of powers. If this would be a good arrangement for the clerics, it promises less for those Eliot terms "the lower orders" (qtd. in Kojecky 248).

Around the time he composed the lectures for *After Strange Gods*, Eliot gave poetic form to his ideal image of the "cleric"—that is, the religious intellectual—as a prophetic outsider in his pageant play, *The Rock* (1934). Eliot's first foray into drama, *The Rock* was written in collaboration with E. Martin Browne of the Religious Drama Society at the behest of the Anglican priest R. Webb-Odell, who directed the Forty-Five Churches Fund (Eliot, *The Poems* 859). Its 1934 production at Sadler's Wells was intended to raise money and awareness for Webb-Odell's fund, which was dedicated to building new churches in the ever-growing London suburbs. Eliot considered himself to have truly authored only the verse "Choruses" of the pageant, and it is in the form of "Choruses from 'The Rock'" in his *Collected Poems* that this work is best known to Eliot's readers. Still, the "Choruses" remain relatively underread compared to Eliot's other poetry, aside from a few lines from the first chorus ("Where is the wisdom we have lost in knowledge?" etc.), which are often quoted in journalistic contexts as shorthand for skepticism toward technology.

In the "Choruses," Eliot bends the project of suburban church-building to his signature social and aesthetic concerns.[6] Suburban sprawl indexes the spiritual hollowness of secular modernity:

> And now you live dispersed on ribbon roads,
> And no man knows or cares who is his neighbour
> Unless his neighbour makes too much disturbance,

> But all dash to and fro in motor cars,
> Familiar with the roads and settled nowhere. (I.44–48)

Instead of the fetid, filthy crowds of *The Waste Land*'s "Unreal City," we see here an Unreal Exurb, where the distance between prosperous middle-class families opens a yawning existential emptiness. Young professionals may try to fill that "waste and void" with those spacious leisure sports, tennis and golf (VII.1). But Eliot prophesies that courts and courses will become desert in an apocalyptic revelation of the fundamental paltriness of suburban life:

> In the land of lobelias and tennis flannels
> The rabbit shall burrow and the thorn revisit,
> The nettle shall flourish on the gravel court,
> And the wind shall say: 'Here were decent godless people:
> Their only monument the asphalt road
> And a thousand lost golf balls.' (III.31–36)

What suburbanites need, Eliot argues, isn't tennis courts and golf courses. They need churches.

Building new churches in the suburbs isn't just an answer to modern spiritual anomie, however. It's also a strategy for ameliorating unemployment in Great Depression Britain. Given an established state church, the project amounts to a kind of ecclesiastical New Deal, a spiritual public works campaign. In the first chorus, a group of "Workmen" chant: "*There is work together / A Church for all / And a job for each / Every man to his work*" (lines 91–93). The Workmen freeze, silhouetted in tableau, and the "Unemployed" respond: "*No man has hired us*" (line 94). Well, the Church can hire you—if the audience members will only give to the Forty-Five Churches fund!

For Eliot, these two problems—spiritual vacuity and economic precarity—were in truth one. He wrote to Webb-Odell in February 1934: "He who is concerned that a church should be built is committed to a concern with all the problems of the community which the church is intended to serve. The problem of church-building is integral with the problem of more and better housing in general. The employment of men for building churches suggests the whole problem of unemployment. . . . We must assert that these are all one need, and that they can all be satisfied" (qtd. in Eliot, *The Poems* 859). This sense of the irreducible intertwinement of the built environment, spiritual quality of life, and economic conditions is the central intuition of Anglo-

Catholic Socialism—an intuition Eliot shared with Cram and Scudder as well as his colaborers on the pageant play. But anyone who has seen a sprawling, ugly, and isolated American megachurch "campus" in a faceless suburb knows that this intuition has not been widely shared among those with the money and power to shape church-building in the twentieth and twenty-first centuries.

The key to the "Choruses" and the play for which they were written is the titular figure of "The Rock": a mysterious personage associated, in different sections, with Nehemiah, rebuilder of the Jerusalem Temple after the Babylonian Captivity of Judah; Saint Peter, "the rock" on which Christ promised to build his church and according to tradition the first Bishop of Rome; and, most significantly, the eleventh-century French preacher Peter the Hermit, whose sharp words instigated the First Crusade.[7] In the eighth chorus, Eliot writes:

> There came one who spoke of the shame of Jerusalem
> And the holy places defiled;
> Peter the Hermit, scourging with words.
> And among his hearers were a few good men,
> Many who were evil,
> And most who were neither. (lines 8–13)

Eliot's aim in *The Rock* is identical with Peter the Hermit's: goad his audience with words to take up the cause of rebuilding Jerusalem—here, typologically representing the Christian Church, itself antityped by suburban Anglican church buildings. But the Crusades are a troubling historical example to raise, to say the least. To ask British Christians, citizens of a modern pluralistic democratic state, to become latter-day crusaders is a complicated business. Eliot paints the Crusades as noble in origin—the preaching of Peter the Hermit—but flawed and sinful in execution:

> Not avarice, lechery, treachery,
> Envy, sloth, gluttony, jealousy, pride:
> It was not these that made the Crusades,
> But these that unmade them. (VIII.36–39)

But this response dodges the fundamental question: whether it's licit for religious authority to compel coercive violent intervention, especially in the age of the state's monopoly on legal violence.[8]

Ultimately, the figure of "The Rock" escapes identification with any of his historical avatars in the "Choruses." Eliot gives him more abstract titles: "the Stranger" and "him who knows how to ask questions" (III.57–58). (The latter title recalls Eliot's delineation, in "Catholicism and International Order," of the Catholic's social responsibility to ask fundamental ethical questions of all social theories.) Perhaps the most telling pseudonym for "The Rock" is "The Critic" (I.44). At first glance, this might seem merely Eliot's flattering self-portrait of the religious poet-critic as social prophet. But in the correspondence surrounding the play, Eliot speaks of The Chorus, not The Rock, as his authorial mouthpiece. The Rock is an image of Eliot's vocational ideal, embodying clerical "counsels of perfection," to refer to his later Moot lecture. The Rock is "The Witness. The Critic. The Stranger. / The God-shaken, in whom is the truth inborn" (I.44–45). Eliot, through the Chorus, remains a mere witness to this archetypal Witness.

The utopian energies of the "Choruses" concentrate in "The Rock," Eliot's figure of the idealized Critic. Eliot's other writings from 1933–34 forgo picturing his positive social ideal, which he waits until 1939 to formulate even partially. But in the "Choruses" Eliot goes beyond mere reticence about his ideal; instead, criticism *becomes* the ideal; negativity usurps Utopia. No longer are these two moments in a dialectic of social criticism and imagination, as they were for Cram and Scudder. Criticism for Eliot is not a propaedeutic but a good in itself. Perhaps this illuminates the persistence of class distinctions in his best vision of the future: with the fundamental structures of inequality abrogated, what would The Critic prophesy against? Eliot's idea of a Christian society guards against political heresy at the cost of its resemblance to the Body of Christ and its true community of equals.

W. H. AUDEN: MONASTICISM VERSUS EMPIRE

"The waste is a suburb of prophets," W. H. Auden writes in his 1940 poem "The Dark Years," a gloomy rumination on life during wartime (*Collected Poems* 248, line 47). It's an unusual image. Where for Eliot (and a host of urbanist critics after him) suburbs are the targets of the prophet's ire, for Auden, a suburb could be a dwelling in the desert for a community of critics. One needs distance from the city to be able to cry against it, and it isn't good for a man to be alone. In the untitled dedicatory poem to his 1951 volume *Nones*, addressed to the theologians Ursula and Reinhold Niebuhr, Auden praises what he calls "the suburb of dissent," a haven for a "civil style" of speech in the debased media capital of New York City. Auden's suburbs, then, are spatial metaphors uniting critical distance and friendly community, a sort of monastery outside the city limits. Auden and the Niebuhrs lived in Manhattan. Together with fellow New Yorker and Catholic Worker cofounder Dorothy Day, they all frequented an ecumenical theological discussion group hosted by the Russian émigré Helene Iswolsky called the Third Hour; Auden and Day also published in the group's magazine of the same name.[9] Perhaps Auden had Third Hour discussions in mind when he hymned those "golden hours" and set-apart spaces in which civil speech was still possible (*Collected Poems* 621).

After Auden broke with Marxism in the late 1930s and returned to Christian faith, he found himself in need of a new political reckoning with time and space. Much like his queer Anglo-Catholic predecessors Cram and Scudder, Auden found medieval monasticism a useful language of political imagination in his reclaimed tradition. Monasticism allowed Auden to think of history outside of the temporal framework of progress. It also enabled him to conceive of political community beyond the classical model of "the City"—the *polis*—and the ideal of citizenship it implies. Ultimately, monasticism gave Auden a new model for political action by cultivating suburbs of dissent: communities at the margins, constituted by the personal bonds of friendship rather than the impersonal laws of citizenship, equipped to intervene in the present by communion with the past, which generates a hopeful vision of the future.

Auden isn't usually considered a medievalist poet. Edward Mendelson, in his introduction to Auden's *Selected Poems*, argues that it's one of the marks of his greatness that Auden, unlike Eliot, wasn't given to romanticizing any historical age (xv). Yet the later Auden consistently identified his temperament as Arcadian in contrast to Utopian; a partisan of a beautiful past rather than a perfect future, he dreamed of the Garden of Eden and not the Radiant City. Auden took medieval Anglo-Saxon alliterative verse as the model for his long dramatic poem *Age of Anxiety* (1947) and was the most prominent literary booster of the medievalist fiction of the Catholic fantasist J. R. R. Tolkien (Mendelson, *Later Auden* 243, 294). In 1941, he identified the thirteenth-century poet William Langland, of *Piers Plowman* fame, as one of his top three poetic influences (Auden, "Criticism" 132). While Alan Jacobs asserts that it would be impossible to draw a concrete connection between Auden's verse and Langland's, I don't propose anything so specific here (*What Became*

62

of Wystan 35). Instead, I suggest that Auden's general interest in medieval monasticism can help us rethink what is probably the most recognizable commonplace of Auden criticism: what I'll call the "Two Audens Thesis."

The Two Audens Thesis holds that Auden's career ought to be understood
in halves divided by the watershed period of 1939–41, when Auden moved
to the United States, fell in love with Chester Kallman, and returned to the
Anglo-Catholic Christianity of his youth. The basic design of Mendelson's
monumental two-volume literary biography of Auden embodies the Two
Audens Thesis. But it was established much earlier by poets under Auden's
influence such as Randall Jarrell and Philip Larkin. In a review of Auden's
1960 collection *Homage to Clio,* Larkin defined the two Audens this way: the
pre-1940 Auden was "a tremendously exciting English social poet full of energetic unliterary knockabout and unique lucidity of phrase," whereas the post-
1940 Auden was "an engaging, bookish, American talent, too verbose to be
memorable and too intellectual to be moving" (24). That split judgment—a
vexed and limited appreciation for Auden's later work combined with a clear
preference for the earlier stuff—has been widely shared up to the present,
even by critics who hold Auden's later work in higher esteem than Larkin did.

One big reason critics have had for insisting on the Two Audens Thesis
is to affirm the left-wing politics of the early Auden while distancing themselves from the supposed conservatism of the later Auden. This political value
judgment is implicit in Larkin's review: the early Auden is "energetic," "unliterary," and "social" (not to mention "English") whereas the later Auden is merely
"engaging" and "bookish"—that is, intellectually rich but disconnected from
the working class. He's no longer "social," and he's thoroughly Americanized.
As Aidan Wasley sums it up in *The Age of Auden: Postwar Poetry and the
American Scene* (2010), the later Auden of much academic criticism is "a devoutly apolitical aesthetic and cultural conservative" (164). "*Devoutly* apolitical": Wasley nestles that tricky adverb next to the adjective. Does it mean that
Auden was devoted to not-being-political? Or does it mean that Auden was
apolitical in a devout—that is, in a *religious*—manner? Wasley's ambiguity at
this point seems paradoxically precise, even poetic. He suggests that Auden,
by devoting himself to Christianity, ceased to challenge and indeed implicitly
endorsed the social status quo. Auden's later poetry is often explicitly religious in content, devoted to the ethical scrutiny of the individual, and devoid
of confidence in the eventual victory of the proletariat over the bourgeoisie.

But to describe it as "conservative" would be wrong, especially if one takes "conservative" to mean "apolitical," as Wasley glosses the term.

Monasticism offers a good lens through which to see the later Auden's politics afresh because the charges that Auden faced during this period, and which his work from this period continues to draw—of irrationality, frivolity, and withdrawal from the social project—are precisely those faced by monks from the third century until today. In his *History of the Decline and Fall of the Roman Empire* (1776–89), for example, Edward Gibbon eloquently derided the monks as "unhappy exiles from social life . . . impelled by the dark and implacable genius of superstition" (qtd. in Brown 1). But as the historian Peter Brown notes, by and large contemporary historians no longer think of monasticism in Gibbon's contemptuous terms. "Far from being weird and wonderful drop-outs," Brown explains, monks are now seen to act "as a catalyst for the social imagination of an entire society" (1). The social imagination of the later Auden is ripe for a similar reappraisal.

Auden presents his idea of monasticism most clearly in "The Fall of Rome," an essay written in 1966 for *Life Magazine* but later rejected by it. This essay completes Auden's comparative study of life in late-imperial Rome and in the modern West—a project that preoccupied him throughout the later part of his career, from the watershed of 1940, when he first read Charles Cochrane's *Christianity and Classical Culture*, onward. "The Fall of Rome" enumerates parallels between late-antique and modern cultural institutions with crotchety vigor: "Instead of gnostics, we have existentialists and God-is-dead theologians, instead of neo-platonists, devotees of Zen, instead of desert hermits, heroin addicts and beats (who also, oddly enough, seem averse to washing)," and, instead of the Colosseum, television (227–28). This list recalls Auden's poetic technique of collapsing modernity and antiquity through stylistic anachronism. His retelling of the Christmas story *For the Time Being* (1942), for example, has the Christ-child arrive just when "Committees on Fen-Drainage / And Soil-Conservation will issue very shortly / Their Joint Report" (*Collected Poems* 374, "The Summons" IV.4–6). Auden's 1947 poem "The Fall of Rome"—quoted in full at the end of the rejected essay with which it shares a title—observes that

> Caesar's double-bed is warm
> As an unimportant clerk
> Writes I DO NOT LIKE MY WORK
> On a pink official form ("The Fall of Rome" 228, lines 17–20)

Both poetic works rewrite Roman imperial decadence in the language of mid-twentieth-century bureaucracy. What Mendelson calls Auden's "historical double focus"—his quality of keeping late antiquity and the present in vision simultaneously—determined both the themes of his prose and the aesthetics of his poetry (*Later Auden* 184).

The two points of Auden's historical double focus are linked by what the great humanist Erich Auerbach calls a "figural interpretation of history." In *Mimesis* (1953), one of Auden's principal sources for his "Fall of Rome" essay, Auerbach defines figural interpretation as a hermeneutical method practiced by early Christians which forges "a connection between two persons or events ... such ... that the first [in Auden's case, the fall of Rome] signifies not only itself but also the second [in Auden's case, the demise of technological civilization], while the second involves or fulfills the first" (Auerbach 73). For Auden, as for Cram, Scudder, and Eliot, "the here and now is no longer a mere link in an earthly chain of events, it is simultaneously something which has always been, and which will be fulfilled in the future; and strictly, in the eyes of God, it is something eternal, something omni-temporal, something already consummated in the realm of fragmentary earthly event" (Auerbach 74). Auden's figural interpretation posits a hermeneutic relationship between his own midcentury moment and that of late antiquity in order to foster understanding and criticism of his present. Although Auerbach's *Mimesis*, as its title implies, concerns itself with imitation, for Auerbach this means *the literary representation of historical reality*. But Auden's late-imperial typology turns on the ethical sense of imitation as *following a moral exemplar*. As Auden saw it, modern technological society imitates, and in some way *participates in*, the hubris and corruption of the late Roman Empire. As a result, modern people of goodwill—and Christians in particular—ought to imitate, and thus participate in, the monastic revolt against Empire.

The call to imitate the monastics as moral and political exemplars is implicit in the language Auden uses to describe monastic life in "The Fall of Rome": "The problem [of the monastic movement] was one of devising a kind of social organization which would be neither totalitarian, based on collective egoism, nor competitive, based on the egoism and ambition of the individual. At its best, the monastic movement solved this problem better than any other social form before or since" (226). These anachronistic monks with their Freudian vocabulary of "egoism" expressing distinctly twentieth-century political concerns are close kin to the Herodian bureaucrats of *For the Time*

Being or the Roman clerk with his "pink official form" in the poem "The Fall of Rome." Auden presents monasticism as an alternative political tradition that should appeal to anyone on the postwar, post-Stalin, mid–Cold War scene disenchanted with the consumer capitalism of the so-called free world but unwilling to countenance Soviet-style Communism. By diagnosing liberalism and totalitarianism as suffering from variants of the same moral malady—"egoism"—Auden cements political systems to ethical failings. He urges that "more attention" be given to the monastic project of building a religious community of mutuality without the dubious benefit of state coercion (227). Here, Auden's monastic "idea of a Christian society" departs from Eliot's neo-Constantinian "Christian State."

The monastic vow of celibacy, however, presents an obstacle to widespread imitation of the monks. For Auden, as for Cram and Scudder, celibacy challenges conventional family life as much as active sexuality; it is the *queerness* of celibacy that makes it a stumbling-block to latter-day would-be monastics with heterosexual family ties. Auden speculates that this obstacle may, however, be a productive one: "perhaps family life and communal life are incompatible, except under catastrophic conditions" (226–27). The contexts in which Auden had himself experienced "communal life"—such as "February House" in Brooklyn Heights, where he lived for a year with Benjamin Britten and Carson McCullers, among others—were groups of friends bound not by a vow of celibacy, nor even by common faith, but instead by their shared difference from sexual and social norms.[10] Behind Auden's conjecture that community is best found outside the heteronormative family, then, lies the question of the relationship between his queerness and his Christian radicalism.

Beginning in the late 1940s, Auden described himself as an orthodox Christian, "doctrinally and liturgically conservative" (Ursula Niebuhr 116). At the same time, his marginal position as a gay man enabled him to apprehend radical political implications in this conservative theology. As he put it in a 1963 letter to Christopher Isherwood, "though I believe it sinful to be queer, it has at least saved me from becoming a pillar of the Establishment" (qtd. in Mendelson, *Later Auden* 455–56). Auden imagined queerness as a mixed blessing—or what Olivia Bustion calls an "enabling disability"—that keeps his theology and his politics in their properly paradoxical relationship (Bustion 100). One way that queerness did this is by making Auden, like Scudder, feel askew of progress narratives like the heteronormative bourgeois family script of job, marriage, children, house, etc. By engendering a sense of anachronism or belatedness, Auden's queerness offered him a special receptivity to the forms of counterimperial community traditionally enacted in the same-sex celibate communities of monasticism. Bustion indeed argues that "Auden's work gets *queerer, more radical* after he converts" to Christianity (24n74). One way this claim seems true to me is in the matter of time: the progressive temporality of his 1930s poetry seems awfully chrononormative compared with the temporality of recurrence on display in "The Fall of Rome" and elsewhere.[11]

Auden's political poetry of the 1930s discloses a progressive theory of history that underwrites political action. "Spain" (1937) is the most noteworthy example: stanzas beginning "yesterday" and "to-morrow" enumerate the small victories of science, art, and learning over superstition (*Selected Poems* 54–57). The normal order of things is steady, if uneven, progress. However, the poem's stanza-ending refrain "but to-day the struggle," repeated three times in the opening sequence of the poem and twice more at its end, announces a crisis in the temporal order of advancement: the Spanish Civil War. Progress is a rational order—"To-morrow . . . / the gradual exploring of all the / Octaves of radiation" (57, lines 78–80)—but the crisis is irrational, an aberration in which "our" fever-dreams and "fears" are incarnate as "invading battalions" of fascists (56, lines 69–72). The middle section of the poem, a dialogue between "History the operator, the / Organiser, Time the refreshing river" and "the nations" that are at History's mercy, labors to reconcile progress and crisis (55, lines 35–37). The poem defines political action by conflating individual choice in the moment of crisis with the necessity of historical progress. "I am your choice, your decision," History declares to the nations (56, line 56). This identity between necessity and choice effaces individual ethical responsibility: a line Auden would later disown avows "the conscious acceptance of guilt in the necessary murder" (57, line 95). The price of serving progress, of bringing something really new into the world, is the forfeiture of morality.

Auden's later writings similarly reveal a vision of history that motivates political action. But it is a vision of recurrence rather than progress, and it preserves the unity of politics and ethics, rather than severing them, through the principle of imitation. Auden works out his typological temporality of recurrence in perhaps the most celebrated of his later poetic works, the sequence "Horae Canonicae" (1947–54). The formal device that structures this sequence—a poem for each of the "canonical hours" of prayer in the Daily Office—is itself monastic in origin. The monks developed the Office as a scheme for partitioning the day into periods of prayer pegged to the time of crucial events in Christ's passion. Auden had read about this in *The Shape of the Liturgy* (1945) written by the Anglican Benedictine monk Dom Gregory Dix, a particularly influential book for Auden's theology and a likely inspiration for "Horae Canonicae" (Dix 323–28; Mendelson, *Later Auden* 279).[12] As in Dix, each section of Auden's poem demonstrates how everyday human actions—waking up, working, feeling bored, walking home—are implicated in the death of Christ.

In its philosophy of time and of human action, "Horae Canonicae" is a sort of extended rejoinder to "Spain." This emerges most clearly in the prose-poem section titled "Vespers," where two men meet one another while walking the streets of "our city" at evening (*Selected Poems* 234). Their meeting is close to a cruising encounter, except what the two men wordlessly recognize in one another is not their shared sexual orientation but their opposed political temperaments. The poem's speaker is "Arcadian," and his opponent "Utopian." "[B]etween my Eden and his New Jerusalem," the speaker explains, "no treaty is negotiable" (235). With Auden's political history in mind, the poem seems to dramatize a meeting between two of his selves—not a past and a present self so much as two competing tendencies always within himself, with the Arcadian lately taking the upper hand.

Whereas in "Spain" "to-day" is a unique crisis within the regular progress of "yesterday" and "to-morrow," in "Horae Canonicae" today—just like yesterday and tomorrow—reenacts the crux of Good Friday. And whereas "Spain" originally avowed "the conscious acceptance of guilt in the necessary murder" as the unique political imperative of "to-day," "Horae Canonicae" makes the recognition of one's shared guilt in the unnecessary murder of the Christ, "on whose immolation . . . arcadias, utopias, our dear old bag of a democracy, are alike founded," as the imperative of every day ("Vespers," *Selected Poems* 237). By making ever-present this sense of shared guilt, the typological time of the Daily Office disarms the righteous anger of political opponents so that, "for a fraction of a second" at "civil twilight," the possibility of a civil exchange opens up between them (237, 235). In the poem's final section, this possibility blossoms. "Lauds," named for an office said in the middle of the night or early morning, is written as an antiphonal communal prayer over the sleeping city. "God bless the Realm, God bless the People," the speakers intone; may they become "sensible of" each other as "neighbors"—each with the obligation to love the other—rather than opponents (239, lines 11, 5).

In its spatial dimension, "Horae Canonicae" deconstructs the walls of the City in the hope that neighborhood can be found outside.[13] "Vespers" begins by naming "our city" and ends with the admission that "without a cement of blood . . . no secular wall will safely stand" (237). This marks a shift in Auden's spatial imagination. Previously, Auden had relied upon the figure of the City as his recurring poetic abstraction for human community (Deer 24). The great hope of "Spain," for example—a hope put forward and then retracted in its dialogue between History and the nations—is "to build the just city" (line 53). But "Vespers" denies the possibility of building "the just city" altogether, since all such building is premised on violence. If "Horae Canonicae" abrogates building, it does not, however, abrogate justice; it relocates critical energies from the city to the suburb of dissent. In "Lauds," neighborhood becomes possible in a community of prayer located outside the city and its economy of ambition.

Auden's monastic spatial imagination, which imagines retreat as a form of engagement—a political rather than antipolitical act—emerged from his reading of Charles Cochrane's account of monasticism in *Christianity and Classical Culture* (1940). According to Cochrane, monasteries in the fourth century became centers of "Christian democracy," even of "Christian communism" (341–32). Under the leadership of Saint Basil the Great, the monasteries were "organization[s] embodying principles which made it a model, not so much of, as for the *polis*," proximate utopias where "economic and moral interdependence," "equality of the sexes," "communal self-sufficiency," and "hospitality" were practiced (341–42).[14] In other words, in these religious communes, the relationship between the monastery and the City was pedagogical rather than oppositional.

A quasi-monastic pedagogical community at the margins of the City is the subject of Auden's very late poem "The Garrison" (1969), first published in the magazine of the Third Hour discussion group. In the poem, a group of friends gather to eat, drink martinis, listen to (and perhaps sing along with) music, and talk. Among friends, "personal song and language / somehow mizzle," or confuse, "Time" and "Nemesis" in their slow but ineluctable destruction (*Collected Poems* 845, lines 7–8; 5). Eating and drinking, singing and talking: when *personal*—neither propaganda nor advertising copy—these acts open a rift in deterministic time, which, in this poem, advances not toward universal beneficence but universal ruin, for "Time crumbs all ramparts" (line 5). These time-shattering personal acts echo the liturgical actions of Christian worship—the eating and drinking of the Eucharist, the singing of psalms and hymns, the speech of prayer and preaching—transferred here to the context of a party.[15]

The first word of "The Garrison"—"Martini-time"—announces a temporal rift by invoking a repeated, ritualized act of martini-drinking in deceptively lighthearted language (*Collected Poems* 845). There's a certain brashness or even decadence in according political significance to such genteel pleasures as drink and records. But, as Bustion notes, "the community elevates fun . . . to a serious ethic" (10–11). "The Garrison" is more than a cozy shelter from the storms of history. The personal acts of the gathered friends make it

> possible for the breathing
> still to break bread with the dead, whose brotherhood
> gives us confidence to wend the trivial
> thrust of the Present (*Collected Poems* 846, lines 9–12)

The friends' communion with each other and with the dead—"break bread" intensifies the poem's Eucharistic allusion—arms them to change the present. The verb "wend" means to change, but it also carries connotations of turning or twisting, which brings the word into the semantic orbit of "crookedness," a consistent figure of queer sexuality in Auden's poetry (Bozorth 223). In "The Garrison," then, to make the Present less trivial is to make it more queer. The Present's "trivial thrust" is its emphasis on or trend toward the trivial, but "thrust" also names a violent forward motion that the friends' communion forestalls. The poem cracks open the linear-progressive time of technological civilization to let the past come rushing in, and it understands this temporal sabotage as at once queering and sacralizing time. At this belated moment, in line 14, the poem reveals its addressee as "Chester": Auden's longtime companion and sometime lover Chester Kallman. "The Garrison" communicates its political theology through the vectors of same-sex love and friendship.

A garrison, like a suburb of dissent, embodies both retreat from and engagement with "the City" (line 17). The queer couple and their friends "have been assigned to / garrison stations," enclaves which house soldiers within a city's boundaries for the purpose of defense (lines 15–16). But these soldiers' way of defending the City is to practice "loyal opposition" to its leaders, no matter who is in power (line 18). Rejecting capitalist greed and the desire for celebrity ("never greening / for the big money, never neighing after / a public image" [lines 18–20]) but also abstaining from "rebellions" (line 21), the friends' political vocation is like that of Cochrane's monastics: modeling human flourishing from the City's margins. Having already opened the present to communion with the dead, in its closing lines the poem breaks fully into Auerbach's vertical dimension of history, where past, present, and future are co-present to each other: "to serve as a paradigm / now of what a plausible Future might be / is what we're here for" (lines 22–24). In the queer temporality of martini-time, the present sacraments of personal song, language, food, and drink give the dead a flourishing life in a plausible future. Auden's word "paradigm" invokes a typology in which the friends' community is both modeled on the past and provides models for the future, in a dialectic of example and improvisation.

The historical example of radical community that remains implicit in "The Garrison" is the monastery. The poem's impulse to save the City by retreating from and even opposing it is the same one that animated the monastic protest against Empire that Auden identified in his essay "The Fall of Rome." The politics of friendship and abundance modeled in "The Garrison" match Auden's description of monasticism "at its best" as neither totalitarian nor competitive. And by serving as a social paradigm for the City, the community of "The Garrison" fulfills the pedagogical function of the monastery identified by Cochrane. What might be missing in "The Garrison," compared to Cochrane's monasteries, is hospitality. Auden's friends seemingly neglect to share their abundance with anyone outside the circle of friendship.

It's in this question of the extent of hospitality—rather than in the religiosity of the poetry, its rejection of linear-progressive time, or its monastically inspired strategies of withdrawal—that we might find a true limit to the later Auden's social imagination. Trading the ideal of citizenship for friendship gives Auden a suburb of equals, but its borders may not be porous to the City it wants to teach. To truly reflect the body of Christ, these garrisons must extend their welcome not just to friends but to strangers and even enemies. We can see this ideal given flesh in the Catholic Workers' "houses of hospitality," modeled on medieval hospices, which I take up in the next chapter.

Beginning in the 1930s, Anglo-Catholicism ceased to exert such a strong attraction for U.S. literary intellectuals who sought to unite sacrament and social justice. At least two factors contributed to this shift by erasing Anglo-Catholicism's distinctiveness vis-à-vis other Christian traditions. The first factor is chronicled by Mark Thomas Edwards in his 2012 book *The Right of the Protestant Left*. Mainline ecumenical Protestant intelligentsia of all denominations, he shows, disappointed with the thinness of Social Gospel–era Protestant liberalism, discovered a Catholic and liturgical consciousness, and this discovery inflected their worship, their politics, and their forms of thought. Anglo-Catholics were no longer the only game in town for those seeking a socially conscious middle way between Roman Catholicism and Protestantism. H. Richard Niebuhr's writings are a great example of this Protestant catholicizing tendency: for instance, the nineteenth-century Anglican Socialist F. D. Maurice is the hero of Niebuhr's landmark *Christ and Culture* (1951).[16]

But by time of the Great Depression, many were no longer seeking a middle way between Catholic and Protestant. Al Smith's 1928 presidential candidacy signaled Roman Catholics' move toward the American mainstream. In 1933, Dorothy Day and Peter Maurin founded the Catholic Worker movement and its associated newspaper, which became the heart of what historian James T. Fisher calls the "American Catholic Counterculture," sustained mainly by the intellectual energies of adult converts. The Workers' movement was, among other things, a literary enterprise. As I'll argue, Day and Maurin are important writers in their own right, and the movement drew a number of other authors into its orbit, including Auden and Claude McKay. This counterculture incubated the midcentury flowering of U.S. Catholic literature by Flannery O'Connor, J. F. Powers, Thomas Merton, and, most important for my purposes, Walker Percy, whose debts to Catholic radicalism become clear in chapter 5.

THE MYSTICAL BODY IN CRISIS

The Catholic Worker Movement and the
Challenge of Pluralism

In January 1956, the New York City Fire Department slammed Dorothy Day (1897–1980) with a $250 fire-safety fine for the Chrystie Street Catholic Worker house. When she appeared in court empty-handed, the judge gave her five days to raise the funds. "Miss Day will pray to St. Joseph, whom she credits with meeting the bills through good-willed people all these years, for the money," the *New York Times* reported (Lissner 25). Day's friend the poet W. H. Auden, an assiduous reader of and sometime contributor to the *Times*, was the answer to her prayer. Neither rich nor particularly goodwilled (at least by his own exacting standards), the poet nevertheless hatched a beguilingly bizarre plan to foot the bill. At the time, "NBC Television was producing a broadcast of *The Magic Flute*, for which Auden, together with Chester Kallman, had translated the libretto" (Mendelson, "The Secret Auden"). Auden "stormed into the producer's office, demanding to be paid immediately, instead of on the date specified in his contract. He waited there, making himself unpleasant, until a check finally arrived" ("The Secret Auden"). When Day left again for court, still lacking the money, Auden was waiting outside in a group of needy men, dressed shabbily enough to pass unnoticed by the preoccupied woman. Day felt someone press "something into her hands, muttering, 'Here's two-fifty.' Only on the train did she discover she'd been handed a cheque, not for $2.50 but $250, and that the hobo [who'd given it to her] was the pre-eminent poet of the age" (N.M.).

Almost a poem in itself, this stunt offers a window onto the aesthetics of the *Catholic Worker* newspaper and movement. Auden's abrasive act of gift-giving embodies the spirit of Catholic Worker cofounder Peter Maurin (1877–1949), who lived in voluntary poverty modeled on Saint Francis of Assisi (also the medieval hero of Vida Scudder). Begging, after a fashion, for the wages he was owed, Auden turned those wages into a gift by endorsing the check, translating the money as if by magic from the postindustrial media economy to the economy of personal exchange. Auden enters into what Kelly Johnson identifies as the voluntary beggar's "creative . . . cycle of gift which does not exclude work or exchange, but orders them to serve the good of proclaiming Christ" (36). This cycle was launched at the *Catholic Worker* by Maurin and continued by Day's appeal in the *New York Times*. But where begging was a vocation for Maurin, it was a costume for Auden—something he slipped into, obscuring his identity, then slipped out of. Auden flips the hierarchy of need by reversing the roles of beggar and donor, blurring the distinction between them. This Catholic carnivalesque, this camp Franciscanism, illustrates both his bond with and difference from Day, Maurin, and the Workers.

The Catholic Worker movement was the most important American outpost of what the historian James Chappel identifies as "a transnational network of Catholic antifascists" that developed in the 1930s in response to looming totalitarian threats (109, 135–36).[1] Founded in New York City in 1933, the Worker was the joint brainchild of the radical journalist Day and the French-born hobo-philosopher Maurin. The movement's eponymous newspaper stumped for "sacramental radicalism" with a "revolutionary symbolism" drawn from the Middle Ages and the Catholic medievalist tradition (McCarraher, *Christian Critics* 77, 82–88).

Day and Maurin launched the Catholic Worker movement into the teeth of the Great Depression on May Day 1933, when the first issue of their paper hit Manhattan's Union Square. This movement was at once a publishing project and a social project. The original goal of the *Catholic Worker* newspaper was twofold: first, to report on social justice issues from a Catholic radical perspective drawn from the social encyclicals of the popes, beginning with Leo XIII's 1891 *Rerum novarum* ("On the Condition of the Working Class"), and the predominantly French and English Catholic social thinkers, including the neo-Thomist Jacques Maritain, personalist Emmanuel Mounier, and distributist G. K. Chesterton, who sought to apply the encyclicals' teachings. The popes and the lay Catholic social thinkers alike often appealed to medieval sacred history as a way of criticizing the modern capitalist order.

The second aim of the paper was to publicize Maurin's threefold plan for Catholic social action: founding urban houses of hospitality, inspired by the medieval hospice, to care for the poor in the city; instituting roundtable discussions at which answers to pressing social questions could be sought through civil dialogue; and establishing rural farm communes where "workers can become scholars and scholars can become workers" in a context of self-sufficient communal life on the land (Maurin, *The Green Revolution* 27). The Catholic Workers had great success with the first part of Maurin's plan, the houses of hospitality, and they took considerable steps toward achieving the second two, though those steps were plagued with difficulty, especially on their farm communes. As an immigrant worker and organic intellectual, Maurin carried early twentieth-century Catholic social thought from the France of his birth and young manhood to the United States. Maurin's vision was, in his words, "to create a new society within the shell of the old," with "a philosophy so old that it looks like new" (83).

In her January 1970 "On Pilgrimage" column, Day made clear the larger aims of the Catholic Workers, writing of the early days that "we were a revolutionary headquarters rather than a Bowery mission, as most newspapers like to picture us." The *Catholic Worker* newspaper too was a strange hybrid of avant-garde little magazine and newspaper for the unemployed. With its integration of the religious, the social, and the aesthetic, the *Catholic Worker* was a primary organ for the literary Christian Left in the 1930s.[2] In this chapter, I aim to give an account of the Catholic Worker movement in literary history, focusing not only on Day and Maurin but also the preeminent poet the paper attracted in its initial phase of the 1930s–1940s: Claude McKay (1889–1948), Harlem Renaissance veteran and ex-Communist Catholic convert. But I begin with Day herself, believing that Catholic publisher Maisie Ward's striking assessment of her is correct: "the truth about Dorothy is that she is a great poet" (Fisher 47).

POETRY OF THE CHRISTIAN REVOLUTION:
DOROTHY DAY'S MEDIEVALIST MANIFESTO

Dorothy Day was a radical writer first—before she became a Catholic, before she became a social reformer, before she became a Servant of God (that is, a candidate for canonization as a saint). Day was born in Brooklyn, but her father, a sportswriter, moved the family to San Francisco in 1903 (Allaire and Broughton). The 1906 San Francisco earthquake destroyed her father's newspaper plant, forcing the family to move to Chicago. After a couple of desultory years at the University of Illinois, spent mostly reading Russian novelists and U.S. radical writers, at eighteen years old she returned to New York (Elie 15–16). Day soon made a name for herself as a journalist writing for radical publications and as a rounder in the Greenwich Village bohemian scene, a comrade of Village radicals including Max Eastman and Claude McKay. She plays a small role in her friend Malcolm Cowley's Lost Generation memoir *Exile's Return: A Literary Odyssey of the 1920s* (1934, 1951). At a Village dive called the Hell Hole, "the gangsters admired Dorothy Day because she could drink them under the table; but they felt more at home with Eugene O'Neill, who listened to their troubles and never criticized" (Cowley 69). It was in the back room of the Hell Hole, Day recounts in her 1938 conversion story *From Union Square to Rome*, that O'Neill, with whom she was at one point romantically involved, read to her Francis Thompson's Christ-haunted poem "The Hound of Heaven," and she "was moved by its power" ("Chapter 1: Why" 4).[3] Day would describe this period of her life as at times "Baudelairean . . . choosing 'the downward path which leads to salvation'" ("Chapter 1: Why" 1).

Day not only ran in literary circles; she nurtured literary ambitions. After a harrowing love affair that issued in a pregnancy terminated by an abortion, Day married a wealthy man and went "to Europe to write a novel" about her experiences—traumatic autobiography gilded with a touch of fiction, after the early-1920s fashion exemplified by Fitzgerald's *This Side of Paradise* (Elie 36). The marriage didn't last long, but the novel, *The Eleventh Virgin*, was published in 1924. When Hollywood gobbled up the salacious tale's movie rights, Day was comfortably well-off for a short time (Elie 38–39). Day later wished the novel unwritten and all copies destroyed, but a remnant still lingers today among used book dealers.

Though it curdled her affections for *The Eleventh Virgin*, Day's conversion did not destroy her literary ambitions. Into the 1930s, "she 'still dreamed in terms of novels,'" and plotted a work of Catholic social realism (Elie 66). She never finished this second novel, though she published excerpts from it over the years in the *Catholic Worker*. In the late 1920s, Day moved into a cottage on Long Island where she would eventually give birth to her daughter Tamar and convert to Catholicism. Malcolm and Peggy Cowley moved into another cottage next door and drew Day into a wider literary milieu that included Kenneth and Lily Burke, Hart Crane, John Dos Passos, Allen Tate, and Caroline Gordon (Elie 44). Later, she would attract the poets Auden and Robert Lowell (Fisher 48). Day poured her writerly talents into her eloquent memoirs and her tireless journalism for the *Catholic Worker*. She led the movement until her death in 1980.

We can see Dorothy Day's evocative writing style on display in her first editorial for the *Catholic Worker*, published May 1933 and entitled "To Our Readers." It opens with the following lines: "For those who are sitting on park benches in the warm spring sunlight. For those who are huddling in shelters trying to escape the rain. For those who are walking the streets in the all but futile search for work. For those who think there is no hope for the future, no recognition of their plight—this little paper is addressed." Though it points to other "radical sheets" as its near neighbors, "To Our Readers" is not radical reportage, or even an editorial statement. The first three sentences especially, with their anaphoric syntax ("For those who are . . . For those who are . . . For those who are . . .") and their concrete imagery, are poetry or prose-poetry, the cadences not too far removed from those of, say, Carl Sandburg (a favorite of Day's).[4] In the invocation of the cruel spring rain, there may even be an oblique reference to the opening of Eliot's *The Waste Land*.

If it's a stretch to liken these plainspoken lines to high modernist poetry, "To Our Readers" fits more neatly into the major genre of revolutionary poetry—that is, the manifesto. In his study of the manifesto form, *Poetry of the Revolution: Marx, Manifestos, and the Avant-Gardes* (2006), Martin Puchner documents the manifesto's roots as a sermonic and catechistic form of radical religious communities (12–17). In the pages of the *Catholic Worker*, the manifesto gets back in touch with those roots. "To Our Readers" is the self-conscious rallying cry of a religious avant-garde. The editorial's bullet-point structure and its statements of aims recall the founding documents of many a modern artistic sect. It prods its reader with rhetorical questions:

It's time there was a Catholic paper for the unemployed. The fundamental aim of most radical sheets is the conversion of its readers to radicalism and atheism. Is it not possible to be radical and not atheist? Is it not possible to protest, to expose, to complain, to point out abuses and demand reforms without desiring the overthrow of religion? In an attempt to popularize and make known the encyclicals of the Popes in regard to social justice and the program put forth by the Church for the "reconstruction of the social order," this news sheet, *The Catholic Worker*, is started.

In the fiat-like passive voice of that final sentence ("this news sheet . . . is started") there's a curious elision of the sentence's subject, for the "Catholic Worker," as the communal subject that could authorize the pronouncement, does not yet exist except as the vision of a couple of ragged journalists. In this sense, I liken "To Our Readers" to what Puchner calls a "Marxian speech-act": "The speech acts of the manifesto . . . are launched in the anterior future, claiming that their authority will have been provided by the changes they themselves want to bring about. But this future perfect construction is nothing but a hope, a claim, a pose, a desire that often comes to naught" (24). The words of Day's editorial are community-creating words, but their effect is uncertain, a gamble.

In other ways, "To Our Readers" differs from the typical manifesto, stretching the boundaries of the form. Like Scudder, Cram, and Henry Adams, Day drew on the medieval past in particular when she put forth her hopes and claims for the future. The idea for the Catholic Worker movement's most enduring institution, for example—"houses of hospitality" where the urban poor could receive food and shelter—was explicitly derived from the model of the medieval hospice ("Maurin's Program"). This historical debt sets the Catholic Worker movement at odds with other avant-gardes. Most modernist manifestos come to bury the past not to praise it, as in F. T. Marinetti's archetypal "Futurist Manifesto" (1909), which condemned museums as cultural cemeteries. And just where you would expect to find the manifesto's central ideological content, "To Our Readers" points away from itself to church tradition—"the encyclicals put forth by the Popes" and "the program put forth by the Church." This sets it apart from the "self-authorizing" character of Marxian speech-acts on Puchner's account (19). The Catholic Worker movement was not a self-authorizing community; it was more like a new and semiautonomous religious order within the Roman Catholic Church—what Day called a "lay apostolate"—that depended on the Church's authority. Despite these differences owing to its distinctly religious character, the family resemblance between this editorial and other manifestos is strong. In short, "To Our Readers" is a manifesto that connects its reader to the past and then takes her to church.

The Catholic Worker movement is often criticized, even by sympathetic observers, for its failure to "translate the sacramental vision into a durable politics of work, technology, and social relations" (McCarraher 88). While these criticisms address the movement's political technique, I want to focus on its aesthetic significance. Through writings like "To Our Readers" Day crafted a social icon that we might call "the idea of the Catholic Worker," a creative project drawn from the materials of the religious past but imbued with future hope that helps us to imagine social relations differently—much like Cram's Walled Towns, Scudder's Franciscan Christian Revolution, Eliot's idea of a Christian Society, and Auden's suburbs of prophetic dissent. But what sets Day's "idea" apart is its incarnation. No mere *logos asarkos*, the Catholic Worker ideal was chastened and enlivened by a community life of entwined political, literary, and religious practice in Catholic Worker houses of hospitality, farms, and publishing. The historian James Fisher alleges that "an air of deconstruction and death hung over the [Catholic Worker] movement," that its embrace of suffering and holy foolishness predisposed it to failure and to count failure as success (46). But a politics of self-destruction was perhaps a fitting rejoinder to the various politics of self-fulfillment and other-destruction that surrounded the Catholic Workers in the 1930s—a prophetic alternative that still speaks today.

Peter Maurin, French immigrant to the United States by way of Canada, unwashed eccentric and itinerant laborer, philosopher-poet and cofounder of the *Catholic Worker*, was Day's strongest link to the medieval past, and, for her, the embodiment of the idea of the Catholic Worker. Maurin's threefold plan, embodying a kind of working-class Catholic agrarianism, was, he always insisted, based on medieval models. A profile of Maurin published in the May 1946 number of the *Catholic Worker* begins: "'I am neither a proletarian nor a bourgeois. I am a peasant. I have roots.' . . . By roots Peter Maurin means that he has a philosophy of life based upon the Faith of the Middle Ages. He also calls himself a Medievalist." Much like a medieval manuscript, the profile begins with an illuminated first letter (see fig. 3). Maurin brought with him ideas from turn-of-the-twentieth-century French Social Catholicism, propounding what he called a "Green Revolution" of farm communities, an anti-industrial vision not unlike that of John Crowe Ransom and the Twelve Southerners discussed in chapter 4 (Fisher 38, 41). Unlike the Twelve Southerners, however, the Catholic Workers *did* actually start some new, if sometimes ill-fated, farms.[5] Meanwhile Maurin indoctrinated anyone he could corner with his "phrased essays" of homespun poetry, the style of which I analyze at length in the next section. Maurin was the Catholic Worker movement's gnomic ideologue and untidy exemplar. In his ramshackle person he effected an astounding synthesis of intellect and labor, of ideology and piety,

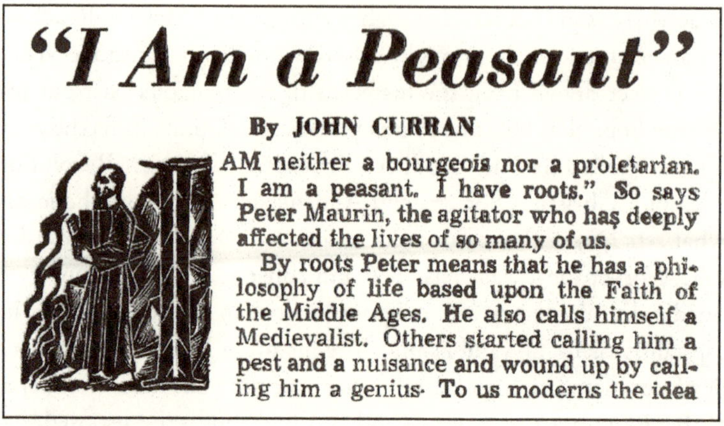

"I Am a Peasant"

By JOHN CURRAN

AM neither a bourgeois nor a proletarian. I am a peasant. I have roots." So says Peter Maurin, the agitator who has deeply affected the lives of so many of us.

By roots Peter means that he has a philosophy of life based upon the Faith of the Middle Ages. He also calls himself a Medievalist. Others started calling him a pest and a nuisance and wound up by calling him a genius. To us moderns the idea

Fig. 3. John Curran's profile of Peter Maurin. Image courtesy of the Thomas Merton Center, Bellarmine University.

of history and modernity, in an aesthetic form designed not to please but to shock. Or at least Day's textual Peter Maurin effects such a synthesis.

Whenever Day wrote about Maurin, she composed his life typologically, writing him as a repetition of figures from sacred history. Whether as "another St. Francis of modern times," a Mary who "brought to us Christ in the poor, as surely as the Blessed Mother brought Christ to Elizabeth," or a homeless and suffering Christ himself, the idea of Peter Maurin in Day's writings takes on a paradoxical relation to Peter Maurin the historical person (qtd. in Fisher 34). Other Catholic writers soon adopted what Fisher calls this "figural method" when speaking of Maurin; in a 1938 essay for *Commonweal*, for example, journalist Joe Brieg figured Maurin as a new Saint Peter presaging a reborn church (Fisher 35). From 1939 on, as he increasingly absented himself from the Catholic Workers' Bowery headquarters on unannounced rambles, Maurin took on a fully fictionalized life in the pages of the movement's newspaper. First Day and then other Catholic Workers wrote stories about a "present day working class saint" called Ben Joe Labray, an Americanized Maurin figure (Fisher 64–66). Day held up Maurin as the prophet of a new, but also very old, kind of subjectivity, one that reversed the traditional American script of the self-made man. Indeed, Day's Maurin was an unmade man: "The essential difference between Maurin and the classical model of American selfhood was in his acceptance of poverty as a goal in itself, even as one to be worked toward.... Day introduced American Catholics to a prophet in their own midst who emulated not the leadership qualities or moral excellence of Christ but his vocation to suffering" (Fisher 34).

In her portrayal of Maurin, Day put forward a Christian leftist alternative to fascist and Communist critiques of the bourgeois self of American rugged individualism. In this sense, Maurin was the Catholic Worker model of what the French Communist philosopher Alain Badiou calls the "new man," a type which "haunted" the twentieth century (8). For Badiou, this idea of the new man "circulates between the various fascisms and communisms," and "their statues are more or less the same": "Creating a new humanity always comes down to demanding that the old one be destroyed. A violent, unreconciled debate rages about the nature of this old humanity. But each and every time, the project is so radical that in the course of its realization the singularity of human lives is not taken into account" (8). Badiou acknowledges that the language of the "new man" is biblical in origin; it comes from the writings of Saint Paul, whom Badiou elsewhere takes as the archetype of the political subject, the one who bears militant witness to an overwhelming Event.

Day's new man also draws from these biblical sources, but he differs from fascist and Communist models in his nonviolence. She explicitly invokes the passage from the book of Ephesians in which the concept of the new man originates in her obituary for Maurin: "The fact was he had been stripped of all,—he had stripped himself throughout life. He had put off the old man, to put on the new. He had done all that he could to denude himself of the world, and I mean the world in the evil sense.... He loved people, he saw in them what God meant them to be. He saw the world as God meant it to be, and he loved it" ("The Story of Three Deaths" 2). Day's rhetoric interiorizes the violence of political transformation into the "stripping" of the self. Day merges her subjectivity with Maurin's in this rhetoric of gracious self-unmaking and self-making. She struggled throughout her life to put off the "old man" of her middle-class all-American upbringing and put on the "new man" of the poor Catholic immigrant sufferer. Day's Maurinesque "new man" is, however, also an "old man"—an anachronism, a medievalist: the Catholic Worker's orientation to history itself is ultimately nonviolent. Taking Maurin as a model of subjectivity, Day imagined "the Catholic Worker" as a self-in-community productively engaged with history, voluntarily subject to poverty, absolutely committed to pacifism, and relentlessly considerate of what Badiou calls "the singularity of human lives," which other models of the new man trampled (8). For this reason, among others, both she and Maurin used the term "personalism" to describe their political ideology ("Day after Day" 2).[6]

The idea of the Catholic Worker was also intimately bound up with Day's all-embracing concept of "the Mystical Body of Christ"—the true community of equals forged by Christ's life, death, and resurrection, here imagined as a universal collective subject whose existence is currently occluded from human vision but whose arrival is always imminent. As Fisher explains, the Mystical Body of Christ was a kind of invented tradition of doctrine, posing as an inheritance of the medieval church but in fact a modern Catholic polemical response to Protestant individualism (48–51). Again drawing on Pauline texts like the book of Ephesians, the doctrine of the Mystical Body indicates the individual Christian's intimate communion with Christ which is always immediately supra-individual; all Christians are caught up as members in the greater unit of Christ's body. In her writings, Day equivocates on the denotation of the term, often stretching it radically. Sometimes it seems to mean the Church worldwide; sometimes it seems to mean all humanity, as in her wartime article "The Mystical Body and Spain" (1936). But perhaps this discrepancy is best understood not as an equivocation but as an analogy. Day saw the Church as united to all humanity in the humanity of Christ, and she saw every human being as a bearer of Christ's image and a potential part of the Church. For Day, the Worker is the Sufferer, and the Sufferer is Christ.

The values of particularity and catholicity that jostle uneasily in Eliot's theological criticism find paradoxical concord for Day in the universal Mystical Body of the one Christ. This paradox offers not a discursive but an imagistic resolution to the problem of pluralism, one embodied in the Ade Bethune–designed masthead of the *Catholic Worker*, showing a Black worker and a white worker shaking hands within Christ's embrace (see fig. 4).[7] Here, too, however, Day's political vision of universal connection is predicated upon

Fig. 4. Ade Bethune's masthead for the *Catholic Worker* (1946). Image courtesy of the Thomas Merton Center, Bellarmine University.

theological limits. It depends upon seeing people as members or potential members of a body in which they may not desire to share. The doctrine of the Mystical Body disciplines the Catholic Worker's perceptions to see each person as connected to Christ, but it also privileges that perception over the perceived person's self-understanding. Yet these limits were at the same time the conditions of possibility the enabled both the Catholic Worker movement and the career of Peter Maurin.

"LOGIC WITH CRACKS": PETER MAURIN'S "EASY ESSAYS"

Peter Maurin carried his poems in the pockets of his overcoat. Like the books and papers and broken eyeglasses that also filled those pockets—and like the tattered thirdhand overcoat itself—the poems seemed a part of him, all the more inseparable from the man for their down-at-heels ephemerality. Maurin would lose the poems or the coat or the glasses, or he would give them to someone who needed them more than he did. But in giving these items away, he endured not a breach but an expansion; he held them more durably in his tenuous way than a more grasping man would have. He memorized his poems, declaimed them during lulls in radical meetings, or recited them to willing and half-willing listeners in New York's Union Square. He printed them on mimeographed sheets and handed them out on street corners. Born in France in 1877, he came to North America in 1909 and began writing in English in the 1920s. After 1933, he published his poems in the *Catholic Worker* newspaper and in Catholic Worker books and in related publications as far afield as Germany, Australia, and the United Kingdom. Maurin was never remunerated for this work. A beggar and a prodigal, he gave his writing as a gift—just as he gave all his labor from the late 1920s onward. But the more he gave his poems away, the more they were his. The logic of his authorship is the paradoxical logic of the Gospels: "Whosoever shall seek to save his life shall lose it; and whosoever shall lose his life shall preserve it" (Luke 17:33). The life he gave away was in the poems he gifted.

Maurin's life and his poems are so indissolubly connected that to analyze them apart from his biography would be impossible. But just for this reason, his poems have not received the attention they deserve as art. The literature on Day dwarfs that on Maurin (although Day studies almost always have something to say about him in connection with her). Biographical and ethical studies of Maurin tend to treat the poetry as an adjunct to his life and philosophy, to be mined for illustrative quotes rather than closely analyzed. By contrast, I am interested in Maurin's life and philosophy primarily as they illuminate his technique. I've chosen to call his writings his poems to emphasize his writerly craft, even though he called them "phrased essays" or "easy essays." If Maurin's adjective "phrased" suggests that the pieces push what T. S. Eliot once called "the borderline of prose," his noun "essays" accents their philosophical content rather than their poetic form. By reading Maurin as a poet, I read him against the grain of his own self-understanding. But such a reading might help us to appreciate his achievement as a *literary* Christian leftist.[8]

The subordination of Maurin's poems to his life makes some sense given their distribution as gifts. Sociological theorists of gift exchange point out that gifts carry the personality of the giver with them.[9] Personal presence was the keystone of Maurin's practical philosophy, which he called "personalism."[10] All three planks of his social "program of action" depended upon it (Day, "Maurin's Program"). At "roundtable discussions for clarification of thought," people met face-to-face to work through philosophical and political questions together. In "houses of hospitality," people living among the poor personally ministered to their needs. In "agronomic universities"—communal farms and study-centers—scholars and workers lived, farmed, and studied together. Maurin's bedrock principle of personal exchange made face-to-face gift distribution his favored channel for his writings.

Maurin's commitment to personal presence also complicated his attitude toward traditional publishing. When he first began writing, he was reluctant to publish his poems at all "because that crystallized what should be open to further clarification" (Ellis 35). By 1933, however, the desire to give his ideas a wider reach overwhelmed his qualms, and he began searching for Catholic publishers to print his poems. An editor at *Commonweal* connected him to Dorothy Day, and soon after they "broadcasted his ideas through the new medium" of the *Catholic Worker* newspaper (Day, "On Peter Maurin" 42). Through the paper, Maurin and Day sought to extend Peter's personal presence, rather than depersonalize his message. Putting their antimodern personalist message into the modern mass medium required some modifications to the newspaper form. The *Catholic Worker*, as published in New York in the 1930s, looked different from other papers. Where you might expect to find cartoons or photographs, for instance, the Workers printed woodcut icons of saints dressed as modern working people.[11] Picking up an issue of the paper was almost like picking up one of Maurin's castoff overcoats, each column a pocket filled with some unexpected, and potentially holy, thing.

If Maurin's personalism influenced his publishing practices, it also definitively shaped his poetics. Maurin proclaims his commitment to Catholic tradition in a startlingly original style. He praises the Middle Ages in the plainest of modern speech—the vernacular English the Frenchman learned only as an adult. His rural peasant roots sprout up through cracks in metropolitan concrete. His poems give form to an imagination shaped by his period of discernment with and departure from a monastic community, his experience in turn-of-the-twentieth-century French Social Catholicism, and his midlife conversion to a Franciscan ethic of voluntary poverty. Ultimately, Peter Maurin forged a distinctive poetic voice by adapting the ideology and style of fin-de-siècle French Social Catholicism to the twentieth-century American urban vernacular.

Maurin was born in a village in the Languedoc region of southern France in 1877. One of twenty-four children, he lived a traditional peasant life on his family's ancestral farm. He grew up on a rustic diet chiefly of vegetables and cured pork and bread baked in the village's communal oven (Day, *The Long Loneliness* 176). Later, his course took him to wealthy Paris suburbs, to the Canadian wilderness, and finally to the New World megalopolises of Chicago and New York City. But village life was never far from his mind. "I was always interested in the land and man's life on the land," he told Day ("On Peter Maurin" 4). His agrarian and communitarian criticisms of isolated urban capitalist existence grew out of this early farm experience. In his Languedoc childhood, Maurin lived a form of life still in touch with the Middle Ages at the edges of the modern world.

As a young man, Maurin sought a vocation that would enable him to bring the medievalesque peasant life of his childhood into the modern world in a new and durable form. He hoped to reconnect the immiserated industrial proletariat to Christ and to the land. Maurin spent five years discerning a vocation with the Lasallian Christian Brothers, a monastic order devoted to teaching and building schools. Though he left the novitiate without becoming a Brother, he always remained an educator. He repeatedly indoctrinated Dorothy Day and many other Catholic Workers in "a Catholic outline of history" and in the three-part social program he trumpeted in person and published in the paper (Day, *The Long Loneliness* 172). Maurin's poems likewise take a frankly instructive tone. Day attributed their technique of repetition, on which I expand below, to his pedagogical training. Peter "was the kind of teacher who believed in repetition, restatement, and the continual return to first principles," she recalled ("On Peter Maurin" 5).

After leaving the Christian Brothers, Maurin found his footing among the writers, activists, philosophers, and cranks of turn-of-the-twentieth-century French Social Catholicism. This "romantic milieu" featured a wealth of strong personalities, including "the bourgeoisie-hating 'ungrateful beggar and author,' Léon Bloy; the Maritains, Jacques and Raissa, who dramatically converted on the brink of carrying out a double suicide pact; [Charles] Péguy; and later Gabriel Marcel" and Emmanuel Mounier (Fisher 44).[12] Two generations of French Christian thinkers bristling with manifestos, they presented a challenging aspect of radical holiness. Bloy refused to work; the Maritains lived in a celibate marriage; Péguy published long righteous screeds against his ideological enemies and died a martyr's death on the battlefield early in World War I. In their extremities, each of these representative Social Catholics followed medieval exemplars. Bloy strove to become a beggar-saint in the mold of Francis of Assisi (only more irascible). In his numerous philosophical works, Jacques Maritain recapitulated the thought of Thomas Aquinas for the modern world. Péguy folded his passions for nationalism, Socialism, and Catholic mysticism into his devotion to Joan of Arc.[13]

In many respects, Maurin was cut from the same cloth as these writers. But he was attracted to the democratic rather than the reactionary side of Social Catholicism. Maurin worked for five years for Marc Sangnier's Le Sillon (The Furrow), a movement that attempted to integrate Christianity with the French Republican tradition (Ellis 25–28). Among other duties, Maurin helped to distribute Le Sillon's newspaper. In its educational and political aims, Sangnier's group foreshadows the American Catholic Workers. As Le Sillon increasingly emphasized political over spiritual goals—a shift that earned it a papal condemnation in 1910—Maurin became disenchanted with the movement. By 1908, he was adrift (28–29). His mandatory French military service loomed. Unlike the martial Péguy, Maurin was a confirmed pacifist. To escape the requirement, he left for Canada to join a homesteading project in rural Saskatchewan (29–30).

It was in North America that Maurin made his own romantic move toward radical holiness. After his homesteading partner died in an accident,

Maurin, "still speaking only French," came to the United States in 1911 (Ellis 31). Over the next twenty years, he lived as an itinerant laborer, working a succession of manual jobs across the country, with the exception of one crucial period. In the early 1920s, he achieved a comfortable level of prosperity working as a French teacher in Chicago (33). In 1925, he moved his teaching practice to upstate New York. Soon after, he underwent a religious conversion (34). He never spoke about this experience directly, though his close associates recognized it as the crux of his vocation (Sheehan 83). Apparently motivated by the example of Saint Francis of Assisi, Maurin ceased to accept payment for teaching or any other labor, though he did accept return gifts of food, clothing, and shelter (Ellis 35). He involved himself in labor activism and began composing his phrased essays for delivery at radical meetings. Eventually he found work as caretaker of a Catholic boys' camp in return for room and board. On the weekends, he came down to Manhattan, where he harangued listeners in Union Square and slept in Bowery flophouses (35–44). He was living in this manner when he met Dorothy Day in 1933, and together they launched the *Catholic Worker.*

When he arrived in Canada in 1909, Maurin spoke not a word of English. Twenty years later, he composed his life's work as a writer in his adoptive language. The residue of his history as a French speaker and adult English learner always clung to Maurin's English, though it was fluent and stylized. Even after almost forty years in America, his heavy Languedoc accent, Day noted, made him difficult for other New Yorkers to understand (Day, "On Peter Maurin" 37). This accent shaped the form of his poetry, which was originally composed for spoken delivery, not written publication. Maurin's "short phrased lines" allowed him to pause frequently for breath (Day, Foreword 7). This afforded him maximum clarity and power when speaking in loud radical meetings or in outdoor public settings like Union Square. In this light, I understand Maurin's short lines as experiments in form determined by breath, a staple source of innovation in modern American poetry at least since Whitman's long line. Speaking these short phrased lines in loud public places, Maurin had to keep the ears of his listeners despite his frequent pauses. So he packed each line with jokes, puns, and wordplay. Often these devices play out across breaks in lines that are end-stopped or only subtly enjambed. In this way, they carry the listener from line to line despite the frequent pauses in which he was vulnerable to shouting-down. The constraints of his situation as a second-language speaker in loud public fora helped to shape his distinctive poetic voice.

COMMUNION OF RADICALS

Maurin's short line and skillful wordplay feature prominently in the following excerpt, taken from a piece called "Legalized Usury" Maurin delivered orally at a Catholic Worker "Round Table Discussion" at the Manhattan Lyceum in 1933 and subsequently printed in the *Catholic Worker* newspaper:

> Two years ago, I went to see Professor Moley,[14]
>> Former head of President Roosevelt's Brain Trust,
>> and said to him:
>> "I came here to find out
>> if I could make an impression on the depression
>> by starting a rumpus on the Campus.
>> But I found out
>> that agitation is not rampant on the Campus.
>> Only business is rampant on the Campus.
>> May be, said I
>> history cannot be made on the Campus.
> And turning toward his secretary, Professor Moley said:
>> "That's right, we don't make history on the Campus,
>> we only teach it."
>> And because history is taught but not made
>> on the Campus of our Universities,
>> THE CATHOLIC WORKER is trying
>> to make history on Union Square,
>> where people have nothing to lose. (lines 1–19)

Maurin constructs the poem through opposition and parallelism, near-parallels, and parallels with a difference. Even its prosy opening implicitly (and when delivered in person, explicitly) opposes Maurin to Moley, *M* vs. *M*, to point up the contrast between the shabby provocateur and the academic bigwig. An irregular metrical rhythm kicks in at line 5 with "*im*pression on the *de*pression," a formulation echoed by "rumpus on the Campus" and "rampant on the Campus." The repetition of syllables in "impression" and "depression," "rumpus" and "Campus," highlights the opposite meanings of the nouns: the hopeful impression made by the agitator contrasts the desperate depression of the economy, as the boisterous rumpus contrasts the sedate campus. The alliteration and assonance of *Campus* of our *Universities/Catholic* Worker, *Union* Square at lines 16–18 cut to the heart of the poem's otherwise implicit

88

message: the Catholic Worker movement is actually an educational institution, in parallel opposition to the university. The movement offered a rumpus education, not a campus education—one founded upon agitation rather
than business, for making history rather than studying history, led by a Maurin rather than a Moley. Here we can see Maurin carrying forward a teaching
vocation like that of the Christian Brothers, in the Catholic Worker rumpus
where "scholars must become workers so the workers may be scholars" (Maurin, *The Green Revolution* 27).

Despite its rhetorical density, "Legalized Usury" is not a difficult poem at
the level of words or sentences.[15] It represents the speech of a common person for common people. Maurin incorporates into the poem the slang words
("rumpus") and everyday American idioms ("nothing to lose"), of which he was
notoriously fond (Day, "On Peter Maurin" 20). In another education-themed
poem, Maurin makes his commitment to vernacular language explicit, attrib-
uting the principle to that most American of writers, Ralph Waldo Emerson:

> [E]ternal principles
> must at all times
> be presented
> in the vernacular
> of the man on the street.
> Emerson says
> that the way
> to acquire the vernacular
> of the man of the street
> is to go to the street
> and listen
> to the man of the street.
> The way to become dynamic
> and cease to be academic
> is to rub shoulders
> with the men on the street.
>
> ("Agronomic Universities," lines 9–20, in *The Green Revolution* 127)

The Catholic Worker rumpus was to be a site of dynamic education in religious agitation—an education for the working class offered by a working-
class pedagogue.

When Dorothy Day wrote, near the end of Maurin's life, that "Peter is a Frenchman (for those of you who do not know him) and a peasant, and he has his own way of saying things," she summed up the language and class determinants of Maurin's style ("On Peter Maurin" 28). At the same time, she acknowledged that those very constraints helped to produce his unique voice. "The content of Peter Maurin's program was not original" but drawn from a host of medieval and modern social thinkers (Novitsky 87). Maurin always telegraphed this. He often set others' ideas (especially those of Eric Gill and Jacques Maritain) in his phrased essay form. His goal was to articulate "a philosophy so old that it looks like new" (Maurin, *The Green Revolution* 83). This observation about content also applies at the level of form. Many of his poetic tricks are rhetorical commonplaces, devices attested from antiquity. But they feel strange in modern writing—so old they sound like new.

Beyond his old-new originality, Day also gestured to something else in Maurin's language, something more affective, perhaps more fundamental. In addition to the concentrated rhetoric of the propagandist and the class-conscious diction of the agitator, I hear pleasure in Peter Maurin's unmistakable voice, "his own way of saying things." The delight of linguistic discovery, as experienced by someone learning the language even as he wrote in it, expresses itself in the irrepressible humor of the verse.

Maurin's style also testifies to his mysticism. Fisher contends that "Maurin's essays and sayings often resembled Zen koans; he loved puns and American idioms, and used language to suggest a mode of consciousness beyond the reach of ordinary discourse" (Fisher 36). Yet Maurin's "puns" and idiomatic expressions were the very stuff of "ordinary discourse." They are not difficult to decipher. And just because these linguistic building blocks are ordinary, "the vernacular of the man on the street," Maurin found them fit, when arranged in his characteristic way, to express "eternal principles."[16] Maurin's mysticism is emphatically sacramental in its perception of spiritual meaning in and through the ordinary—in this case, through ordinary language.

What sets Maurin's appropriation of ordinary discourse apart from ordinary discourse itself is his ceaseless repetition. This style led some readers, including Day, to compare him to Charles Péguy (Day, Foreword 7). Though he knew Péguy's work, Maurin disclaimed any direct influence from or acquaintance with the man (Day, *The Long Loneliness* 177). Nevertheless, Maritain, who knew both men well, wrote to Maurin, after he visited the Catholic Worker in November 1934, that "it seemed as if I had found again in the

Catholic Worker a little of the atmosphere of Peguy's office in the Rue de la Sorbonne" (qtd. in Ellis 79).[17]

In a recent essay on Péguy, the French philosopher and anthropologist of modernity Bruno Latour connects Péguy's repetitive style to his polemical campaign against "the temporal power of capitalism" ("Charles Péguy" 51).[18] Capitalism, according to Latour, "nullifies the discontinuity of time . . . by making us believe that what will happen in the future is already so determined by the past that we can always calculate its *yield*" (51). The model for this "temporal logic" is compound interest: "a bank savings account . . . causes the past to be propelled toward the future like a ball rolling down an inclined plane" (51). Against the capitalist temporality that joins past and future by skipping over the present, Péguy appeals to the Christian dogma of the Incarnation. This inscription of the eternal into the temporal, of God made into a human being—paradigmatic in its historical uniqueness—insists on what Latour calls "the irreducible hiatus of the present" (54–55). The Incarnation allows Péguy to think in terms of the repleteness of the now, rather than a future rate of return.

It was in his poetic style, "*by means of repetition alone,*" that Péguy "was able to communicate the hiatus of the present for the time-dimension of the world," Latour argues (56). Yet he maintains that Péguy's repetitions do philosophical, and not only stylistic, work; repetition is no mere "effect" but a "concept generated by style" that makes it "possible to inhabit an entirely different space-time from the rest of the moderns" (57). In an earlier piece on Péguy, Latour describes in greater detail just how repetition forces this temporal rift:

> An author who does not repeat himself short of one phrase or another, in a progressive fashion, heals over transitions, and imposes in this way upon the reader the image of a temporal flow or of a movement of meaning that proceeds straight through from the beginning to the end. An author who repeats himself suspends this movement, deflects this current, and weakens the confidence habitually put in the temporal framework of progress. Further, if he repeats arguments and restarts incessantly, he produces an effect of breathlessness and restlessness, specifically to serve other purposes than those of the world of representation. ("Pourquoi Péguy se répète-t-il?" 2, my translation)[19]

According to Latour, Péguy's repetition disrupts the effortless flow of the past into the future demanded by the temporality of compound interest. His sentences confront the reader with a nonprogressive "temporal framework"; their syntax argues that thinking in terms of progress is no more inevitable than progress itself. Péguy's style in this way forces an existential confrontation with the present.

Latour's analysis of Péguy leads me to read *Maurin*'s kindred repetitive style as a poetics of present confrontation, just as his personalism is a philosophy of that confrontation—a theory for the practice of shared personal presence with the poor and suffering in space and time. By reordering ordinary discourse, Maurin challenges the assumptions about time that structure ordinary discourse. He frustrates the smoothly consequent progression from one item to another that Latour identifies as the syntactical form of the temporal logic of the bank account. At the level of style, Maurin's poetry argues that the past does not inevitably determine the future, that causes can be unraveled, that the history of capitalism's rise can be rewritten.

"Big Shots and Little Shots," first published on May Day 1934, is Maurin's tour de force of repetition:

1. America is all shot to pieces
    since the little shots
    are no longer able
    to become big shots.

2. When the little shots
    are not satisfied
    to remain little shots
    and try to become
    big shots,
    then the big shots
    are not satisfied
    to remain big shots
    and try to become
    bigger shots.

3. And when the big shots
    become bigger shots
    then the little shots
    become littler shots.

4. And when the little shots
    become littler shots

> because the big shots
> become bigger shots,
> then the little shots
> get mad at the big shots.
>
> 5. And when the little shots
> get mad at the big shots
> because the big shots
> by becoming bigger shots
> make the little shots
> littler shots
> they shoot the big shots
> full of little shots.
>
> 6. But by shooting the big shots
> full of little shots
> the little shots
> do not become big shots;
> they make everything all shot.
>
> 7. And I don't like
> to see the little shots
> shoot the big shots
> full of little shots,
> that is why
> I am trying to shoot
> both the big shots
> and the little shots
> full of hot shots. (lines 1–46)

This is Maurin's authorial mission statement—his *ars poetica*—and the single best example of his style of "logic with cracks" (Day, "Background for Peter Maurin" 7).[20] The line breaks mark pauses for breath, and they hammer home, visually and aurally, the repetition of "shots." The mesmerizing alternation of "big shots" and "little shots" waxes both ridiculous and sublime: the poem feels like a slang litany. But the ceaseless univocal repetition of these phrases in the first five stanzas builds a weight of significance behind the moment when their meaning shifts. Structurally, the poem turns on the antanaclasis (repeating the same word but changing the meaning) at line 32, where the "little shots" of the proletariat metamorphose into bullets. It turns for last time at line 43, where Maurin's rhetorical shooting emerges as the pacifist alternative to violent class warfare. When the poem's punch line trades little shots and big shots for Maurin's poetic "hot shots," its form clicks into place with all the finality of a Shakespearean sonnet's ending couplet.

If such repetition was the form Maurin's "Catholic outline of history" took, medievalism defined its historical content (Day, *The Long Loneliness* 172). By means of his repetitive "Easy Essays," Maurin indoctrinated his listeners and readers into a narrative inimical to the progressive story of capitalism. Medievalism in the Catholic Worker movement and in the transnational Catholic Left more generally provided an interpretation of history on which to base a critique of modernity. The "Easy Essay" appearing in the inaugural issue of the *Catholic Worker* under the title "Wealth-Producing Maniacs" exemplifies the historiographical importance of medievalism for the Catholic Workers:

1. When John Calvin legalized money lending at interest, he made the bank account the standard of values.
2. When the bank account became the standard of values, people ceased to produce for use and began to produce for profit.
3. When people began to produce for profit, they became wealth-producing maniacs.
4. When people became wealth-producing maniacs, they produced too much wealth.
5. When people found out that they had produced too much wealth, they went on an orgy of wealth destruction and destroyed ten million lives besides.
6. And fifteen years after a world-wide orgy of wealth and life destruction, millions of people find themselves victims of a world-wide depression brought about by a world gone mad on mass production and mass distribution.[21]

The tightly interlocking syntax of these stanzas lends a feeling of inevitability to Maurin's historical narrative, linking the schism of the Reformation to the twentieth-century catastrophes of World War I and the Great Depression. But Maurin was no historical determinist. Rather than a causal interpretation of history, Maurin offers a figural interpretation of history, much like Auden's postwar typology of crumbling empire.

When Maurin looked back to Calvin's legalization of usury, he didn't exactly see the primary historical cause of the Great Depression of the 1930s United States. He didn't even necessarily impugn Calvin's motives for acting as he did. Instead, Maurin saw a historical type of which the Depression was but the latest antitype—a promise of social degradation that found one eventual and partial fulfillment in the seeming collapse of the liberal capitalist world order in the 1930s. The cultural results of Calvin's legalization of usury were never assured; and in fact, Maurin's ultimate goal in relating this historical narrative is to undo its consequences. But in New York City in 1933, Maurin believed he could see the inherent potentialities of Calvin's act anew, glimpsing within time another piece of the eternal meaning of this "fragmentary earthly event" (Auerbach, *Mimesis* 74).

On the streets of Chicago and New York City, Maurin's French medievalist sensibility picked up new influences in his new language. Along with the American slang he incorporated into his poetry, Maurin also engaged deeply with Anglophone religious intellectuals. He often published digests, in phrased essay form, of their works in the *Catholic Worker*. These connections fix his crucial place in the literary history of American Christian leftism. In his "Easy Essays," Maurin quotes the nineteenth-century British social prophets—Carlyle, Ruskin, and William Morris—so dear to Vida Scudder. To help translate his vision into the twentieth-century American vernacular, Maurin also incorporated voices from the American tradition of social idealism, from the Puritans to Emerson (*The Green Revolution* 127, 202). Maurin likewise drew upon American antimodernist intellectuals including Henry Adams, the Nashville Agrarians, and Ralph Adams Cram. "Back to Christ!—Back to the Land!," first published in the November 1935 *Catholic Worker*, argues for farm communes as an antidote to the ills of industrialism (1, 8). The poem quotes from a wide variety of sources, including Carlyle, Gill, Cram, and the southern novelist and essayist Andrew Lytle. Maurin appended a recommended reading list to the piece, as he often did; this one includes the Twelve Southerners' *I'll Take My Stand* (1930) ("Back to Christ!" 8). This same poem appeals to Lenin, Gandhi, and another person identified only as "a Chinese," according them the same authority as Cram, Lytle, Carlyle, and Gill. Cram—and Lytle, too—would have been scandalized to keep such company. But the pockets of Maurin's overcoat joined strange members to the Mystical Body, their disparate insights held together by the intensity and catholicity of his vision.

In May 1934, this catholicity of vision led Maurin to take the Catholic

Worker uptown to Harlem (Ellis 82). In a donated storefront on Seventh Avenue, he launched an educational outpost to counter the growing Communist influence in the Black Metropolis. Maurin displayed a Black Madonna in the window, recruited Black speakers, and held classes on French, art, theology, and personalist agitation. In the Harlem context, Maurin appealed especially to the example and theology of the North African bishop and Doctor of the Church, Saint Augustine of Hippo (83–84). Despite these efforts, the Harlem branch of the Catholic Worker never gained much traction. When World War II approached, a patriotic landlord kicked the pacifist Maurin back to the Bowery (86). As quixotic and short-lived as some Catholic Worker farming communes, the Harlem experiment was vintage Maurin.

Yet Maurin's hope for a Harlem beachhead of Catholic action did not remain disappointed for long. In 1938, the Jesuit priest and racial justice activist John La Farge invited the Russian émigré Catherine de Hueck to establish a house of hospitality in Harlem (Karen Johnson 55). De Hueck's Toronto-based Friendship House apostolate, allied but not formally affiliated with the Catholic Workers, had opened several such houses in Canada before conservative pressures forced them to close. The Harlem Friendship House would go on to minister to Claude McKay, Jamaican-born sonneteer and Afromodernist novelist, in a time of great need. McKay's contact with Friendship House workers helped to facilitate his eventual conversion to Catholicism. Soon after, his sonnets appeared alongside Maurin's "Easy Essays" in the pages of the *Catholic Worker*.

"DARK LIKE ME": CLAUDE MCKAY'S BLACK MEDIEVALISM

Claude McKay was in a bad way when, in 1942, his friend Ellen Tarry found him alone in his Harlem apartment. A terrible case of the flu, complicated by his long-standing high blood pressure, congestive heart failure, and poverty, had left him unable to care for himself (Cooper, *Rebel Sojourner* 351). A proud man, McKay would not reach out for help. He had alienated many former allies in years of intellectual combat and, contrary to his pride, by repeatedly asking them for money. In such straits, Tarry, an African American journalist and writer of children's books, was a good person to have in his corner. A devout Catholic laywoman, she called on her fellow volunteers at de Hueck's Harlem Friendship House to help nurse McKay back to health. He "was grateful for the help, and he was extremely impressed that they offered their assistance without asking him to accept their religion" (351). Neverthe-less, these Catholics made an impression on a weary sojourner longing for community. By June 1943, McKay wrote to Mary Jerdo Keating, a white Cath-olic intellectual friend he had met at Friendship House, that he was consid-ering joining the Church. "I am quite aware that my act would be of more so-cial than of religious meaning, if you can differentiate between both," McKay hedged (357). He went on to compare his motivations to those of "T. S. Eliot, who became an Anglo-Catholic from purely intellectual and social reasons" (357). But McKay, like Eliot, found it finally impossible to differentiate the religious and the intellectual and social, especially as his health continued to deteriorate.

On June 25, 1943, just ten days after writing to Keating, McKay "suffered a disabling stroke while on the job" as a riveter at the federal shipyard in Port Newark (Cooper, *Rebel Sojourner* 356). Friends had warned him off the phys-ically demanding work, but McKay took the job anyway. After his hospital-ization, Keating and her husband put McKay up in their Connecticut cottage to recover. He lived there through the summer and into the fall, mulling over his religious questions and working up his venomous sonnet sequence "The Cycle" (357–58). While never published as a whole in his lifetime, some of these poems eventually appeared in the *Catholic Worker*. Through the Keat-ings, a partially recovered McKay secured a research position with the activ-ist Bishop Bernard Sheil in Chicago, where he moved in April 1944 (359–60). Along with de Hueck and, for a time, Tarry, the Keatings had moved to Chi-cago to establish a Friendship House there. The Catholic Workers already had a house in Chicago as well. In these circles, McKay joined a vibrant, if not always harmonious, community devoted to interracial, anticapitalist Catho-lic action (Karen Johnson 55–64). He began taking instruction from local priests. Months later, McKay announced his conversion in a letter to Max Eastman: "On October 11, 1944, the Feast of the Maternity of the Blessed Virgin Mary, I was baptised into the Catholic (Roman) Faith" (Cooper, *Pas-sion* 304).[22]

A few weeks after his baptism, Day reconnected with McKay and invited him to a Christmas retreat at the Catholic Worker farm in Easton, Pennsyl-vania (Cooper, *Passion* 306). It is likely that McKay met Peter Maurin at this retreat, as Maurin had been living primarily at the farm since the summer of 1938, and he continued to live there at least through the winter of 1945 (Ellis 123, 159). But McKay was most struck by the changed religious aspect of his old friend Day. He described her to Eastman as "something like a saint" and floated the idea of profiling her for the Socialist and anti-Communist magazine *New Leader* (Cooper, *Passion* 306–7). It is no wonder if Maurin made less of an impression. By this point, he was but a shell of the fiery agitator who had held court in Union Square in 1933. Returning to him in October 1944 after a sabbatical, Day determined that Maurin had suffered a stroke in the preceding months (Ellis 159). Dispossessed at last, he began to forget his "Easy Essays." In January 1945, Maurin handed in a few more pages and announced that he was finished writing for good (160).

Their mutual endurance of strokes and subsequent physical (and in Maurin's case, mental) deterioration were but the final acts in the parallel lives of Maurin and McKay. Both men grew up in contact with agrarian peasant societies that indelibly shaped their mature imaginations. The communal life of his native Languedoc was always the implicit background of Maurin's agrarian leftism. Similarly, McKay often hymned the simplicity of rural Jamaica from his later urban vantages. He was to return to the landscape of his childhood one last time in his final autobiographical manuscript, "My Green Hills of Jamaica."[23] Both men lived itinerant transnational lives that braided together improvised labor, political activism, and literary production. Both increasingly depended on others' generosity for their livelihood—Maurin willingly, McKay unwillingly. And both underwent religious conversions as adults. These profound experiences spurred each man to write a body of social-critical poetry published primarily in the *Catholic Worker*.

In these postconversion poems, McKay develops what I call a "Black medievalism." McKay revises Catholic Worker medievalist discourse to better account for the concerns of Black people, as he had done with radical ideologies throughout his career. Through this medieval imagery, McKay also reworked his relationship to history—his own spiritual history as well as the history of civilizations. This Black medievalism was far from a tired radical's coming to rest in the comforts of tradition. McKay joined his voice to a chorus of Catholic leftists from many nations who expressed their criticisms of modern society—in its capitalist and fascist as well as Communist forms—and their hopes for future brotherhood in medievalist strains. This idiom, radical yet committed to tradition, was a strangely compelling fit for a political poet whose combinations of Marxism and Black nationalism had long fired his skepticism toward progressive schemes for human betterment.

McKay's late poems have not always received the critical scrutiny these fas-

THE CATHOLIC WORKER MOVEMENT AND THE CHALLENGE OF PLURALISM

cinating documents deserve. Indeed, assessments of McKay's late career can be charged with a whiff of suspicion that his religious conversion marks his intellectual expiration date, a slackening of aesthetic standards or a diminution of poetic powers for which religion is either to blame or for which it succors the aging writer. Here we can feel the implicit pressure of secularization theory on literary criticism: one narrative shape readily available for describing the career of a poet who undergoes adult conversion is that the convert poet backslides, lapses, falls away from the thrust of secular progress. Or at least that is how McKay's critics have sometimes read him.[24]

McKay's longtime friend and editor Max Eastman (1883–1969), a strident secularist, set the tone for this influential strain of reception when he scolded McKay in a letter: "All these years, at such cost and with such heroism, you resisted the temptation to warp your mind and morals in order to join the Stalin church. Why warp it the other way now for the Catholics? Why not die firm, free and intelligent as you have lived?" (Cooper, *Rebel Sojourner* 360). In the same letter, Eastman analogized McKay's conversion to his deteriorating health, lamenting that his friend should come to "so sick a finish," intellectually and politically as well as physically. As editor, Eastman would go on to keep most of McKay's Catholic poetry out of the *Selected Poems*, published posthumously in 1953, and to erase McKay's conversion from the biographical note he wrote for the volume. Since Eastman, critics have weaved a thorny nest of questions around these Catholic poems about how McKay's ill health, poverty, and often-paranoid opposition to Communism in the 1940s bear on the sincerity of his newfound religious beliefs (Deshmukh 149). As a result, it can be difficult to separate critical evaluations of McKay's late poetry from critical judgments on his religious conversion.

Lately, however, this has begun to change. The *Complete Poems* (2004), published in the University of Illinois Press's American Poetry Recovery Series and edited by William J. Maxwell, made McKay's Catholic poetry widely accessible, complete with in-depth commentary, for the first time. In his introduction, Maxwell acknowledges the continuities as well as the changes in McKay's outlook after his conversion: "McKay's turn to Catholicism, though prodded by [a] paranoid anticommunism developed in the late 1930s, was no negation of a life of political insurgency," as McKay continued to "mix socialism and anti-imperialism into his censure of the godless Soviet Union" (McKay, *Complete Poems* xxv). Madhuri Deshmukh's 2014 *Callaloo* article "Claude McKay's Road to Catholicism" paves the way for a wholesale revaluation of McKay's late career. "Critics have been wary, to say the least, of Mc-Kay's final conversion to Catholicism" Deshmukh charges, "suspecting him of an intellectual abdication or exhausted rejection of his nomadic and radical youth" (148–49). Unlike these critics, however, Deshmukh finds that McKay's Catholicism provided him a steady base for the enchanted anticapitalism of his formal poetry: "The need for Church dogma, Church doctrine, to help mediate one's way in the world is akin to the need for traditional poetic form. Both provide structure, moderation, and the wisdom of the past to help organize the teeming disorder of the modern present" (164–65). To this I would add that McKay saw traditional forms primarily as his own peculiarly lawful form of lawlessness; meter and rhyme were his vehicles for revolution. In the author's note to his 1922 collection *Harlem Shadows*, McKay explains his seemingly anachronistic attachment to formal poetry this way: "I have adhered to such of the older traditions as I find adequate for my most lawless and revolutionary passions and moods" (xx). Such a revolutionary spirit would not be subject even to the expectation that a truly modern poet would write in free verse. McKay's Catholic poems maintain this penchant for rebellious traditionalism and take it in a new, medievalist direction.

I build on this ongoing revaluation of the late Catholic McKay by proposing that we understand the Black medievalism of his postconversion poetry as the surprising fruition of his career, rather than a regrettable slip from secular leftist militancy.[25] By "fruition," I don't mean a providential enfolding that gathers all of McKay's life to its inevitable conclusion, as if no other outcome were possible than his ending as a Catholic apologist in verse. McKay made his leap to faith as a Roman Catholic with a deep awareness of the historical and geographical contingency that conditioned the process, as I will demonstrate. Rather, McKay saw fragments of his past—and of the past writ large—blossom into partial fulfillment in his final, Catholic phase. I aim to illuminate how what Tracy Fessenden calls "the patterning of secular time"—a linear and progressive movement from a full religious past to a diminished religious present—has shaped the way we narrate writers' lives, and to offer an alternative mode of narration (Fessenden 157).[26]

Writing under conditions of exile both geographical and spiritual, McKay's late works embody a kind of politically committed, worldly religiosity we can better understand in the wider context of the literary Christian Left. The *Catholic Worker* published most of Claude McKay's late poetry that saw the light of day in his lifetime. This body of work witnesses that McKay's late reconciliation with God left him all the more unreconciled to the great race and class injustices of his time. In his 1922 volume *Harlem Shadows*, McKay had employed "old . . . poetically overworked and dead" words whenever he "could make them glow alive by new manipulation" (*Harlem Shadows* xxi). In his late poems, McKay took up medievalist tropes that had wide currency in the discourse of the transnational Catholic Left he joined with his conversion, and he newly manipulated this medievalist discourse to engage anti-Black racism.

The most concentrated example of McKay's Black medievalism is his sonnet "The Middle Ages," published in the *Catholic Worker* on May Day 1946.

> The Middle Ages which they say were dark
> Like me, were lit up with Thy grace, oh Lord!
> And rare with music like a singing lark
> Rising with notes of Thy divinest word!
> Averrhoes, Aquinas and Maimonides,
> Mohammedan and Christian and Jew,
> Interpreted the richness of their creeds,
> Thy Church brooding over all points of view,
>
> Like a grand tree, rooted in faith supreme,
> Its glory and its strength protecting all,
> Illuminating earth with heaven's beam
> Of the Brotherhood of Man without the Fall!
> Hermits and princes, men with wisdom's rods
> With which they walked abroad and talked to gods.

The stunning enjambment of the first two lines—"dark / Like me"—dramatizes the collision of medievalist speech with McKay's Black body: not the poet's persona, his lyric "I," but the poet-as-object (like *me*), the poet's body. By cribbing a line from Langston Hughes's well-known poem "Dream Variations" (1926), McKay also suggests continuity between the different stages of his career as bellicose troubadour of Harlem's Renaissance and Catholic neomedievalist: McKay's Black medievalism remixes the Renaissance dynamic of historical recovery.[27]

Under the black-letter Gothic script of its title, the first line of "The Middle Ages" could be announcing an abstract defense of the medieval against the moderns' chronological snobbery—the sort of defense that Peter Maurin undertook time and again in the pages of the *Catholic Worker* (see fig. 5). But

---

The Middle Ages

THE Middle Ages which they say were dark
Like me, were lit up with Thy grace, oh Lord!
'And rare with music like a singing lark
Rising with notes of Thy divinest word!
'Averrhoes, Aquinas and Maimonides,
Mohammedan and Christian and Jew,
Interpreted the richness of their creeds,
Thy Church brooding over all points of view,

Like a grand tree, rooted in faith supreme,
Its glory and its strength protecting all,
Illuminating Earth with Heaven's beam
Of the Brotherhood of Man without the Fall!
Hermits and princes, men with wisdom's rods
With which they walked abroad and talked to gods.
                                        CLAUDE McKAY.

Fig. 5. McKay's "The Middle Ages" as it appeared in the *Catholic Worker*. Image courtesy of the Thomas Merton Center, Bellarmine University.

the poem's second line makes medievalism personal: dark are these ages, and beautiful in their darkness, as McKay's skin is beautiful—dark, "they say," with the presumption of ignorance, but in truth as bright with art and learning as a McKay lyric. (If there is a volta in this sonnet, it is here, between lines 1 and 2, rather than at the end of the octave or before the final couplet.) In the same breath, McKay unites two great prejudices of the enlightened rationalism of the modern white West—against the Catholic Middle Ages and against the supposedly savage Black body—and, by combining them, disposes of them simultaneously. Medievalism ought to imply antiracism, McKay suggests, and antiracism ought to occasion a second look at those purportedly dark Middle Ages.

Yet the lines' enjambment resists a too-quick assimilation of the plight of the Middle Ages to that of the Black body, instituting a visual and sonic rift between the two as well as a connection. McKay seems to be trying on a medievalist discourse, unsure whether it suits him. The remainder of the first quatrain comes too easily; the images of the light of grace and the ascending lark are conventional in the extreme, lacking any *Harlem Shadows*–style "new manipulation" to set them aglow. But things get interesting again at line 5, where a mouthful of philosophers tumbles out in an ungainly rhythm, breaking with the (mostly) iambic pentameter of the first quatrain. These names limn Mc-Kay's medieval vision, not of a unified Christian Europe, but of a multicultural Mediterranean.

McKay gives his readers Abrahamic "creeds," plural, and even, as the last word of the poem has it, multiple "gods." Twelfth-century contemporaries Averroës and Maimonides were both products of the Al-Andalus, the medieval Islamic empire that stretched from North Africa into present-day Spain, a fact McKay perhaps acknowledges by naming the "Mohammedan" philosopher first. Born in the Andalusian intellectual center of Cordova (Córdoba), each thinker spent considerable portions of their careers in North Africa (Seeskin; Hillier). McKay also lived in North Africa during "his mature expatriate decade, 1923–1933," as Maxwell notes—a choice he made under FBI pressure as well as out of his affinity for the place (McKay, *Complete Poems* xvii). A few months before he was baptized, McKay even confessed to Max Eastman that if he had "remained in Morocco," he "most certainly would have become a Moslem" (*Complete Poems* 384). Sensitive to exclusion based on race and political affiliation and alive to differences of culture and religion because of his travels, McKay shifts Catholic Worker medievalism into an insistently cultural-pluralist register in this sonnet.

But the poem also struggles to contain pluralism within Catholicism by putting the Church at both its center and its boundaries. "Aquinas" and "Christian" take the middle spot in the sonnet's list of philosophers and their creeds. This placement at once relativizes and accentuates the favored philosopher of Maritain. On the facing page, a fragment from the French Social Catholic poet Léon Bloy under the title "Spiritually We Are All Semites" appears in English translation as well (see fig. 6). Bloy insists on the Jewishness of the bodies of Jesus, Mary, and the apostles, and this insistence lights up McKay's invocation of the Jewish philosopher Maimonides. The rhetorical effect of juxtaposing McKay's text with Bloy's is complex; it acknowledges Jewish difference while also claiming a special Catholic kinship to the Jews. At the same time, it acknowledges a fraught but shared history of oppression and of sacred texts between Jews and African Americans. Together, these texts subtly assert Christian superiority by privileging Gentile Catholic thoughts *about* Jewishness over Jewish self-understandings. Yet McKay's cultural pluralism helped to push the *Catholic Worker's* reckoning with difference further within the frame of the paper's Catholic confessional commitment.

McKay's grappling with religious difference in "The Middle Ages" fits in

Spiritually, We Are All Semites

GOD'S WORD is enough for me. Even if all Jews—what an absurdity!—were rascals with the exception of one alone who would be righteous beneath the velamen, this single man would bear upon him the Promise, God's word of honor in its fullness and power, and nothing in it would be changed.

In addition, let me tell you that each morning I partake of the Body of a Jew named Jesus Christ, that I spend a part of my life at the feet of a Jewess whose heart was pierced and of whom I have made myself the slave, and finally that I have put my confidence in a band of Sheenies—as you call them—one offering the Lamb, another bearing the Keys of heaven, a third commissioned to teach every nation, etc., and I know that it is only with such feelings that one can be a Christian. Anything else one might say is trite and contingent and absolutely does not exist.

From "Le Pelerin de l'Absolu," by Leon Bloy.

Fig. 6. Léon Bloy's Catholic argument against French anti-Semitism in the Dreyfuss Affair era, here repurposed for a post–World War II American Catholic audience. Image courtesy of the Thomas Merton Center, Bellarmine University.

with, and advances, a larger pattern of Catholic Worker responses to the challenge of pluralism.[28] In articles published throughout the 1930s, Day sought to resolve the conflict between her religiously specific doctrinal commitments and her religiously plural cultural context by appealing to the idea of the Mystical Body of Christ: "We believe that we are all members or potential members of the mystical Body of Christ," Day wrote in a representative editorial. "*All* men are our brothers, Jew or Gentile, white or black, since God created us *all* and since His Son died to atone for the sins of *all* men. Since Christ is our Brother, *all* men are our brothers, the communist, fascist, the red baiter and the 'capitalist'" (Day, "Catholic Worker Celebrates" 1, emphasis in original). McKay also invoked the Mystical Body to at once resolve and suspend religious difference. In the same June 30, 1944, letter in which he admits to Max Eastman that he would have become a Muslim had he stayed in North Africa, McKay affirms his belief "in the mystery of the symbol of the Mystical

Body of Jesus Christ, through which all humanity may be united in brotherly love" (Cooper, *Rebel Sojourner* 361).

McKay's sonnet "The Middle Ages," however, imagines the corporeal Catholic Church, and not the Mystical Body of Christ, as the vehicle of universal reconciliation. A sheltering tree "brooding over all points of view," like a mother bird on her nest, McKay's idealized Church nurtures and protects religious intellectuals in their engagements with secular wisdom. (Averroës, Aquinas, and Maimonides are all known for synthesizing the teachings of their respective religious traditions with the philosophy of Aristotle.) But the idiomatic sense of "brooding" as melancholy thought unsettles the comforts of the matronly image; it recalls McKay's years of difficult seeking leading up to his conversion. The image of the brooding tree speaks less to any actually existing medieval society than to McKay's efforts to reconcile his attraction to the Church with his intellectual and material needs while recognizing the intractability of cultural differences. In a September 1946 letter, he reminds Eastman that "there is a formidable left wing within the Catholic church [*sic*] because it can accommodate all, even you" (Cooper, *Passion* 314). Whether or not the Church could truly accommodate all, writers in the *Catholic Worker*, from Day's early editorials onward, strove to imagine ways in which it could. McKay's poetic efforts to imagine a "Brotherhood of Man" went further than nearly all of his fraternal Catholic contemporaries.

McKay's medievalist turn, much like his primitivist appeal to rural Jamaican life, exemplifies a signature move in the discourse of the Black Atlantic that Deshmukh, drawing on Paul Gilroy, calls "a backward glance that carves out space for a critique of the modern present" (Deshmukh 163). But why, at this point in his career, would a specifically medievalist form of "backward glance" appeal to him? McKay had long been disillusioned with the optimistic progressivism that undergirded many leftist approaches to social change. But such skepticism toward progress doesn't necessarily imply affection for the premodern past.

During his expatriate decade, McKay's skepticism jostled with his excitement toward cosmopolitan modernity. In his 1929 novel *Banjo*, a work bristling with doubts about the cultural value of material progress, the Haitian-born intellectual Ray, usually taken as a spokesman for McKay, confesses that the grandeur of European Christendom leaves him unmoved. The port of Marseilles excites him only as a staging ground for a polyglot, kaleidoscopic profusion of international Blackness:

Here [in the Black crowd] for Ray was the veritable romance of Europe. This Europe that he had felt through the splendid glamour of history. When at last he did touch it, its effect on him had been a negative reaction. He had to go to books and museums and sacredly preserved sites to find the romance of it. Often in conversation he had politely pretended to a romance that he felt not. For it was America that was for him the living, hot-breathing land of romance. Its mighty business palaces, vast *depots* receiving and discharging hurrying hordes of humanity, immense cathedrals of pleasure, far-flung spans of steel roads and tumultuous traffic—the terrible buffalo-tramping crush of life, the raucous vaudeville mob-shouting of a newly-arrived nation of white throats, the clamor and clash of races and the grim-grubbing position of his race among them—all was a great fever in his brain, a rhythm of a pattern with the time-beat of his life, a burning, throbbing romance in his blood. (68–69)

Ray is no medievalist: the "sacredly-preserved sites" of the European Middle Ages leave him cold, whereas American "cathedrals of pleasure" ignite his desire in syntax that burns through clauses like prairie fire.

The one time Ray invokes the Middle Ages by name, in the other novel in which he appears, *Home to Harlem* (1928)—McKay's first—he does so in a thoroughly conventional manner, as the "other" of enlightened modernity. Ray visits Jake, *Home to Harlem*'s protagonist, a working-class African American driven by instinct and joie de vivre, when the latter is laid up with venereal disease. The intellectual castigates his rough-and-tumble friend for not using prophylactics: "This is a new age with new methods of living. You can't just go on like a crazy ram goat as if you were living in the Middle Ages." Jake replies: "Middle Ages! I ain't seen them yet and don't nevah wanta" (McKay, *Home to Harlem* 206). Yet this exchange finds Ray defending the sterility and safety of his educated modern perspective that, elsewhere in the book, he feels as a straitjacket. "Civilization is rotten. We are all rotten who are touched by it," Ray spits in words fit for a staunch medievalist like Cram (243). In their last conversation, Ray confesses to Jake: "You are happier than I as you are. The more I learn the less I understand and love life" (274). It is precisely Jake's naïve love, and perhaps even understanding, of life that Ray desires and envies in him. Naïveté, intuitive understanding, and a joyful embrace of life free from overintellectual anxiety are classically attributed to medieval life under the paradigm of conventional medievalist nostalgia, so it makes sense that Ray associates Jake with the Middle Ages. But just as Ray could not surrender his intellect, though it made him miserable, to take up Jake's spontaneous way of life, McKay would never have been able to embrace the unthinking comforts of mere nostalgia for the premodern condition.

In one essay about his conversion, McKay calls himself "a fanatic lover of the truth in history," and we can see this aspect of his personality reflected in the Ray of *Home to Harlem* as well ("Why I Became a Catholic" 32). In their first conversation on the train to Pittsburgh on which they're both working, Ray amazes Jake by telling him about the glories of African civilization and the courage of the Haitian Revolution; such historical knowledge is the liberating, rather than misery-making, part of Ray's education. Then Ray digs down beneath this scientific history to school Jake in sacred history, too, recounting the origins of Ethiopia's royal line in the ancient liaison between King Solomon of Israel and the Queen of Sheba, and of Ethiopia's later stature as the first Christian nation (*Home to Harlem* 131–37). Even in 1928, McKay's craving for historical truth would not be satisfied by scientific history alone; it also had a spiritual dimension. And this hunger was the deepest intellectual need sated by his conversion—which is not to say that historical truth, in a disciplinary sense, is exactly what he found. What McKay grasped was more like a satisfying historical myth.[29] Catholic Left medievalism supplied him a historiography that empowered social radicalism without buying into the pretensions of progress.

Alan Jacobs, in his recent study of Christian humanism during World War II, calls the intellectually elaborated form of medievalism that McKay encountered among Catholic leftists "the neo-Thomist account of modernity" (*The Year of Our Lord* 41). Jacques Maritain—French Social Catholic philosopher, friend and mentor to the Catholic Workers, and sometime expatriate in America—was its most important exponent. Jacobs summarizes the neo-Thomist story this way:

> The scholastic culture of the Middle Ages built an increasingly complex but also harmonious and orderly intellectual edifice that reached its greatest amplitude in the thought of Thomas Aquinas—the philosophical and theological equivalent of the great cathedrals of the period, especially Chartres. In Thomas, biblical and pagan wisdom found their unity and were set in right relation to each other. But this great achievement was soon undermined by the destructive philosophy of the nominalists (Duns Scotus, William of Ockham), which paved the way both for a revival of un-Christian paganism and for the anti-intellectual and egocentric enthusiasms of the Reformation. (40–41)[30]

Peter Maurin digested for a working-class audience precisely this narrative in the "Easy Essay" "Wealth-Producing Maniacs," bridging intellectual and economic history and pointing up in the process its contemporary political relevance. James Chappel reminds us that what was at stake in telling the neo-Thomist story in the 1930s and 1940s wasn't just scoring points in a philosophical debate but forming an antitotalitarian politics. Taking for his example Maritain's 1936 opus *Integral Humanism,* Chappel insists that the volume is more than a history of philosophical anthropology—of reflection on what it means to be human—since the High Middle Ages; it is also "a furiously antifascist, antiracist, and anticapitalist tract" (111). The neo-Thomist story of modernity was an engine of the Catholic Left's radicalism, including McKay's. In the *Catholic Worker,* his Aquinas-invoking sonnet "The Middle Ages" is printed directly above a translated excerpt from the *Summa theologica* condemning usury.

The Catholic critique of capitalist modernity founded on the neo-Thomist account, brought to fruition in late nineteenth-century France, and imported to the United States by Maritain, Maurin, and others, supplied McKay with a figural interpretation of history that rooted modern dysfunction in the Protestant Reformation. In his late manuscript "Right Turn to Catholicism," unpublished in his lifetime, McKay emphasizes the intuitive appeal of this interpretation of history: "As I continued to get enlightenment, it just flashed upon me that Agnosticism, Atheism, Modernism, Capitalism, State Socialism and State Communism were all children of the Pandora Box of Protestantism" ("Right Turn" 4).[31] But this old-school "new knowledge" was also shaped geographically by his years of expatriation and exile, "informed by my travelling in Europe and North Africa, especially in Spain. Spain appeared to me not only as a link between Africa and Europe, but also between Asia and Europe" (4). The Catholic McKay saw himself—much as he saw Spain—as a bridge not only between the West Indies and the United States, but also across the Atlantic and Mediterranean, spanning the New World, Africa, Asia, and Europe.[32] Perhaps most important, fraternal Catholic neo-Thomism also helped McKay bridge rifts inside himself. Its brainy medievalism helped McKay to reconcile primitivism and intellectualism—the sort of synthesis he had been looking for since *Home to Harlem*'s split between Jake and Ray and even earlier, in his shift from dialect to formal poetry.

From this new Catholic vantage, McKay judged that many of his racial fellows could stand to possess more fanatic love for the truth of sacred history. In his essay "Why I Became a Catholic," published as part of a feature on Black Catholics in *Ebony* magazine in 1946, McKay chides a largely Protestant African American audience for what he terms their ignorance "about the early growth and traditions of the Christian religion" and their "naive acceptance of the materialistic Protestant god of Progress" (32). McKay asserts that "like the Mohammedan religion today, there never was any race and color prejudice in the Roman Catholic Church from its beginning up until the Reformation"—a tendentious claim that nevertheless demonstrates his ongoing penchant for connecting Catholicism to Islam (32).

In such statements, McKay criticizes his Protestant brethren and, at the same time, revises the medievalism of the Catholic Left to better account for Black history and support Black struggle. McKay takes pains to highlight the role of people of color in pre-Reformation Christianity, recapitulating and amplifying the sort of church history lesson that Ray gives Jake in *Home to Harlem.* In "Why I Became a Catholic," McKay points out that "three of the early popes" and "early church fathers, such as St. Athanasius and St. Augustine[,] were Negroid in the American sense of the word" (32). An untitled sonnet McKay published in the October 1945 *Catholic Worker* adds to this roll of black saints:

> Oh, one was black of the wise men of the East,
> Who came with precious gifts to Jesus' birth,
> A symbol all men equal were at least,
> When Godhead condescended to the earth.
> The Ethiopian in Jerusalem
> Was human to the preacher of our Lord,
> Who drawn to him as to a precious gem,
> Bestowed on him the message of the Word.
>
> Yes, and a great Black Empire was the first,
> To change itself into a Christian nation,
> Long before Rome its pagan fetters burst
> And purged itself for Jesus Christ's oblation.
> From the high place where erstwhile they grew drunk
> With power, oh God, how gutter-low have black men sunk!

Here McKay depicts the Black Magus of medieval iconography of the Epiphany alongside the Ethiopian eunuch converted by the Apostle Philip—the event which, tradition has it, led to the nation's Christianization.[33]

McKay's most trenchant revision of Catholic Left medievalism in "Why I Became a Catholic" ties the rise of Protestantism to the institution of Black chattel slavery:

> There were three great events which coincided to give impetus to the rise of Protestantism in the 15th and 16th centuries: (a) the looting of the Roman Catholic Church, (b) the discovery of America, (c) the transportation of African Negroes as slaves to America. There were slaves, white and black, in ancient times and in the feudal ages. The seven-centuries old Mohammedan conquest of Spain had introduced African slavery in Europe. But such slavery was mild and the slaves had certain rights. It was the Protestant-Anglo-Saxon-American system of slavery which brutalized the Negro and reduced him to a subhuman being. (32)

In his haste to commend his new faith to *Ebony* readers, McKay downplays the role of individual Catholics, Catholic nations, and Catholic theologies and ways of reasoning in the construction of the Atlantic slave system.[34] All the same, it seems to me that McKay is on to something when he attributes the particular brutality inflicted by Anglo-American slaveholders to the ruthless efficiency of the Protestant work ethic. Most importantly, when McKay shifted this medievalist discourse to account for racism and slavery, he tackled matters outside the purview of the white defenders of Western Christendom who have often espoused it. Indeed, such medievalism has sometimes shored up an explicit or implicit commitment to white supremacy.[35] But McKay drafted medievalism into service for Black liberation.

As he sought to understand his conversion and explain it to his Catholic readers, McKay applied a similar method of figural interpretation to his own personal history. McKay was already known for retelling his story to suit his current commitments: he had written his later anti-Communism back into his 1937 autobiography *A Long Way from Home*, for example (Tillery 75). But there's more going on in McKay's Catholic writings than just a kind of self-serving self-revision. Now McKay perused the fragmentary earthly events of his past for signs of divine presence, and experiences he had glossed one way earlier took on new shades of meaning.

In an essay for the Catholic magazine the *Epistle*, McKay pointed especially to his aesthetic experiences in the cathedrals of Western Christendom he had visited in England, France, and Spain as preparation for his conversion. During his 1919–21 trip to England, the agnostic writer George Ber-

nard Shaw had schooled McKay in medieval aesthetics and Fabian Socialism, training his perceptions for his later Continental travels: "Years before in
London, Bernard Shaw had impressed me with a long talk about the beauty
of medieval cathedrals and how to look at them. Now on the continent of Europe, in France and in Spain, I had leisure for visiting and contemplation in
the cathedrals. I lifted my head up at the great Gothic arches and was overwhelmed by their beauty. It was in Europe that I saw the vision of the grandeur and glory of the Roman Catholic religion" ("On Becoming a Roman
Catholic" 106). Elsewhere in the essay, McKay projects his later historio-
graphic quest back onto his Spanish travels: "As a pagan I had always accepted
without thinking clearly about it, that Catholic countries were the most backward and un-progressive in the world. But Spain taught me that progress was
not with the 'progressives'" (106). Here, Ray's disdain for Europe's "sacredly-
preserved sites" in *Banjo* gives way to a medievalist sublime—an aesthetic perception of architecture and history that seals spiritual truths.

Perhaps the most telling example of McKay's figural interpretation of his
own past is another sonnet. Originally published in the famed "New Negro"
issue of Alain Locke's *Survey Graphic* in 1925 under the title "Russian Cathedral," McKay published a slightly revised version as "St. Isaac's Church, Petrograd" in the October 1947 *Catholic Worker*. In its *Survey Graphic* form, the
poem hymns the divine ingenuity of human art and suggests that the proletariat—those men and women of woe—are the modern antitype of Christ.
However, in its *Catholic Worker* iteration, "beauty" is demoted to lowercase,
while "Man of Woe" and "Divinity" are capitalized, focusing the praise on
Christ himself, God incarnate as suffering man. The poem's new title point-
edly returns the eponymous church—in fact converted, in 1931, into the Soviet State Antireligious Museum—to its ecclesial origin as a Russian Orthodox cathedral ("Museum History"). Likewise, it rewinds the city of Leningrad
to its pre-Stalinist name of "Petrograd." The republished version of the poem
subtly laments the suppression of Russian Christianity under Soviet rule. But
it also locates the first inklings of McKay's faith in his aesthetic experiences
of Christian architecture—here, of the Eastern Church—during his expatriate decade. Further, it draws those experiences together with his conversion
in such a way that, to return to Auerbach's formulation, they signify not only
themselves but also his conversion, while his conversion involves or fulfills his
earlier expatriate experiences. In this, McKay is not just changing his story to
suit his current convictions; he's drawing on a long Christian tradition of fig-

ural interpretation that connects events across and, in some sense, outside of time. Yet I want to emphasize that McKay did not see his Catholic conversion as a foregone conclusion. His awareness that things could have turned out differently shows up in the pluralist way he inflects Catholic Left medievalism in his postconversion writings.

McKay's Black medievalism is part of the story of the postwar emergence of a kind of rudimentary American religious pluralism that the historian Kevin Schultz calls "Tri-Faith America," the three faiths in question being Protestant, Catholic, and Jewish.[36] We can see McKay's "The Middle Ages" as imagining a "tri-faith medieval Mediterranean" along similar lines, but swapping out Protestantism for Islam. This pluralism underscores the retrospective, nondeterministic nature of his figural approach to history. The poem's "Mohammedan, Christian, and Jew" stand in for three different construals of the same Abrahamic sacred history: the Catholic one is the one that works for me, he seems to say, and it makes the best sense, to me, of their coexistence, but I can see how you'd come to a different conclusion—I can see how I'd come to a different conclusion, if I'd stayed in Morocco—so we can make space for each other. McKay's experience of writing through exile prompted a sort of complicated worldly religiosity, hospitable toward other faiths yet unreconciled to modernity.

McKay's late Catholic writings stand as an important example of what we can miss as critics when we try to fit a poet's career into the Procrustean bed of secular time. To account for other patternings of time, we will need to find new languages. These new languages might be in some ways old ones: for example, I've suggested that a fresh engagement with Erich Auerbach's humanist criticism might be a good place to start. Along similar lines, we might look to Bruce Holsinger's account of "the sacramental sensibility motivating much medieval historiography," a sensibility that "finds in discrete past events and surviving relics the wondrous promise of an invisible totality it can only occasionally glimpse in the lived present," for another (5–6). I've also shown how queer studies' examination of nonnormative temporalities offers yet another rich possibility. Such vocabularies will not only help to address a longstanding need in McKay studies for a full-orbed account of his Catholic period; they will also enrich the wider study of twentieth-century literature and religion.

4

"BACK TO CHRIST! BACK TO THE LAND!"
The Theological and Political Meaning
of Southern Agrarianism

In the November 1935 *Catholic Worker*, Peter Maurin published an argument for Catholic agrarianism entitled "Back to Christ—Back to the Land!" Like many of his "Easy Essays," it's a bricolage of quotations assembled into a cumulative case. He gives the last word to the Anglo-Catholic architect Ralph Adams Cram, discussed in chapter 1: "Catholics should take up this back-to-the-land problem and put it into operation."[1] Before this, though, Maurin takes his penultimate quotation from a more surprising source: *I'll Take My Stand: The South and the Agrarian Tradition* (1930) by the Twelve Southerners, organized and edited by the Vanderbilt-based poet and critic John Crowe Ransom. *I'll Take My Stand* is a landmark not only of white southern literature but of the intellectual history of reaction in America.

In many ways, the Catholic Workers and the Twelve Southerners are political polar opposites. Where Maurin crossed the color line to bring the Catholic Workers to Harlem, *I'll Take My Stand* endorsed the de jure segregation of the Jim Crow South. The particular piece from the Twelve Southerners' anthology Maurin borrows from in his "Easy Essay" is Andrew Nelson Lytle's "The Hind Tit," a purple prophecy of doom from one of the most dyspeptic and unreconstructed neo-Confederates among the writers Ransom assembled. For Lytle, the Civil War never stopped; it continues as "a war to the death between technology and the ordinary human functions of living" (202). He figures northern industrial capitalism as an invading army of Frankenstein's monsters and robots, the "unnatural progeny of inventive genius." These cyborg carpetbaggers threaten the manhood of the southern yeoman farmer, in danger of being "eunuched" and "enslaved" (201, 203). Lytle doesn't deign to mention that these are the very depredations suffered by Black men in the South for generations. This points to the unacknowledged fear behind his dystopian phantasmagoria: what terrifies Lytle about industrial capitalism is its penchant for making everything solid melt into air, and he's shaken by the possibility of collapsing the legal boundary between races upholding the power structure of the South, in which men like him are on top.

So what's an antiracist Catholic leftist like Maurin doing by quoting from one of Lytle's most race-baiting and reactionary essays? Maurin steers clear of Lytle's most backward opinions and colorful imagery, selecting a few relatively innocuous-sounding sentences about the insufficiency of Communism and the necessity of widespread farming for democracy. These were matters on which the two agreed, and they also are what makes agrarianism *actually agrarian*. The sympathies between the "Green Revolution" of the Catholic Workers and the soil-bound conservatism of the Southern Agrarians ran more than skin deep. For another of the Twelve Southerners—Allen Tate (1899–1979)—and for the novelist Caroline Gordon (1895–1981), Tate's on-again/off-again wife, Maurin and Day's back-to-the-land ethos paved the way for conversion to Roman Catholicism. Conversion in turn helped to lead them away from reactionary nostalgia for the Old South.

In her novel *The Malefactors* (1956), a sort of roman á clef, Gordon fictionalizes her and Tate's respective religious conversions through the characters of Vera and Tom Claiborne.[2] At one point, a character tells the failed poet Tom Claiborne (Allen Tate) that "Joseph Tardieu"—the novel's Peter Maurin character—has ideas "rather like yours. He thinks that agriculture is absolutely basic" (Gordon 41). Claiborne responds, "He's damn right." The novel concludes with the repentant adulterer Tom determining to leave New York City and rejoin his wife, who has become the elderly Tardieu's caretaker, at the "Catholic Laborer" outpost of "Mary Farm": "He could sleep in the hay if there was no bed. He could be sitting there on the bench with the other bums when [Vera] came down in the morning" (338). Claiborne's ancestral plantation in Tennessee has long been underwater, flooded in a New Deal–style federal dam project. His religious conversion requires him to divest himself of his attachments to the fantasy of the Old South, but not to the land itself. The poet ends back on a farm, sleeping with his face in the hay, closer in fact to the actual activity of agriculture than he has been in years.[3]

Because of the outsized influence of *I'll Take My Stand*, which joined Lost

Cause mythmaking and Jim Crow apologetics to its defense of a farm economy, agrarianism has usually been understood as a conservative ideology.[4] But this isn't the whole story. Historically, the politics of agrarianism are ambivalent, and "ideology" probably makes the agrarian position sound too systematic. I understand agrarianism in much the same way I do the medievalism to which it was sometimes joined, as in Maurin's case: as a fungible symbolic vocabulary that can express a whole spectrum of political commitments.

In the next two chapters, I tell the story of agrarianism's political and theological ambivalence by uncovering an alternative Left-agrarian tradition in the South. I hope that when my readers think of Southern Agrarianism, they won't just think of Ransom and the Twelve Southerners. Instead, I hope they will also remember the Fellowship and Committee of Southern Churchmen, James McBride Dabbs, Walker Percy, and Wendell Berry. The ambivalence of agrarianism isn't only found in this alternative tradition, however. It's also evident to some degree in the Nashville Agrarians themselves, most clearly in the writings of their ringleader, John Crowe Ransom.

JOHN CROWE RANSOM AND THE
NASHVILLE AGRARIANS: AN AMBIVALENT LEGACY

In some ways, Ransom's career embodies the process of secularization. "I am the son of a theologian, and the grandson of another one, but the gift did not come down to me," he avers in the "letter of apology" prefaced to *God without Thunder: An Unorthodox Defense of Orthodoxy* (ix).[5] His father indeed was a Methodist minister, a pillar of the southern Protestant establishment. Ransom became a soldier, a poet, and later a critic and a professor—immensely influential in the last two roles as a model and mentor to many midcentury American writers. As one generation of Ransoms gave way to another, they instantiated a larger cultural changing of the guard. While his father was a member of the clergy, John Crowe Ransom was a member of the new secular clerisy, one of the unsanctified sages of the modern world.

On the other hand, in his early work Ransom made it his mission to push back against secularizing forces. He was a peculiarly and ambivalently God-besotted writer, from his 1919 collection *Poems about God* until the 1940s, by which time Ransom had distanced himself from his southern Protestant heritage (Quinlan 4).[6] A countersecular logic inheres in Ransom's early material, launching out from institutionalized scientific expertise back toward the unmolested mystery of Creation. As a professor, Ransom points away from the institution of the university to the activity of the critic. As a critic, he points away from the critic's analyses to the poem's "desperate ontological or metaphysical manoeuvre" ("Criticism, Inc."). As a poet, he points toward the "inexhaustible fullness or particularity" of the details of the world, which is for him "the body and manifestation of an inscrutable God" (*God without Thunder* 68). Ransom had a peculiar vantage from which to contest secularization as an English professor and man of letters. He wasn't quite one of the technocratic social scientists that Eugene McCarraher identifies as the new moral arbiters of therapeutic consumer culture (*Christian Critics* 14–15). But neither was he a priest of the old faith. The early Ransom saw it as his duty in this in-between vocation to uphold the claims of mystery against the too-clear vision of the social scientists, and for this purpose he creatively appropriated the authority of Christianity.

Taking Ransom's reputation-making critical output of the 1930s as a whole, we can see that its keynote is a rebuke of industrial modernity on behalf of the religious past. His Agrarian writings look back to the Old South in search of a religious sensibility; it is the religiousness of the past that makes the past particularly valuable to Ransom. Even his early articulation of a New Criticism that preserves the poem's unique ontological status engages directly with secular historiography by resisting the secularization of literature, making the poem an arena of transcendent readerly experience rather than an artifact to be explained away by historically trained experts. Ransom's 1937 essay "Criticism, Inc." marks an important turning point in this respect, for even while it seeks to shield the poem from professorial historical explainers, it delivers poetry to a new class of technical experts versed in the complexities of literary form. Ransom's model here is explicitly industrial (the "Inc." in "Criticism, Inc."). Applied science, always art's foe in his earlier work, had by 1937 become criticism's older brother, regarded with jealous admiration.

Ransom's earlier religious criticism, the key text of which is *God without Thunder*, published in 1930—the same year as the much more well-known Southern Agrarian collection *I'll Take My Stand*, which Ransom edited—took theology for its model rather than science. But theology was more than *just* a model for Ransom. Even as he considered his post–"Criticism, Inc." formalist approach to be an actual science of poetry, not merely science-like, similarly, in writing *God without Thunder*, Ransom was actually doing theology, though as a layman. His argument in the book proceeds from claims about the nature and character of God. Across his career, then, Ransom moved from literary criticism *as* applied theology to literary criticism *as* applied science.[7]

Any reader expecting Ransom to conform to the stereotype of the New Critic—a man wrapped up in the formal play of high literary art, disdaining the cultural conflicts of his own day as well as the historical context of the poem—will be surprised by his early criticism's explicit engagement with current cultural and political questions. Like Eliot's contemporaneous *After Strange Gods*, which also deploys language of "orthodoxy" to widen his critical purview, Ransom's *God without Thunder* takes literature for just one parcel of the field of cultural conflict. Ransom intervenes in the religion-science debate of the 1920s as well as the fundamentalist-modernist controversy in Protestant theology, throwing in a critique of economic industrialism to boot. He draws on all kinds of textual resources with no particular literary pedigree to make his argument. Ransom gives an interpretation of the Scopes trial as part of his sympathetic account of Protestant fundamentalism, and he disputes the "anthropological view" of religion represented by H. L. Mencken's "Treatise on the Gods" (97–109). The alliance between scientists like R. A. Millikan and liberal clergymen like Harry Emerson Fosdick embodied in the Washington Agreement of 1923, a document expressing a religion of human moral betterment by technocratic means, comes in for even harsher treatment. "As a religious scheme," Ransom writes, "this is 'Hamlet' without the Prince of Denmark" (14). In *God without Thunder*, Ransom covers a vast cultural territory from the pronouncements of popular preachers, to *Paradise Lost*, to then-contemporary philosophical polemics.

Ransom's religious criticism engages with popular forms and political conflicts because on his definition of "religion" it could do nothing else. He defines religion thus: "*The religion of a people is that background of metaphysical doctrine which dictates its political economy*" (*God without Thunder* 116, emphasis in original). This definition rejects individualism from the jump: "religion" here belongs to "a people" collectively rather than to "*individual men in their solitude*," as William James puts it in the *Varieties* (James 31, emphasis in original). Ransom's definition also fundamentally entangles religion, economics, and politics, preparing the way for a critique of industrial capitalism on behalf of the religious past:

There are in the main just two economies: the one is the religious, and the other is the secular. The former is the conservative and the latter is the pro-

gressive.... Philology represents religion as looking backward rather than forward: *re*, back, plus *ligo*, bind. Religion enlarges the God and limits the man,
telling the believer incessantly to remember his limits, and be content with his
existing condition.... [Secularism] is defined by a total attitude, which abandons the idea of limitations. Secularism is a wartime economy, and the war is
the one which man has declared against nature. (116–17)

Alongside crotchety platitudes about contentment with one's "existing condition," which likely rang hollow in the book's early-Depression publication
context, as well as echoes of Lytle's unceasing war of northern industrial ag-
gression, we should be careful to hear the more radical notes in this passage.
When Ransom criticizes "progress," he takes aim at the insanity of a capitalist economy premised on limitless growth. Indeed, this passage brings to
light the common roots of "conservatism" and "conservation": in Ransom's language of embracing limits and his metaphor of a war against nature there's a
premonition of the more recent "green" ecological critique of capitalism and
its watchword of "sustainability"—an agrarian thread picked up by Wendell
Berry, whom I discuss in the next chapter.

Ransom's critique of industrial capitalism in *God without Thunder* binds
itself back to the religious past primarily by recovering the Hebrew Bible as
the Christian Old Testament. He recommends especially the book of Job for
a bracing tonic of the inscrutability of God. Modern scientists and theologians have concocted a tame new God in their own image to authorize their
industrial pursuits: "God as a Great Man . . . is the modern scientist glorified
and apotheosized," friendly, rational, and humane (20). This new God has
made nature immediately knowable and infinitely malleable for human good;
under his dispensation industrial humanity can rest easy in its control over
the world and its resources. "The God of Israel," as Ransom puts it, however,
is not so easily reckoned with. Ransom focuses on this God's qualities "which
seem most peculiarly Hebraic, and the most foreign to the temper of our Oc-
cidental modernism" (28).[8] The God of the Old Testament is mysterious; he
demands sacrifices which brook no compromise with economic efficiency;
and he brings evil as well as good of his own accord.

Acquaintance with such a God darkens the easy dream of ceaseless progress in human knowledge and welfare, instilling what Ransom calls "the tragic
spirit" (47). "Tragedy exhibits always the inevitable failure of the secular enterprise," he writes (47). "In tragedy the mind makes the critical confession

that human goodness, and intelligent work, a combination popularly supposed to be the sufficient cause of prosperity, do not actually produce their
triumphant effect upon the material world" (47). The tragic spirit is the rebuke of the religious past to a modern temper overconfident in the certainty
of industrial progress, and it expresses a skepticism apposite to the dire economic situation of 1930.

Appealing to the Old Testament, Ransom was forced to deal with the ob-
jections to its authority leveled by biblical criticism since the early Enlightenment period. Particularly the "higher criticism," which flourished in Germany
in the nineteenth century and had a lively and hotly debated Anglophone reception in the second half of that century, presented a major stumbling-block
to intellectuals of Ransom's generation. The 1908 Catholic Encyclopedia, for instance, found the higher critics' two most Bible-shaking claims to be the multiple authorship of biblical books (especially the Pentateuch, traditionally ascribed to Moses), and the historical implausibility of many biblical narratives
(Reid). Splintering the author-figure who mediates God's authority and undermining the text's relationship to historical fact, the higher criticism joined
psychological and ideological explanations of faith, along with evolutionary
biology, to form a phalanx of modern challenges to religious belief.

To rescue biblical authority in light of these challenges, Ransom develops
a theory of "myth." Myth, for Ransom, is a general category for nonliteral discourse, embracing everything from lovers' outlandish declarations to poems
to sacred texts: "The myth of an object is its proper name, private, unique, un-
translatable, overflowing, of a demonic energy that cannot be reduced to the
poverty of the class-concept. The myth of an event is a story, which invests the
natural with a supernatural background, and with a more-than-historical history" (65). Within this category, myths vary widely in significance; the myths
with the most staying power and social clout are, by Ransom's lights, religious. Further, as Francesca Aran Murphy argues, such myths have the practical value of making moral choices possible: myths turn the raw human experience of the world into "a structured cosmos . . . from which ethical action
emerges" (90). They help us to judge whether an action, or an economic system, fits or clashes with the world's form.

Ransom's invocation of "myth" in defense of orthodoxy closely parallels the
contemporary search by post–liberal Protestant theologians like Karl Barth
and the Niebuhr brothers for a hermeneutic alternative to Scripture's eviscer-
ation by historical critics and literalization by fundamentalists. Critical ob-

servers often referred to this theological trend as "neo-orthodoxy," though neither Barth nor the Niebuhrs (who in any case all disagreed vehemently with one another) accepted the label.[9] Both Ransom and the neo-orthodox theologians diverge from the fundamentalists by rejecting empirical history in favor of a kind of spiritual history as the ground of Scripture's meaning (Brackney 214). Reinhold Niebuhr, for example, used the category of myth to denote "a foggy but creative zone between fiction and literal truth" in which religious symbols could motivate political action (McCarraher 66). In his 1937 address to the ecumenical Oxford Conference on Life and Work, Niebuhr argued that "all orthodox Christian theology has been guilty of the sin of profanity. It has insisted on the literal truth of its myths, forgetting that it is the function and character of religious myth to speak of the eternal in relation to time, and that it cannot therefore be a statement of temporal sequences" (*The Essential Reinhold Niebuhr* 89).[10] Niebuhr criticizes the "orthodox" who insist on the "literal truth" of the Bible—that is, Protestant fundamentalists—from the neo-orthodox position of those who correctly understand that the mythic history of the Scriptures is more-than-historical.

Ransom and the neo-orthodox were equally contemptuous of liberal theologians' winnowing of Scriptural content to a few moralistic principles. H. Richard Niebuhr's famously biting epitome of liberal theology from 1937 even paraphrases, probably unintentionally, Ransom's title: "A God *without wrath* brought men without sin into a kingdom without judgment through the ministrations of a Christ without a cross" (*The Kingdom of God in America* 193, my emphasis). According to Ransom, this liberal attitude spelled death for a myth: "A myth which has flourished once will perish when its devotees become too squeamish, and begin peeling off its wrappings of concrete detail, saying that they are interested only in the 'heart' of its mystery—but finding in the end that the heart which they arrive at is only an abstract essence that has no blood in it" (*God without Thunder* 88). Despite this polemic against squeamishness, however, Ransom himself exhibits some squeamishness toward "religious myth" by kowtowing to the logic of authenticity (85).

In the middle of his argument against individualism and consumerism, Ransom the ornery producerist economist capitulates to them. In a revealing passage under the heading "*But the myth, on the whole, must be in keeping with our taste*," he writes that "we cannot hope to find our religious expression in a religion which causes us to blush. And this is most embarrassing. I do not know of situations much more painful than that of wishing to take part in a religious institution and feeling not quite able to go through with it, because of some massive but indistinct repulsion or disgust, which comes we do not know why" (88–89). It takes the fire out of his defense of an inscrutable and wrathful God if, when asked why one should accept this myth, Ransom can only say, "Because it is in keeping with my taste." The critic Denis Donoghue pinpoints the problem when he writes that "Ransom, too, becomes a psychologist of religion in his dealings with God the Father, even if the psychology he practices is a grim one" (27). Despite its rhetorical bluster, its warm account of fundamentalism, and its jibes at technocratic optimists, there's an incipient theological liberalism at work in *God without Thunder*. As Murphy argues, Ransom's reduction of religion to psychic need gives "the religious imagination a suggestive, but insufficient base" (91).

The book's seemingly most contrarian moment, Ransom's Job-inspired apologia for "the tragic spirit," bears out my account of his hermeneutic liberalism. Ransom can only make Job a tragedy by excising the book's "happy ending," undoing the redemptive arc of its narrative and divesting it of eschatological hope on the far side of tragedy (50–51). He picks and chooses his way through the biblical canon just like any higher critic looking for the authentic core of scripture; he's just a biblical critic with particularly dour taste. And it is this taste for tragedy that's at the root of his most conservative pronouncements in the book, like his insistence on accepting one's lot despite injustice. Hewing to the dictates of his taste, Ransom refuses the kind of eschatological hope that motivated civil rights agitation. Ransom could not bring himself to believe that, as Martin Luther King Jr. put it, "the arc of the moral universe is long, but it bends toward justice" ("Our God Is Marching On"). Ransom's morbid delectation of tragedy belongs more to what Walker Percy called "Southern Stoicism," which Percy bemoaned as the besetting sin of southern writers of Ransom's generation, than to the Christian orthodoxy Ransom ostensibly defends. The irony is that if Ransom had been more theologically conservative, he may have been more politically liberal.

The religious past Ransom invokes in *God without Thunder* is not so much the time of the Old Testament itself as a time when the Old Testament could still be naively believed—that is, a time before the higher criticism of the Bible threw its authorship in doubt in the later nineteenth century. It was the young Ransom's encounter with the higher criticism that profoundly shook his own youthful faith and pointed him to poetry instead of the ministry as a vocation (Quinlan 4–7). When Ransom tries to get around the higher critics by deploying the category of myth, he's actually arguing a for a kind of time travel: to go back before the higher criticism and return to the orthodox Protestant South of the early nineteenth century—that is, the antebellum South, as the breakdown of Protestant orthodoxy roughly coincided with the Civil War and Reconstruction. But this wished-for return is of course impossible for Ransom, born in 1888, even in memory.[11]

It is at this juncture that Ransom's two publications from 1930 link up into one larger critical project that leverages the religious past against industrial modernity in the name of both spiritual and ecological health. The Old South sketched in the pages of *I'll Take My Stand* is, in the terms of *God without Thunder*, a myth. Where *God without Thunder* attempts to ground a "religious" economy of human limitations in Christian theological myths like the Fall and the doctrine of the Trinity, *I'll Take My Stand*'s introductory manifesto, "A Statement of Principles," projects a social icon of a past "religious" economy as both a yardstick for the present and a program for future.

In "A Statement of Principles," Ransom, speaking on behalf of the Twelve Southerners, sets "a Southern way of life against what may be called the American or prevailing way" (xxxvii). From Ransom's point of view, both "Americanism" and "the Communists," far from being opposed, share the same problem (xl–xli). Each ideology proposes "more industrialism" as the solution to social ills for which industrialism is responsible in the first place (xli). Because it rejects the industrial system wholesale, Ransom argues, agrarianism is the truly radical alternative. Despite its avowed anti-Communism, however, "A Statement of Principles" conforms strikingly to Puchner's definition of "the Marxian speech-acts" of the manifesto form: "launched in the anterior future, claiming that their authority will have been provided by the changes they themselves want to bring about" (Puchner 24). As Ransom put it in a sequel to *I'll Take My Stand*, the unfinished economic treatise entitled *Land!*, unpublished except in pieces in his lifetime, "I am justifying a[n agrarian] movement which does not yet exist on any conscious or concerted scale" (*Land!* 3).

Ransom's "Statement" also announces its aspiration to a more dynamic genre than the essay by its distinctive visual appearance. It is laid out on the page in thematic paragraph-blocks, each separated by a triple-space on either end—a typographical acknowledgment of limitation, like the margins a careful farmer, bent on caring for the land rather than maximizing productivity, leaves at the edges of a field. Pages have always had margins, too, but here the margins vie for consideration with the text itself. This space, like the *Selah* that punctuates the Psalms, invites the reader to pause and reflect, to imagine the communal past into the present crisis. Such a measured pace contrasts sharply with the breakneck cadences of the manifestos of the avant-garde: "A Statement of Principles" is an unorthodox manifesto.

The literally conservative act of imagination called for by this spacious document nevertheless required a radical spirit. Reading *I'll Take My Stand* together with *God without Thunder* reveals that, for Ransom, industrialism's error is ultimately theological. As industrial systems, both liberal capitalism and Communism are species of "secular" economy that make humans into gods, beings without limits. Industrialism is life without margins, and margins are necessary to creaturely flourishing. Industrialism, thus, is heresy; agrarianism is orthodoxy. Yet Ransom acknowledges that his orthodox agrarian "principles [are] rather at variance with the orthodox doctrines of the American economic society" (*Land!* 3). Ransom's agrarian orthodoxy is paradoxically unorthodox—a marginal orthodoxy.

Land!, only recently published for the first time, demonstrates an interesting shift in Ransom's rhetoric of orthodoxy. As the passage just quoted shows, in *Land!* he tends to deploy "orthodox" to describe the then *currently accepted* economic theory of industrial capitalism, rather than the *theologically correct* theory of agrarianism. Yet Ransom holds out hope that agrarianism might become "orthodox in theory"—that is, widely accepted as true and correct—and "justify itself in practice" (*Land!* 106). In some ways, this later project is more pointed in its anticapitalism and less concerned with anti-Communism than is *I'll Take My Stand*. Ransom's preface to *Land!* states that the "villain" called "industrialism" in the Twelve Southerners' collection is "in the present book . . . generally called 'capitalism,' but he is the same character"—though Ransom also admits, "I would not want to put my villain to death if I knew how" (*Land!* 4). In his contribution to *Who Owns America? A New Declaration of Independence* (1936), also conceived as a follow-up to *I'll Take My Stand* and organized by Allen Tate and the Louisville journalist Herbert Agar (a proponent of Chestertonian distributism), Ransom further softens his radical critique of industrial capitalism into a protest against "the frenzy of Big Business" ("What Does the South Want?" 181). Instead of seeing capitalism as inveterately heretical, as in *God without Thunder*, Ransom here envisions "an orthodox capitalism for the South" on quasi-distributist, petit bourgeois lines: "an economy with a wide distribution of the capital properties . . . many owners, little businesses" (181). By this point, Ransom was well on his way to the appreciation of industrial society fully evident by 1937's "Criticism, Inc."

Despite his insistence that industrialism take account of its environmental and cultural costs, Ransom's incisive synthesis of historical fantasy, theology, and economics fails to adequately reckon with the depredations borne by Black southerners both before and after the Civil War in order for white southerners to enjoy what they did of grace and leisure. Ransom only addresses the subject with the evasive and factually inaccurate claim that "slavery was a feature monstrous enough in theory but, more often than not, humane in practice" (*I'll Take My Stand* 14). Though his style lacks the sheer rhetorical indigestion of Lytle's, Ransom falls prey to the same failures of political imagination and neighborly charity.

Ransom is most compelling when he reminds us of the value of "political genius," the intellectual will to conceive social relations differently from the status quo and the courage to try to change them ("Introduction" xlviii). "To think that this cannot be done," he writes, "is pusillanimous" (xlviii). Nevertheless, the Nashville Agrarians' vision entrenches the very aspects of the southern social order circa 1930 that most cry out for change. In 1934, however, a different group of southern religious intellectuals equally dedicated to caring for the land—the Fellowship of Southern Churchmen—offered a more thoroughgoing critique of American society, North and South, one deeply cognizant of the imbrications of racism and capitalism.

JAMES DOMBROWSKI AND THE FELLOWSHIP OF SOUTHERN CHURCHMEN: A LEFT-WING AGRARIANISM

The Fellowship of Southern Churchmen began on May 27, 1934, when Protestant clergymen, educators, and social activists gathered at the Monteagle Sunday School Assembly in Monteagle, Tennessee, for the Conference of Younger Churchmen of the South.[12] A sleepy-sounding affair, to be sure—somehow, this bumptious band of prophetic southern orators lacked a flair for naming and branding. Later, the portentously named journal *Prophetic Religion* was birthed on the mimeograph machine of Executive Secretary Howard "Buck" Kester's and his wife, Alice (Burgess 4). Despite a name redolent of wood-paneled ecclesiastical bureaucracy, the 1934 Conference of Younger Churchmen was not an affair of church politics alone. It was instead an attempt to articulate the church's political witness in the context of capitalism's seeming collapse. The "Findings" published by the Conference after this first meeting made manifest, from both a Christian theological and a southern regional perspective, that New Deal programs were half measures in a time of total social crisis.

But the Conference not only witnessed against the dysfunctions of secular economy and the federal government's attempts to patch it up. It also reflexively criticized the Church in the South for its failure to take the part of marginalized Blacks and poor whites—and for its ostracism of left-leaning leaders. According to the historian Robert F. Martin, the Conference and subsequent Fellowship "fostered a much needed sense of community among a small group of radical Christians who otherwise might have labored in isolation and eventually have been silenced by loneliness and frustration" (66). They were southern voices crying together in a southern waste—a suburb of prophets, to use Auden's phrase.

On the grounds of the Sunday School Assembly where these southern Socialists gathered sits the family cabin in which Andrew Nelson Lytle lived out his long post–*I'll Take My Stand* career, writing and editing the respected *Sewanee Review* (Sullivan 63). Monteagle, Tennessee, lies hard by the Cumberlands, right on the border of Middle and East Tennessee—legal as well as geographical distinctions in that state. Middle Tennessee is the home country of Ransom's whole Agrarian cohort; Nashville is its cultural as well as political capital. East Tennessee is more densely populated than Middle Tennessee, a country of both heavy industry and Appalachian wilderness, where the Tennessee Valley Authority set up in the 1930s. On this terrain, the Monteagle Conference brought hard-nosed neo-orthodox Protestant theology that was developed in the urban North together with southern practices of rural farm radicalism.

The leading organizers of the conference, including Kester (1904–1977), James Dombrowski (1897–1983), and Myles Horton (1905–1990), who would go on to found Tennessee's Highlander Folk School, were southern churchmen who had gone North for education. At Union Seminary in Manhattan, they came under the sway of the Socialist theologian Reinhold Niebuhr (1892–1971), whose mythic approach to the Scriptures echoed that of the conservative agrarian Ransom. (Dietrich Bonhoeffer, the German Lutheran pastor executed by the Nazis for his part in a plot to kill Hitler, was their classmate.) Neo-orthodoxy came to Monteagle in person, as it were, when the conference hosted Niebuhr as their keynote speaker. The Fellowship of Southern Churchmen (FSC) promulgated a sort of Christian Left agrarianism as a rebuke both to capitalism and to the New Deal programs that were attempting to mitigate capitalism's failure.

The Churchmen's first "Executive Secretary" and lead exponent of this leftist agrarianism was Kester, who made an unsuccessful bid for Congress on the Socialist ticket in 1932 and organized for the Southern Tenant Farmers' Union (STFU) (Salmond 115). Through their "Friends of the Soil" arm, Kester and the Churchmen distributed informational and liturgical documents to southern ministers that "proclaimed the sacred trinity of God, man and the earth and called upon the church of the living God to practice good husbandry, to stop the wanton waste of human and natural resources and to give the children of men their immemorial 'earthright'" (Burgess 4). FSC member Sam H. Franklin headed up Mississippi's Delta and Providence Farm Cooperatives, and a "Friends of the Soil" talk by Kester influenced Clarence Jordan to begin Georgia's Koinonia Farm—all interracial experiments in communal life and work, in a similar spirit to the Peter Maurin–inspired "agronomic universities" of the Catholic Workers up North (Burgess 2, 5; Jacklin 308).[13]

Fellowship members also helped to organize southern textile workers, and they supported, through writings, speeches, and financial contributions, the efforts of the STFU to organize agricultural laborers on the industrial model (Martin 72, 75). Taking a southernized version of Christian Socialism from the city to the country, the FSC attempted to awaken the Protestant churches of the South to their responsibility to build a humane agrarian-industrial order. While their efforts did not produce a widespread liberalization of southern Protestantism, they fostered an important strain of religious dissent in the southern tradition.

The moving spirit behind the 1934 Monteagle Conference was Dombrowski, a Christian Socialist activist and Methodist minister from Tampa, Florida (Dunbar, *Against the Grain* 59).[14] Dombrowski held degrees from Emory University in Atlanta and Union Theological Seminary in New York City, as well as a Ph.D. in philosophy from Columbia University. He came to Monteagle to help direct and teach at the Highlander Folk School alongside Horton (Salmond, "Depression Decades" 115; Martin 68). Highlander would later become crucial to the civil rights movement, hosting workshops that "helped lay the groundwork for many of the movement's most important initiatives, including the Montgomery bus boycott, the Citizenship Schools, and the founding of the Student Nonviolent Coordinating Committee" (Highlander Research and Education Center). At Columbia, Dombrowski wrote his dissertation under Herbert Schneider, a close colleague of the liberal pragmatist philosopher John Dewey, with additional advising from Union Seminary's Harry F. Ward, a fellow Methodist and Socialist and the first chairman of the board of the American Civil Liberties Union, and Niebuhr, who founded the Fellowship of Socialist Christians in 1932 (Dombrowski vii; Waggoner; Duke 109; Rice 22).

Published as a book in 1936, Dombrowski's dissertation *The Early Days of Christian Socialism in America* is a critically charged intellectual history of late nineteenth-century Social Christianity in the United States. It devotes a chapter to the Rev. W. D. P. Bliss of Boston's Church of the Carpenter, on which he quotes Vida Scudder as an authority, and Scudder herself plays a bit part in the book's narrative (Dombrowski 97, 138, 160, 200).[15] Like Scudder, Dombrowski found fault with the liberal theological thinness and bourgeois political timidity of the Social Gospel; its "optimistic interpretation of history" and "dependence on good will alone as a technique of social change," he complained, "led to futility" (Dombrowski 22, 24). As a result, "the Social Gospel exhibited less political realism than either proletarian radicalism or profound prophetic religion" (25). Dombrowski's invocation of the criterion of "political realism" here evinces Niebuhr's influence. The realist, Niebuhr argued in *Moral Man and Immoral Society* (1932), must face up to "the fact . . . that political opinions are inevitably rooted in economic interests . . . and only comparatively few citizens can view a problem of social policy without regard to their interests" (5). This tough-minded acknowledgment of self-interest, both as economic fact and as sinful failure, disqualifies an optimistic reliance on goodwill or the mere progress of time to bring positive political change. In its "confidence that God will form a better society out of the ashes of the present world," realistic, prophetic religion, according to Dombrowski, is at once more pessimistic and more durably hopeful than the Social Gospel's naïve optimism (Dombrowski 26).

While holding Social Gospel thinkers accountable for their often-tepid politics of charity, Dombrowski's *Early Days* nevertheless sought out the prophetic potential in the Christian Socialist tradition, even to the point of countenancing "revolution by violence, provided it promised a more just society" (193). For Dombrowski, though, the accent does not fall on violence per se but rather on the rejection of automatic social progress through the passage of time alone and the recognition of ineluctable class conflict. By means of the 1934 Monteagle Conference, Dombrowski aimed to galvanize southern church leaders who shared his paradoxically dour but hopeful vision to pursue economic and racial justice without the luxury of easy optimism. The "prophetic Christianity" of Dombrowski and his fellow Churchmen in the 1930s underwrote a tragic sensibility much like that of Ransom and Niebuhr. But like T. S. Eliot, the Churchmen leavened their tragic sense with slow hope, taking up their political task with tragic optimism.

Reinhold Niebuhr was both the invited keynote speaker for the Monteagle Conference and "the spiritual father of the Churchmen" (Martin 69).[16] His address to the 1934 gathering on "Religion and the New Social Order" electrified the gathering (Dunbar, *Against the Grain* 60). The performance earned Niebuhr the nickname "Judgment Day in britches" from Churchman T. B. "Scotty" Cowan, "a flamboyant preacher and recent arrival from Scotland" (Burgess 1; Salmond, "Depression Decades" 115; cf. Dunbar, *Against the Grain* 60). Besides Kester, Dombrowski, Horton, Burgess, Cowan, and their northern guest Niebuhr, the other well-known Southern Churchman who attended the Monteagle Conference, unfailingly mentioned by historians of the event, was James Weldon Johnson (1871–1938), author of *The Autobiography of an Ex-Colored Man* (1912) and *God's Trombones: Seven Negro Sermons in Verse* (1927), Harlem Renaissance dynamo, field secretary of the NAACP, former diplomat, and, at the time, professor of creative literature and writing at Nashville's Fisk University (Burgess 1; Martin 66). Johnson was one of a handful of African American leaders at this integrated event.

The principal accomplishment of the Monteagle Conference, besides bringing a sense of community to lonely and beleaguered radical churchmen, was drafting the Conference's "Findings," which were "published in nearby papers under the caption 'Politics Needs Radical Party, Churchmen say. Program of Socialism Urged by Young Ministers at Monteagle'" (Cowan). The Conference's "Findings" recall Dorothy Day's Catholic Worker manifesto "To Our Readers," written a year previous to the Monteagle Conference, as a projective document of Depression-era Christian leftism (although the Churchmen did not match Day's lyricism).

"Findings" begins by damning the New Deal with faint praise, singling out the Tennessee Valley Authority for particular approbation. The document goes go on to criticize federal programs as insufficient to the economic crisis and sometimes damaging to the most vulnerable southerners. The Churchmen claimed that the New Deal "discriminates unjustifiably in the wages of northern and southern workers" and that the Agricultural Adjustment Act "led to the dispossession of share croppers [sic] in the South" ("Findings"). It was just this dispossession that provoked Churchman Sam Franklin's Delta Farm Cooperative experiment. According to the Churchmen, the New Deal's biggest shortcoming was that it regulated capitalism instead of rejecting it: the New Deal's "objectives," they wrote, "can not be achieved under the profit economy, and . . . these short-comings of the New Deal are inherent in the capitalistic system."

The New Deal also failed to adequately address racial inequalities. In their "Findings," the Churchmen enumerate a Jeffersonian declaration of persisting anti-Negro outrages: "We condemn the manifest injustices to the Negro, as evidenced in discrimination by employers and trade union [sic] in the matter of wages, in the exclusion from skilled trades and in the courts, in the dispro-portionate sums expended for education, in restricting the right of suffrage, in the operation of Jim Crow laws, and the inadequacy of housing, recreation, and health facilities." Having made clear their anticapitalism and antiracism, as well as their sympathetic but critical assessment of the New Deal, the Churchmen then swing over to constructive proposals. Like many manifes-tos, "Findings" is stronger at articulating what its authors execrate than what they support. Nevertheless, the first positive statement of the "Findings" ex-alts the churches, rather than the state, as potential sites of political and eco-nomic transformation: "We call upon the church groups to make the principle of brotherhood concrete in the relationships between the races, especially in the economic area" ("Findings"). Here, the Churchmen envision a time where churches in the South would no longer give ideological aid and comfort to segregation, but would instead become fields for the cultivation of interracial friendship and channels for a more equitable distribution of resources. They are never more truly churchmen—prophetic, on the ground leaders of Chris-tian communities—than at this moment.

The Southern Churchmen, like Scudder before them, emphasize the des-ignation of churchman/churchwoman as a political identity.[17] Frequently or-dained ministers, but more often academics or parachurch principals than parish pastors, churchwomen and churchmen exercised commitment to and leadership of the churches from their margins rather than their centers. In this sense, churchwomen or churchmen constitute something like what Eliot, in *The Idea of a Christian Society* (1939), would call "the Community of Christians," a church-within-the-church of elite intellectuals who help to clarify and direct the cultural and political life of regular churchgoers (28–29). But churchmen and churchwomen often found themselves an elite on the fringes. From his or her position on the edge of the church, the churchman or churchwoman mediated between the church and other groups fighting for their own vision of justice. While Scudder negotiated principally with the Socialist Party, the FSC navigated alliances with the STFU and other unions, cooperative farms, and New Deal agencies. In Scudder's time and case, of course, only the churchwoman's role of unofficial intellectual and moral suasion— not a formal clerical position—was open to her. But Scudder strove to make a virtue of this necessity. Like her, the members of the Fellowship of Southern Churchmen creatively leveraged their positions of marginal leadership to argue and act on behalf of forms of social justice that formal ecclesiastical positions might have precluded.

Alongside their vision of ecclesial politics, the Churchmen articulated a broadly democratic party politics. "We are convinced of the need of developing a radical political party of all races, composed of farmers, industrial workers, and members of the middle class," a Popular Front with a southern accent, espousing a kind of minimal Socialism ("Findings"). In this closing paragraph of the document, the Churchmen traverse the church/state divide, and, as a result, some confusion troubles their vision. "Findings" concludes that "such a party should recognize the revolutionary tradition of America, and the higher values of patriotism and religion." This talk of "higher values," which nests "patriotism" and "religion" so cozily together, threatens to hollow out the Churchmen's prophetic Christianity into a bland Socialist civil religion.

The 1934 Monteagle Conference of Younger Churchmen of the South and the subsequent Fellowship of Southern Churchmen brought together church leaders—men and women, Black and white, ordained and lay—to pursue social justice with a consciousness of the South's particular economic and racial dysfunctions, epitomized by the sharecropping system, and its particular virtues, especially a living religious tradition and a love for the land.[18] The Fellowship offered support to radical church leaders facing hostility from mainstream southern Protestants. At the same time, FSC members hoped to exert their powers of marginal leadership to transform southern churches, by means of parachurch pressure, from hostile to hospitable to prophetic Christianity. At a time of deep social crisis, when government intervention had proved insufficient and had indeed, in the Agricultural Adjustment Act, exacerbated injustice toward tenant farmers, the FSC sought to instill deeper cultural and economic changes than legal means could provide by cultivating Christian brotherhood in southern churches.

WILL D. CAMPBELL AND THE COMMITTEE OF
SOUTHERN CHURCHMEN: A CIVIL RIGHTS EXPERIMENT

In 1965, the Baptist pastor Will D. Campbell (1924–2013), a native son of Mississippi educated at Yale Divinity School, rebooted the Fellowship of Southern Churchmen under the new moniker of the Committee of Southern Churchmen (CSC). In the process, he renewed its vision for his generation. Faced with another social crisis, in the form of what he called "the Negro revolution," Campbell saw that civil rights legislation had failed to stem white supremacist violence against both Blacks and white activists. And legal changes could not bring about the fraternal "reconciliation"—*katallagete* in transliterated New Testament Greek—Campbell saw as the ultimate aim of his ministry. With the editorial assistance of James Y. Holloway (1927–2002), a theology professor at the Christian antiracist Kentucky work college Berea College, Campbell launched a new journal called *Katallagete: Be Reconciled!* to serve as the mouthpiece of the Committee. The ungainly, emphatic title was just one of the ways Campbell sought to defamiliarize for southern readers the radical demands of a gospel to which they had become inured.

Just as in the 1930s, white churches across the South remained centers of reactionary hostility; isolated radical churchmen and churchwomen still needed community and support. The Committee of Southern Churchmen, composed, this time around, of both Protestants and Catholics, continued the FSC's commitment to criticizing southern culture and society from a position at once robustly theological and friendly to the best aspects of the southern tradition. *Katallagete* provided "a radically Biblical critique of social and political institutions" while also furthering "a very Southern tradition of relational politics and grace theology" (Miller 2). Much like their Depression-era counterparts, the Churchmen of the 1960s leveraged their marginal but committed positions of leadership within the church and within southern culture. Campbell and the CSC sought to renovate the southern heritage and put it to work for civil rights. But they also sought a reconciled state of spiritual brotherhood that went beyond the recognition and enforcement of legal rights.

The CSC published their manifesto-like "Statement," counterpart to the

Fig. 7. Cover of the inaugural issue of *Katallagete: Be Reconciled.*

1934 Conference "Findings," inside the front cover of the first issue of *Katallagete* in June 1965. The magazine's cover sported a striking black-and-white design: on a black field, a subtly Gothicized white cross, the vertical bar of which terminates in a circle punctuated by a black equals sign (see fig. 7). In the image, Christianity, represented by the cross, seems to rest on racial unity and equality. Instead of offering a theology of racial equality merely based on Christian teaching, this image argues that Christianity itself stands or falls on the achievement of equal rights. "The Church is the Church," the CSC "Statement" claimed, only when "worldly standards . . . cease to count in relationships among men, or Christ's death and resurrection are mocked" (n.p.).

Where the 1934 "Findings" lashed out at the inequalities of the New Deal, the 1965 "Statement" turns its critical gaze inward, lamenting the Church's support of the Jim Crow regime as just such a mockery of Christ:

> But, we in the South have counted worldly standards and have made distinctions of our own creation between men. Most grievously, men of one race have set themselves apart from men of another, and we in the Church have connived and acquiesced in the profanation of God's will for human life. Thereby, we have contradicted in our faith and life the unity of all men created by God's act in Christ; we have crucified Christ anew; we have led the Church to become like the nations, instead of being a light to the nations. (n.p.)

The "Statement" partakes of several familiar traditions of American theopolitical criticism, mixing a New Testament register of Pauline moral instruction with an Old Testament rhetoric of prophetic denunciation. Arguing that segregation repeats and travesties the crucifixion, it recalls the Christological attack on slavery mounted by New England abolitionists such as Harriet Beecher Stowe. Bemoaning the southern church's failure to be "a light to the nations" on the issue of racial justice, it takes up the exemplarity discourse of John Winthrop's "City on a Hill" sermon.

But other stylistic aspects of the "Statement" make Scripture and its requirements strange to its readers. Campbell's jeremiad hits the existentialist note of neo-orthodox theology when it speaks of "God's act in Christ."[19] By emphasizing God's creative action, this formulation resists the reduction of the Gospel to innocuous truth-statements which may be rejected or affirmed without consequence. The "Statement" begins by quoting in English translation Saint Paul's Second Epistle to the Corinthians, from the Greek text of which *Katallagete* derived its name. The passage pleads for human beings to be reconciled to God and to one another: "One man died for all and therefore all mankind has died. . . . With us therefore, worldly standards have ceased to count in our estimate of any man. . . . In Christ's name, we implore you, be reconciled to God!" In the "Statement," this passage appears in the New English Bible translation, only three years old at the time. This contemporary translation put the Bible in plain English words unfamiliar even to such a thoroughly churched audience as the educated southern white moderates the Churchmen targeted.

To be at once familiar and strange; to bring its readers to admit the contemporary political and ethical implications for racial justice of the ancient Christian doctrines they already held; to move them from what Scudder once called conservative "surface orthodoxies" to a deep orthodoxy that radically reapprehends the tradition; to speak the language of southern heritage but to spin that vocabulary for radical ends: these were the rhetorical goals of the "Statement" in particular, and of the CSC and *Katallagete* in general.

In his inaugural *Katallagete* editorial statement, Campbell mapped out the theological and social context for the formation of the CSC and the publication of its journal in terms that echo the founding of the FSC in the 1930s. Despite Supreme Court decisions and civil rights legislation outlawing segregation, violence and injustice still reigned in the South, just as the New Deal had not, by 1934, mitigated many of the effects of the Depression. Campbell's relentlessly ecclesial attack on segregation in the CSC "Statement" takes up that part of the Monteagle Conference "Findings" that imagines southern churches at sites of on-the-ground social activism, while leaving the earlier document's explicit political Socialism behind. By moving the Churchmen away from a politics of law to a politics of grace, of love rather than legality, Campbell turned their philosophy away from Christian Socialism and toward a Christian anarchism.[20] His vision was in this respect closer to the personalist idealism of the Catholic Workers than the hard-nosed, tragic Socialism Niebuhr and his southern proteges espoused in the 1930s.

Campbell called the churches of the South to a more thoroughgoing radicalism than liberal mainline Protestants sympathetic to the civil rights struggle were ready to countenance at the time. In the first half of the 1960s, the churches' response to Black demands for racial equality ran from outright hostility toward change to tepid support for reform. The latter response, though better than opposition, was both too little and too late. "Today there is every indication that more than social reform is in the offing," Campbell prophesied, pointing to the radicalization of groups like the Student Nonviolent Coordinating Committee ("The Day of Our Birth" 3). By the time that mainline Protestants had warmed up to racial reform, racial revolution was nigh. Engaged southern churchmen now faced a dilemma: "The alternative would seem to be that we either once again serve as Chaplain to the Status Quo . . . or else equate the revolution with the Kingdom of God and join it uncritically and with abandon. Much 'white church' is apt to do the first. Much 'Negro church' is apt to do the latter" (4). Both of these positions had historical precedent. "Southern revivalism," Campbell contended, had "for two centuries" taken up the chaplaincy of the status quo. On the other hand, like Dombrowski before him, Campbell found fault with a "social gospel which did go into the world but took so little of the Church with it [that it] cannot be its present help" (5). Either position would be a failure of what Ransom called "political genius." In the face of this dilemma, *Katallagete* offered a radical third way, a theological politics that Campbell—like Ransom, Eliot, and Scudder—represented as the orthodox alternative among heresies: "a well-defined orthodoxy . . . an orthodoxy which takes it into the streets" ("The Day of Our Birth" 5). The Churchmen would preach Christ's reconciliation, by his death, of all people with each other and with God, and they would plead with their churches to be true to this accomplished act of God.

Campbell's sense of humor sets his rhetoric apart from that of the dour Churchmen of the Great Depression. "There is a sense in which the birth of a journal such as this hopes to be absurd," Campbell opened his first editorial for *Katallagete* ("The Day of Our Birth" 3). Absurdity was a mode of life and speech Campbell treasured; it was his ethos. Where Niebuhr was "Judgment Day in britches," Campbell was Judgment Day in motley—or, more accurately, in cowboy boots and an "Amish sombrero" (Houston 135). "We're all bastards, but God loves us anyway" was Campbell's credo (142). In his dress and in his shocking speech, Campbell presented himself as a kind of backwoods holy fool, "St. Francis of the Rednecks" (Clancy 229).

But Campbell's sense of humor did not come at the expense of his sense of tragedy. Campbell defined "Southern tragedy" in a 1972 interview in terms of the conflict between Blacks and poor whites, whose political interests ought to coincide. These "two groups of people, one black, one white, living side-by-side, both in the same boat, both having come here as servants or slaves, who if they had banded together could have taken over the country. But instead they have continued to this very day to be the enemy of each other" (Clancy 228). Campbell's vision of the tragedy of southern history wrests tragic language from the planter class, with its Lost Cause of the Civil War, and substitutes in its place the lost cause of failed interracial working-class cooperation: Campbell's is the tragedy of redneck history, that race trumped class for poor whites, whose true interests aligned with those of Black southerners.

But tragedy was emphatically not the last word in Campbell's theology. Reconciliation—that comic theological truth, at once accomplished fact and ethical injunction, for which Campbell named his magazine—was his ultimate benediction. Reconciliation is what comes after tragedy, what transmutes tragedy into divine comedy. But Campbell founders on this: is reconciliation a fait accompli or a command? For Campbell, it is indissolubly both. The tension between these truths, between the indicative and the imperative, constitutes his "orthodoxy." Campbell's fidelity to this orthodoxy forced him to break with his former employer, the mainline Protestant National Council of Churches, and its liberal gradualist approach to racial justice (Houston 139). These three elements of Campbell's comic orthodoxy, his practical theology of reconciliation, all hang together: first, his insistence on reconciling with the poor white racist, the redneck, and the Klansman, and not merely with the timid if good-hearted educated white moderate; second, his insistence on using biblical-theological gospel vernacular rather than the sociological technical vocabulary to approach the southern white Protestant in their native idiom; and third, his insistence that reconciliation is primarily a theological reality, an accomplishment of Christ on the cross, rather than a social reality, and thus a task to be performed. For Campbell, reconciliation was a matter of grace, not of works. This message was foolishness to some, a stumblingblock to others, but to Campbell and the Churchmen it was God's own bootleg wisdom.

The Fellowship and Committee of Southern Churchmen constitute a radical alternative to the canonical genealogy that runs from the Nashville Agrarians to the postwar resurgence of intellectual conservatism (Murphy 5–7). In the 1960s, the Committee's loose association of pro–civil rights, anticonsumerist, anarchist-leaning Christian intellectuals took hope and energy from the example of their Depression-era Christian Socialist predecessors. In the first issue of *Katallagete*, James McBride Dabbs's article "Southern Churchmen: Fellowship to Committee" cemented the new group's radical patrimony even as it explained the change in the organization's name and its renewed emphasis on racial justice. As southerners, they bore the various burdens of southern history: the violence against and exploitation of southern Blacks under the slave system and the Jim Crow regime, the ignominious defeat of the Confederacy in the Civil War and Reconstruction, and the ongoing manipulation of poor whites by agricultural and industrial elites. As Churchmen, they took on yet another weight: facing up to what Walker Percy calls "the egregious moral failure of Christendom," by which southern churches have aided and abetted slavery, segregation, and capitalism, defending the interests of wealthy white Christians against Black and poor white Christians ("Notes for a Novel" 14). But in the Fellowship's "radical critique of twentieth-century Southern civilization" immanent to southern Christianity, Campbell and the Churchmen of the 1960s found a tradition of dissent they could claim as their own (Martin 66). In their creative appropriation of the past, they sought a revitalized Christian humanism that wouldn't just rebuke Jim Crow but bring to heel all of Western technological society.

5

FROM SOUTHERN TRAGEDY
TO DIVINE COMEDY

The Committee of Southern Churchmen
Radicalize the Southern Heritage

On September 2, 1965, Will Campbell asked the Louisiana Catholic novelist Walker Percy (1916–1990) to join the Committee of Southern Churchmen (CSC). "I think you know who we are," wrote Campbell, the Committee's founding director. "We think the issues [of race] are theological, not just social or political. We do not oppose the invading moral carpetbaggers (we had it coming) except as we are aware of history and try to understand that love means trust and that if we are to follow our Lord we must hope and work also for white Southerners—not just seek to force them" (1). Calling northern activists "invading moral carpetbaggers" immediately before conceding the justice of the invasion was exactly the kind of humor, at once barbed and self-deprecating, that appealed to Percy. When it came to Reconstruction, Campbell was "aware of history" in at least two senses: he knew the white supremacist historical narrative—adapted by Andrew Lytle, among many others—implied by the term "carpetbagger," used as a slur against northern interlopers. But Campbell also knew the ways in which that narrative was false.

By invoking moral, rather than immoral, carpetbaggers in a tone of ironic humor instead of bitter invective, Campbell switches up the literary genre of that historical narrative. The carpetbagger was originally part of the conceptual armory of the "Lost Cause," the tragic story of the irreparable loss of the society of the Old South and the unbridgeable division—between North and South and between white and Black—wreaked by the Civil War. But Campbell's joke turns that tragedy into an incomplete comedy, a historical narrative that licenses present "work" toward the hoped-for reconciliation of Black and white, North and South, believer and skeptic. Nevertheless, Campbell believed that reconciliation could be achieved only by God's grace, not human efforts. In his comic worldview, events are unpredictable and human schemes always on the brink of unraveling. The worst theology (in his estimation) often produced the best ethics, while the best intentions frequently had the worst results. He thought northern activists could stand to benefit from the skepticism toward human efforts and the faith in God's grace bred by this comic outlook.

Campbell and Percy actively supported the African American struggle for civil rights and, at the same time, fiercely disputed any presumption of northern cultural superiority. Reviewing a book of letters by the young volunteers of the Freedom Summer project of 1964 in Mississippi, Percy observed that "earnest, well-disposed boys and girls from such places as Swarthmore and Westchester County . . . equipped mainly with the post-Christian piety of the sociology major" had found the robust Christianity of Black southerners a "stumbling block" ("The Fire This Time"). Campbell tied this cultural chauvinism to a theological lacuna: the sociology of integration (a legal requirement) lacked a theology of reconciliation (a spiritual reality). Campbell's doctrine of reconciliation was the centerpiece of his theology, enshrined in the title of the journal he founded on behalf of the CSC: *Katallagete: Be Reconciled!* The doctrine of reconciliation offered a Protestant cognate to the Mystical Body of Christ professed by Day, Maurin, McKay, and, indeed, by Percy, too. As for Day, all people are "members or potential members of the Mystical Body of Christ," for Campbell, all people are already reconciled to God and one another in Christ's death and resurrection—whether they like it or not, and whether they live like it or not. Campbell thought the theological sway of reconciliation stood a better chance of winning the "trust" of moderate or even segregationist white Christians than the "force" of northern sociology. He hoped to convince white believers in the South to join their Black brothers and sisters—or, more accurately, to help them see that God had already joined them together in Christ.

To distinguish his theology of reconciliation from secular activism on the one hand and Christian quietism on the other, Campbell adopted the discourse of orthodoxy earlier deployed by Scudder, Eliot, and Ransom. "We are concerned with the primitive and heretical socio-theology of the crusaders as well as the crawl of the church but we do not see ourselves as having the an-

swers in our hands," Campbell wrote to Percy, insisting on theological sound-
ness and ideological openness while affirming the necessity of political engagement (1–2).[1] Elsewhere, he contended that Christian social action should
be "based on a well-defined orthodoxy. And it must be an orthodoxy which
takes it into the streets" ("The Day of Our Birth" 5).

By aligning orthodoxy with humor and reconciliation—that is, with comedy instead of tragedy—Campbell upended the dour scheme of Ransom's
God without Thunder (1930). Where Ransom's tragic orthodoxy counseled
contentment with one's "existing condition," Campbell's comic orthodoxy insisted that reconciliation between neighbors be realized in action (*God without Thunder* 116). Comedy was Campbell's way of expressing a commitment
to religious tradition that longed for the future more than it mourned for the
past. This turn to comedy marks an important shift in the Christian radical
politics of history I'm chronicling in this book. To make a traditioned radicalism salient in his midcentury southern context, Campbell not only had to
oppose the milquetoast progressivism of lukewarm liberals (represented by
his sometime employer, the National Council of Churches); he also had to
break the virtual monopoly over the past held by reactionary segregationists.
The discourse of orthodoxy helped him steer a course for the radical middle.

When he received Campbell's letter, Percy had already committed to write
an essay for the Committee's journal *Katallagete: Be Reconciled!* (In the journal's oddly insistent title, the English to the right of the colon translates the
transliterated Greek to left of the colon, an imperative verb enjoined by Saint
Paul in Second Corinthians.) Percy had joined both the Committee and
Katallagete's editorial board by the time the promised essay appeared in the
December 1965 issue. In the piece, Percy crystallized the ethos of the Churchmen: "At least in one Southerner's opinion, the ultimate basis for racial reconciliation must be theological rather than legal and sociological, and in the
South, perhaps more than in any other region, the civil and secular consciousness is still sufficiently informed by a theological tradition to provide a sanction for racial reconciliation" ("The Failure and the Hope" 18).[2] In Percy's view,
the breakdown of the old southern Stoic tradition, which had authorized a
personal ethic of noblesse oblige among select upper-class whites but stulti-
fied the widespread development of a Christian social conscience in the region, offered southern Christianity a new opportunity to flourish—but only
if the churches repented of their long failure to stand for racial justice.

Percy's novels are an important marker of the emergence of comedy—both

in the lower, slapstick sense and the higher, Dantean sense of spiritual pilgrimage—in the white southern literary tradition. This generic development
in turn reflects a redemptive reading of southern history as ultimately comic,
though riven with ironies and losses, that sets Percy apart from the earlier
tragedians of white southern literature: in fiction, the early Faulkner; in poetry and belles lettres, Ransom and Percy's second cousin William Alexander
Percy (1885–1942), the eccentric Delta planter and writer who raised Percy
and his brothers after their parents' deaths. The comic conception of southern
history that Percy shared with Campbell and the other, mostly white and male
Christian intellectuals—both Protestant and Catholic—who comprised the
Committee of Southern Churchmen and contributed to *Katallagete* during
the mid-1960s and early 1970s, had both political and personal implications.[3]
For these writers, the irruption of a Black-led nonviolent revolution in the
South gave a comic-Christian twist of redemption to the tragic-Stoic Lost
Cause narratives on which they had been raised.[4] This comic approach to
history, I argue, grounded the more hopeful, activist political orientation of
the Churchmen compared with the earlier white southern tragedians. The
Churchmen looked back to the Socialist Fellowship of Southern Churchmen
(FSC) of the 1930s to claim a southern tradition of "prophetic Christianity" to
the left of Faulkner[5] and Ransom's tragic Agrarians.

    While Percy is known for his criticism of American consumer culture and
his transmission of European existential philosophy, his civil rights advocacy
is less often appreciated, though Percy's support of the movement—both as
an essayist and as a citizen of Covington, Louisiana—is well attested, as I
show below. Nevertheless, when Percy is put to explicit political use by interpreters and disciples such as the *New York Times* conservative opinion writer
David Brooks or the late Catholic political theorist Peter Augustine Lawler,
he's most often imagined as a resource for reinvigorating the American Right
(D. Brooks; Lawler and Smith). At most, Percy interpreters of the conservative school read him as a kind of centrist. In their contribution to *A Political
Companion to Walker Percy*, Brendan P. Purdy and Janice Daurio interpret
Percy's civil rights advocacy as a "conversion" from "a segregationist Southern
moderate to an integrationist Southern moderate" (207). By returning Percy's
civil rights–era writing to the context of his membership in the Committee
of Southern Churchmen and his place on the editorial board of *Katallagete*,
I seek to claim him for a more radical tradition. Percy's off-kilter Christian
radicalism could be mistaken for centrist liberalism, but his association with

Campbell clarifies his stance: he sought a radical middle rather than mere moderation.

Percy and the Churchmen found their comic vision difficult to maintain in the latter half of the 1960s when, despite the passage of civil rights legislation, the partisans of Jim Crow continued to oppose Black and white activists alike with violence, while white moderates persisted in dragging their feet on racial justice. The Churchmen responded to white intransigence and the subsequent radicalization and de-Christianization of the civil rights struggle by doubling down on their own radically Christian commitments. They pleaded that southerners, Black and white, be reconciled in a spiritual fraternity beyond what laws could guarantee. In short, the Churchmen transformed the idea of southern heritage, so often a sword and shield of reaction, into rhetorical weaponry to fight for social justice. They sought not to destroy that heritage but to bring it to a new kind of fulfillment.

BRINGING THE DIESEL HOME:
JAMES MCBRIDE DABBS'S PRACTICAL POETRY

In an almost unreadable May 17, 1970, letter to Campbell—one of the last he ever wrote—former Committee of Southern Churchmen president James McBride Dabbs (1896–1970) subjected his old friend to some good-natured ribbing: "I look at this type and figure and I've got to clean it before I write any important letters—I mean to important people—oh, you know what I mean." On his Rip Raps Plantation letterhead—Rip Raps was the South Carolina farm Dabbs inherited and to which he retired from an academic career in the 1940s—Dabbs explained why the type was so bad: "I've about worn out this portable on my book on Southern culture and religion. Tentative title, oh, so tentative, HAUNTED—BY GOD." He had just finished drafting the book and begun revising it. The revision would be his last accomplishment before his death on May 30; *Haunted by God* was published posthumously, sans dash, in 1972. Also excised from the manuscript was its brash final sentence as reported in the letter to Campbell: "If this be paganism, make the most of it."

The letter's ragged type testified to the seventy-four-year-old author's weariness. But if Dabbs had worn out both himself and his typewriter in composing *Haunted by God*, he had also worn out his subject, for, in a sense, he wrote the same book three times. *The Southern Heritage* (1958), *Who Speaks for the South?* (1964), and his final volume all work the same ground—"Southern culture and religion"—to similar ends. By retelling southern history, they give the etiology of southern crimes and southern virtues so that the former may be condemned and the latter continued. Dabbs's other two book-length works—a memoir, *The Road Home* (1960), and the critical study *Civil Rights in Recent Southern Fiction* (1969)—likewise treat the same subject on the comparatively smaller canvases of Dabbs's own life and of literary history. Dabbs may have been haunted by God, but he was also haunted by segregation—a subject he turned over obsessively in his mind and on paper.

That obsession made Dabbs a key member of the CSC. He served as its president from 1966 to 1968, and, along with Percy, he sat on *Katallagete's* editorial board and contributed multiple essays to the journal. Dabbs had been a member of the waning Fellowship of Southern Churchmen in the 1950s; a generation older than Percy and Campbell and a veteran of World War I, he was the Committee's living link to the Fellowship's peculiar brand of modern southern dissent and its 1930s combination of political and religious radicalism. In his "Letter from a Birmingham Jail" (1963), Martin Luther King Jr. named Dabbs among his few "white brothers in the South" who "have grasped fully the meaning of this social revolution and committed themselves to it." A South Carolina planter, Presbyterian elder, Thoreauvian nature mystic, past president of the integrationist Southern Regional Council, and former English professor, Dabbs probed southern history in order to prick the southern conscience.

But that cultural work meant exposing Dabbs's own history and conscience. Percy once likened his literary persona to a Quentin Compson who lived; the southern literary historian Fred Hobson pegs Dabbs with a different Faulkner allusion: "Dabbs, in his musings on the southern past, in his essentially religious view of southern history, resembles no southerner living or dead so much as he resembles Faulkner's Ike McCaslin, who in 'The Bear' sits in the commissary of *his* family's plantation and tries to come to terms with the southern past and his family's role in it" (82, emphasis in original). Hobson locates Dabbs in a tradition of white southern explainers of whom Compson, haranguing his Canadian roommate, Shreve McCannon, in Faulkner's *Absalom, Absalom!* (1936), is the fictional "prototype" (Hobson 83). Real-life explainers in this vein produced nonfiction either defending or excoriating the South and its racist legacy. "It would be to oversimplify to say that the apologists, after 1865, belong to a southern party of remembrance, and the critics to a party of shame and guilt, although something of the sort comes close to the truth," Hobson avers (80). Dabbs unites the two schools of southern explainer as "the only major native southern critic—the only member of the party of shame and guilt—who saw more good than ill in the southern tradition" (95).

For Hobson, Dabbs is more like McCaslin, who repudiates his inherited plantation but lives, than Compson, the tortured suicide, because over the course of his life, Dabbs achieved a hard-won equanimity in his relationship to the past. But even McCaslin was more alienated from his southern inheritance—literally—than Dabbs, who kept Rip Raps and farmed and lived and thought and wrote on the plantation until his death. Despite his social liberalism, "Dabbs was as fully a traditional southerner as one could find, was that purest of traditional southerners, an agrarian," with a better claim to that title, as a working farmer, than most of Ransom's collegiate Nashville Agrarians (Hobson 94). Dabbs prosecuted an in-house critique of southern Christianity, one that drew selectively on the better elements of the southern heritage in order to undermine southern racism and hypocrisy.

Dabbs's most penetrating and widely read book refiguring the southern tradition is his first: *The Southern Heritage*, published in 1958 by Alfred A. Knopf. Early in the book, Dabbs establishes his position as a faithful critic of the South by recounting his family history. His mother grew up "rooted in the past" outside of Mayesville, South Carolina, on the plantation Dabbs would later inherit (6). His father, a Scotch-Irish Calvinist and a newcomer to the Mayesville area, was "on the make," a "man of the future" and "pioneer" without inheritance who raised his family on a small farm bought with his own money, located a mile down the road from his wife's childhood home (4). At the plantation, which he called his "second home," Dabbs imbibed the myth of the Lost Cause from his mother's family. But the influence of Dabbs's father, with his puritanical morality (he was elected to the state legislature in 1906 on a Prohibition ticket) and forward-looking embrace of "new methods of farming," leavened the young Dabbs's sense of nostalgia with an instinct of criticism (5).

For the mature Dabbs, southern history is like a crucial poem, the interpretation of which has been badly bungled by an earlier generation of readers. With this conception, the farmer-professor takes covert aim at the literary Agrarians of *I'll Take My Stand*: "Certainly the lost past never drew me from the vital present—or, at least, not for long. It was rather like a poem in which, strangely, my people had taken part, a tale of old, unhappy far-off things, And battles long ago." Perhaps because of the combined spirit of my father and mother, I criticized it without condemning it, and loved it without being lost in it" (8). The internal quotation is from Wordsworth's "The Solitary Reaper," in which the poem's speaker, an Englishman, overhears a Highland Scottish woman singing in the fields in Gaelic and cannot understand the sense of her words, though they seem to him intensely melancholy; battle is only one of several possible subjects the speaker surmises for her song. Dabbs's book plumbs a southern past that, like the song of Wordsworth's Highland reaper, is one of obscure sadness and unclear import, and beset by a welter of conflicting interpretations. In *The Southern Heritage*, Dabbs sets out to vindicate an integrationist interpretation of that heritage against a segregationist interpretation. His criterion for assigning meaning to the poem of the past is its usefulness for future social growth—a pragmatic criterion drawn from the ethos of his forward-looking father. On this ground, Dabbs pits his antiracist reading of the southern heritage against that of segregationists.[6]

In *The Southern Heritage*, Dabbs develops a theory of "practical poetry," communally authored social symbols that direct the life of a culture, specifically of the South (189). Such symbols "function . . . to clarify and focus life for effective action" (190). Dabbs's method of analyzing southern practical poetry resembles the then-emergent "myth and symbol school" of American studies, and he would rely heavily on Perry Miller's studies of New England in his later book *Who Speaks for the South?*[7] Dabbs's definition of practical poetry likewise recalls Ransom's polemic on behalf of "religious myths" in *God without Thunder*. Dabbs shared Ransom's skepticism toward the excesses of industrialism. But whereas for Ransom religious myth counseled passive contentment with one's present circumstances, Dabbs's practical poetry inspires and directs action. He knew that the Jim Crow regime did not maintain itself, and that either upholding or transforming the racial status quo would require human efforts galvanized by images.

Dabbs's poetic criticism of southern life unmasks the meaning of the symbol of segregation by pointing back to two phases of southern history. First, segregation symbolized the overturning of Reconstruction, and second, beyond that, the antebellum Old South. When white southerners defended segregation, this is what they understood themselves to be defending: a connection to the past salvaged from a brutal war and its punitive aftermath. Dabbs acknowledged that such a connection to the past is vital to the flourishing of a culture, but he disputed whether segregation was a true and useful symbol of the southern heritage:

> We are the products of the entire past. Moved by piety, we wish to preserve that past. Yet, for all his piety, every man has ideals that, though rooted in the past, point toward the future. Some of them he cherishes, others he discards. ... The problem for us now is simply this: to what degree does segregation as a symbol, partly of Reconstruction, partly of the Old South, aid us in interpreting and living in our world? Any obligation we have to the past must be expressed in the present and directed toward the future. We cannot change the past, we can change the future. What help can the symbol of segregation give us as we face the future? (129)

Dabbs answered that segregation can give no help to future flourishing in the South. Some of his reasons are "progressive" in nature, rejecting segregation because it is outdated. For example, Dabbs argued that segregation made less and less sense as the South became more industrialized and Americanized (130). But beyond these forward-looking arguments, Dabbs went on to claim that segregation is a faulty symbol of the southern heritage itself, one that "does not focus correctly our own memories" but rather blurs and blinds them (131). "To hold on to segregation as the essential truth of our past," he averred, "is to make a sad mistake" (131).

According to Dabbs, the practical poetry of segregation gets both of its historical referents wrong. The wrongness in question here is not factual inaccuracy, for Dabbs is frankly invested in what Ransom calls "more-than-historical history," a history consciously mythified and idealized for useful political purposes. Rather, segregation as a selective symbol of historical meaning fails to pick out the values useful to life and cultural flourishing in either of the epochs to which it refers, because segregation privileges the abstraction of race over the concreteness of what Dabbs calls "production" (132). Bringing a sort of sacramental, agrarian materialism to bear on his analysis—in keeping with the tradition of Buck Kester and the FSC's "Friends of the Soil"—he argues that "spiritual values" arise organically from "man's necessary relation to the earth," and that therefore "one has to consider the mode of production of primary importance, not only as livelihood but as life" (133).

In this farmer's ideology-critique, Dabbs concludes that the meaning of the poem of segregation is "confusion of race relations with labor relations," justified by a pathetic appeal to a vanished past (155). By playing Black and white workers off one another, middle- and upper-class southerners depressed wages to their own profit (112–13). As an artifact of so-called "Redemption," the white reconquest of political power in the South that put an end to Reconstruction, segregation redefined southern virtues in terms of racial division per se—a spurious virtue, an ideological screen that allowed well-off whites in the rapidly industrializing South at the turn of the twentieth century to prosper at all other southerners' expense. Dabbs anticipates Campbell's definition of southern tragedy as failed interracial working-class cooperation when he notes that the practical poem of segregation erased the memory of the late nineteenth-century Populist revolution that almost was: "We permitted the unhappy events of Reconstruction to distract us from the basic problem of production and to confuse us with the pseudo-problem of race" (206–7). On Dabbs's understanding, segregation then went on to destroy those Old South values actually worth preserving that had emerged organically from farm life: love of the land, neighborliness, hospitality, leisure, a sense of place and, above all, manners (133–34, 136–37).

For Dabbs to be consistent in his agrarian-materialist method of interpretation, he must acknowledge that the Old South values he defends arose organically from a mode of production dependent on the Black chattel slavery that he abhorred. To his credit, Dabbs did not shy from this challenge, especially with regard to manners: "We ought not to have had slavery; but, given slavery, one either develops the manners suited to it or becomes a barbarian" (139). The elaborate southern code of manners developed alongside, or even as a by-product, of verbal techniques of slave control: "Finding force relatively unprofitable, [the South] developed persuasion. . . . Therefore the South developed words; it developed manners. From this point of view, the manners of the ladies and gentlemen were in part the fine flower of that rough courtesy which got the cotton picked and the cane ground" (140). For Dabbs, however, rooting southern manners in its slave power did not invalidate the value of manners; the code of manners was rather a social good that arose paradoxically out of social evil.

Dabbs even suggests that the social good of manners may even be inextricable from the evil of slavery by comparing the slave system to the industrial free-labor North: "The Southerner had to get along with people all the time; the Northerner mainly in off hours after he'd quit fooling with machines. Now, I suppose our chief necessity in the world, and also perhaps our chief happiness, is to get along with people. . . . The Southern mode of production, however paradoxical it may seem, did prepare for that necessity better than the Northern" (142). The argument here, tendentious in the extreme, falls apart under logical pressure. The claim that practice in verbal techniques of control, on the part of southern whites, and deference, on the part of southern Blacks, would suit those same southerners for relationships of equitable, flourishing human intercourse—or, at least, would better prepare southerners for such relationships than northern practices of mechanical manipulation—is at best unproven. The opposite case seems just as likely to be true: if the northern industrial economy was more impersonal than the southern slave economy, at least it spared personal relations from blatant verbal manipulation undergirded by the threat and the practice of violence. At this point, Dabbs veers perilously close to the bankrupt arguments of antebellum apologists for the slave economy, who insisted that southern slavery was morally superior to northern wage-slavery.

Dabbs's claim that positive southern virtues were paradoxically nurtured by the wicked southern slave economy also exposes the deep theological structure of *The Southern Heritage*. Hobson, noting Dabbs's Presbyterian heritage, has remarked on the influence of a Calvinist theology of providence on Dabbs's narration of southern history: "It was impossible for Dabbs to discuss the South and race without finally coming around to the role of Providence in Southern affairs. The South was destined, he suggests, to show the way to the rest of the world," to be a Winthrop-esque city on a hill in race relations (Hobson 88). "The South is a pilot plant, set up under fortunate circumstances, where the white and colored races can learn how to settle the frontier that now divides them," Dabbs writes in *The Southern Heritage*. "Those who are Calvinists might well believe that the South, like Queen Esther, has come to the kingdom for such a time as this" (215–16).[8] To be sure, such lines betray Dabbs's early-civil-rights-movement confidence that eroded over the course of the 1960s, not to mention a powerful ideology of southern exceptionalism. Dabbs would shed, mostly if not entirely, his more grandiose claims for the South's world-historical mission in later books, shifting his emphasis to specifically religious community. *Haunted by God* ends with the possibility that "the church," rather than the South, "might then become a city set upon a hill, a light unto all the people" (251). Nevertheless, he stuck to the general outline of this providential story when he renarrated southern history in darker tones in his subsequent books.

Hobson downplays the function that Dabbs accords slavery in preparing those southern virtues that suited the region for its new leading role. "Even slavery, [Dabbs] maintains, may have contributed to some Southern virtues—manners and leisure among them," Hobson admits (88). But since, for Dabbs, spiritual values arise organically from the mode of production, in *The Southern Heritage* southern manners and leisure unequivocally owe their existence and character to slavery. A Calvinist theology of divine providence does shape Dabbs's narrative of southern history, but the rod and staff of that providential guidance are rough tools.

Dabbs's arguments rooting southern virtues in the slave economy rely for narrative coherence on foundational themes in Christian theology. Dabbs tells the story of the South as a type of *felix culpa*, or "fortunate fall": the idea that original sin, by making possible the redemption of humanity in Christ, ultimately brought more blessing than continued human innocence would have. Milton's Adam, in book 12 of *Paradise Lost*, expresses the idea most pithily:

O goodness infinite, goodness immense!
That all this good of evil shall produce,
And evil turn to good; more wonderful
Than that which by creation first brought forth
Light out of darkness! full of doubt I stand,
Whether I should repent me now of sin
By mee done and occasiond, or rejoyce
Much more, that much more good thereof shall spring,
To God more glory, more good will to Men
From God, and over wrauth grace shall abound. (lines 469–78)

The rhetoric of the fortunate fall allowed Dabbs to claim a good heritage from a flawed lineage. Stories in which God's providence "good of evil shall produce"—whether through Adam's Fall or Christ's death, to take the two most prominent examples—were familiar to Dabbs, and to his Christian readers, from hearing sermons, singing hymns, and reading their Bibles (and their Milton). That an evil history, like the history of southern slavery, might produce real goods that ought to be preserved and passed on would be unsurprising to readers whose moral sensibilities were shaped by long rehearsal of this theological narrative. In Dabbs's version, the South commits its original sin by enslaving Africans, receives God's punishment in the Civil War and Reconstruction, and then, finding itself endowed by grace with a personable way

of life as a paradoxically good by-product of its vile economy of human manipulation, faces the possibility of redemption in the civil rights movement:
a chance to become an example to the world by building a humane hybrid
agrarian-industrial economy and nurturing interracial understanding.

The narrative typology of the fortunate fall likewise enables Dabbs to bro-
ker the relationship between tragedy and comedy, with the emphasis landing
ultimately on comic redemption. In this, Dabbs drew deeply upon his own experience: the fortunate-fall narrative profoundly shaped the way Dabbs told
his own history as well as the history of his region. In a 1936 article titled "Beyond Tragedy," Dabbs explained his conversion from a tragic to a Christian
view of life through reading the Gospels: "The curtain that falls on the last,
awe-inspiring scene of tragedy rises, if at all, on the first scene of Christianity.
Jesus begins where the tragic hero leaves off" (454). "One goes from tragedy
to Christianity, and it is but a step," he went on to claim, "but it is not an easy
step" (462).[9] With Percy and Campbell, Dabbs shared the sense that redemption or reconciliation can only be approached through alienation, despair, or
failure—that fortune comes only after the fall.

In his autobiography *The Road Home*, Dabbs reveals the personal tragedy
underlying the Bible-as-literature meditations of "Beyond Tragedy": the long-
term illness and eventual death, in 1933, of his first wife, Jessie. In 1932, during
the summer of Jessie's final illness, Dabbs absorbed the Spanish philosopher
Miguel de Unamuno's book *The Tragic Sense of Life* (1912); he calls this period
"the summer of Unamuno" (*The Road Home* 138–39). As he began almost pre-
emptively to grieve his wife in the midst of the global immiseration of economic depression, Dabbs felt himself "initiated into the brotherhood of sor-
row, to which as I felt, all men, consciously or unconsciously, belonged. From
the depth of my own self-pity, as from the depth of Othello's, there welled a
pity for mankind" (138). Out of his experience of personal loss, Dabbs began
to move toward a politics of solidarity.

Dabbs did not merely gloss over evil and suffering when he applied the
narrative typology of the fortunate fall to his life and to southern history.
Dabbs refused to call evil "good" when he subjected the past to his "tragic,
ruthless glance."[10] When grieving Jessie, Dabbs "rebelled at the loss; not bit-
terly, I think, but persistently. I accepted the fact of death without approving
of it. So far as I could see, all things were not for the best, for a flower had been
crushed. . . . Yielding to the logic of events, I yet refused to admit their right-
ness" (172–73). Persisting in this Stoical attitude for sixteen days after Jessie's

death, Dabbs underwent a mystical experience that transcended Stoicism: "I went to bed; and in a few minutes, without warning, and with no surprise, I realized that [Jessie] was with me, a warm and living presence. I had a mental image of her then, asleep and smiling in a still room, and the room was myself" (169). Jessie's resurrection and indwelling came to Dabbs as a deliverance of grace, unearned and unexpected, straining the limits of grammar as well as of belief: "Now, without effort on my part (for how could I strive for what I could not imagine?) she had become I yet had remained herself, I had become she yet had remained myself" (170). Dabbs's constant refrain is "by the grace of God," and he almost rescues the phrase from cliché by intending it literally. For Dabbs, as for Campbell, only God's grace can turn tragic loss toward comic redemption. The same quality of double vision that allows him to rebel at Jessie's death while holding her disembodied presence dear to him also allowed him to see a personable southern culture as the unexpected fruit—by the grace of God—of an oppressive southern history.

In *The Road Home* (1960), Dabbs's inward image of Jessie becomes for him a social icon that, by turning contemplation toward action, guides him to his later civil rights work:

> Wishing my life to consist in and of hers, I wished to think of her all day. Yet I remembered that thoughts which do not pass into actions lose their vigor. I remembered also that she had lived an active social life. Therefore, if I really *thought* her, I should find myself living an active social life, myself a cementing force in the world. My analysis of myself and of the world would be made only that I might come to a more perfect synthesis with the world. My work would not be complete until I had done all that I could to bring men together in that union which is God. (183)

Dabbs's memory of his wife—and not a mere memory, but an animation of her real presence—functions as his own practical poem, a symbol salvaged from a painful past that motivates social action toward reconciliation, "to bring men together in that union which is God." On the personal level, then, Dabbs's image of Jessie is the inverse of the practical poem of segregation, a symbol salvaged from a painful past that motivates social action to maintain division and oppression along the lines of race and class. "I had finally to oppose all division and separation, both within myself and within that picture of myself, the world. When finally I realized what a division segregation was, I had to oppose it too" (*The Road Home* 228). Because Dabbs understood the social world and the inner world as analogically connected, keeping faith with Jessie's presence required him to project her unifying influence outward, in action and in writing.

In *The Southern Heritage*, Dabbs proposes that southerners develop a new practical poetry, a public symbol to replace segregation that would function, on the social level, just as his inward icon of Jessie functioned for Dabbs personally. This new poetry would bring southerners together across the lines of race and class, rather than driving them apart. And it would enable them to conceive of the future in terms of creative imitation, not mere repetition, of the past. The practical poetry of the South, Dabbs argued, from the antebellum plantation through to midcentury segregation, enabled southerners to imagine the future only as a "continuation or extension of the past. The South was a conservative society . . . because it was a slave society that, so far as slavery was concerned, had to repeat in the future what had been in the past" (182). After slavery's demise, "the South simply retreated from the lost line of slavery to the next, and last, line of segregation" (182). Southerners needed instead a symbol that would encourage them to "warp the desirable old into the desirable new" (190). This new poetry would push past the ideological obfuscations of racism and address itself to the mode of production, and it would be flexible enough to connect a usable past to a vital future.

Dabbs crystallized his new southern symbol in a phrase: "the diesel at sundown, rolling home" (206). The image came to him while driving one evening:

> One of those big ten- to twenty-ton jobs passed me and, swinging into the lane ahead, loomed against the sundown sky. It wasn't speeding, it was just rolling easy, the pale smoke drifting from the stack. As I watched it, there came to me the words: "the diesel going home at sundown," and, with the words and with a shock of delighted surprise, a remembered picture, seen many times in the quiet countryside, a heritage of our Western past, immortalized by the Latin poets two thousand years ago: the smoke rising from the peasant's hut at evening. (198)

Here Dabbs references the Latin pastoral tradition as embodied by Virgil's *Eclogues* and *Georgics*; later, he reaches even further back, nodding to the Greek poet Sappho's fragment in praise of evening: "the time that brings all things home, even diesels" (206). Dabbs knew that the actual diesel he encountered was not rolling home, that its driver would soon switch on his headlamps and plunge down the dark highways through the night. But what if the earthy rhythms of farm life—of the seasons, of daylight and darkness—could tame industrial production? What if southerners could bring the diesel home?

Dabbs's proposal for a new practical poetry is a sort of industrial pastoral. Pastoral, as in the case of Virgil—or, for that matter, Ransom's Nashville Agrarians—is often written by sophisticated urban poets, criticizing the corruptions of the city with a romanticized picture of country life. In his industrial pastoral, however, Dabbs, the Columbia-educated country boy, long since returned to the farm, imagines a territory in between metropolis and countryside—a kind of suburb of dissent. In his imagined community, Dabbs aesthetically arranges human dwellings and productive mechanisms to connect livelihood to life. He proposes a setup not unlike the neomedieval Walled Towns of Ralph Adams Cram: "the factory set in the open country or beside a village; the workers settled within that countryside in an area stretching for miles, in homes with gardens and perhaps small farms" (*The Southern Heritage* 203). Like Cram's imagined Beaulieu, Dabbs's industrial pastoral resists the progressive imperatives of economic development—to be always bigger, better, and more profitable—in favor of the imperative of harmonious contextual fit with the environment.[11]

Dabbs didn't recommend getting rid of factories. But he did demand conscious ethical responsibility over unquestioned adherence to the dogmas of industrial progress. He warned against the dangers of "merely grab[bing] the offered factories and plant[ing] them in the fields," of industrializing the South willy-nilly, without considering the historical and geographical particularities of southern contexts (*The Southern Heritage* 197). If his proposed arrangement of home and factory recalled the exploitative mill-villages of the nineteenth century, little better than the plantations, Dabbs claimed that the problem with the mill-villages lay in economic rather than geographical relations. If workers owned their homes and factories, then setting the structures hard by one another would be a blessing, not a curse. A redistribution of ownership, together with careful, conscious planning, could preserve homelike relations of time and space, mitigating the human displacement that characterized previous phases of global economic transformation.

Dabbs's industrial pastoral smuggles in some relatively radical political proposals under the guise of countrified nostalgia. This runs counter to the usual "implied politics" of the pastoral form, which, as William Empson famously noted in *Some Versions of Pastoral* (1935), by associating poor, simple people with unchanging nature, allows the pastoral poet to bemoan social injustice while melancholically forestalling efforts to improve the lot of the oppressed (4–5). Delivering midcentury liberal boilerplate, Dabbs contended that safe labor practices and strong unions could help make industrial work more "homelike" and preserve workers' sense of group membership (*The Southern Heritage* 204). But beyond these measures, Dabbs, drawing on Robert Frost, also called for increasing the workers' share of ownership: "This probably means some sort of co-operative venture. The workers must be drawn more closely into both the conduct and the ownership of business. A man must feel that his place is his own, but partly by free gift of the others: something that in some sense he hasn't to deserve. How can he feel this about a mere wage or salary job? He must have ownership in it" (204–5). Just as Dabbs derives his materialist interpretation of the ideology of segregation from his agrarianism, here he leverages the vaunted southern sense of place to argue for workers' direct control of the means of production. (Or, at least, he militates for *increasing* the workers' share of control.) Dabbs introduces this argument with apologetic good manners—"this probably means some sort of," etc.—a characteristic rhetorical technique he once called "Southern indirection" ("Southern Indirection/The Southerner and Time" 22). But by following his mealy-mouthed opening with a sequence of hard imperatives—"A man must feel that his place is his own . . . he must have ownership in it"— Dabbs exposes his more radical edge. His fidelity to his southern heritage culminates in a kind of genteel anarchism.

It may seem that by turning his imagination to labor relations rather than race relations, Dabbs abandons the ostensible purpose of *The Southern Heritage*: to show that segregation betrayed that heritage, and that a South dedicated to racial equality would better preserve true southern virtues than the Jim Crow regime. But if Dabbs's argument that the ultimate meaning and political function of segregation was to preserve the profit margins of the white middle and upper classes is true, then his industrial pastoral strikes at segregation's heart. His substitution of a practical poetry of economics—of production or livelihood, as he called it—for a practical poetry of race is his strongest volley against segregation. However, when Dabbs asserts that after redressing economic injustice "racial problems will tend to solve themselves," he shows himself to be something of a vulgar agrarian materialist, underestimating racism's power to sustain oppression beyond its function as economic ideology (207).

"The diesel at sundown," though it activated some widely shared southern cultural values, was the invention of a single eccentric, bookish farmer and ex-professor. How could it compete with the symbolic juggernaut of racism or the collectively authored myth of the Lost Cause? Dabbs puts his finger on a real need in the South for a new social symbology, a new canon of practical poetry. But Dabbs himself could not supply that need; probably no one writer could. Soon after he published *The Southern Heritage* in 1958, Dabbs appeared on the prime-time ABC television program *The Mike Wallace Interview*. When asked what his neighbors thought of him, Dabbs couldn't help but snicker. With a wry cock of his head, he replied: "Perhaps I belong to the aristocracy of the damn fools in the South. That's one way of putting it." As his friend Campbell knew, however, there's a certain kind of holy witness that only damn fools can bear.

PUNCHING THE DEPUTY:
WALKER PERCY'S GENTEEL ANARCHISM

Among other ways, Walker Percy bore his witness through the fictional creation of a remarkable damn fool: Will Barrett, the afflicted young scion of a Mississippi Delta planter family who, in *The Last Gentleman* (1966), returns to the South after failing out of Princeton and working as a janitor in Manhattan. During one sixty-page stretch, Barrett takes off on an unhinged picaresque romp that unexpectedly confronts him with the darkest elements of his personal southern past. He stumbles into a race riot on the campus of the State University—an event modeled on the reaction to James Meredith's integration of Ole Miss in 1962—during which he's hit in the stomach with the pole end of a Confederate flag, trips, and knocks his head on a Civil War monument. He comes to in a fugue state in the cab of a Trav-l-Aire camper truck, with nothing but a scribbled-in notebook and a highway map to guide him. The map points unaccountably to New Mexico; the notebook's jottings on pornography and theology leave Will curious but in the dark. In his snug little self-contained home-on-the-go, the amnesiac Barrett, shorn of his past, his relationships, and his "place," becomes a kind of anti-southerner. (Indeed, Barrett is already an inverted agrarian: he has let his inherited plantation go to seed and draws his only farm income from Soil Bank checks. He's a plantation owner paid, by the federal government, *not to farm*.) But Barrett's heritage is not so easily escaped. Will is out of cash, his wallet stolen while he was unconscious. As his memory gradually returns, he realizes he must go down to Ithaca, his hometown on the Delta, to retrieve some savings before he can light out for the territories. In order to fund this existential pilgrimage, Will has to face his father's suicide, the painful trauma at the root of his recurrent dissociative episodes.

All the major themes of classic southern literature are here: racism, family, suicide, mental illness, sex, religion, and the legacies of slavery and the Civil War. Percy handles these weighty and familiar matters with a light touch, his style at once beguilingly oblique and hilariously harebrained. By means of jokes and Dabbs-esque "Southern indirection," *The Last Gentleman* transposes white southern traditions from a tragic to a comic key. And this treatment is representative of Percy's larger body of work. As his biographer Jay Tolson aptly puts it, "If, to paraphrase Karl Marx, history repeats itself, first as tragedy, then as farce, Faulkner has given fine literary shape to its first repetition and Percy (among others) to its second" (15). Percy once remarked that he wanted to begin where Faulkner left off, with a living Quentin Compson, and none of his characters fit that bill more closely than erstwhile Princetonian Will Barrett, who, unlike Compson, "will bear it"—"it" being the vaunted burden of southern history—without succumbing to suicide.

Percy had good reason to hope that Quentin Compson could live. His grandfather, also named Walker Percy, shot himself in the chest with a shotgun in 1917, and his father, LeRoy Pratt Percy, shot himself in the head with the same kind of weapon in 1929 (Tolson 32, 45). Rumors of suicide shadowed the 1932 death, in a mysterious automobile accident, of his mother, Mattie Sue Phinizy Percy, as well (99–100). "Much of Walker Percy's concern with Christian faith," Ralph Wood contends, "springs from his desire . . . for a more liberating vision of life than a venerable past can itself supply. The comic freedom implicit in the Gospel will provide Walker Percy an alternative" to the tragic vision he inherited from his forebears (143).[12] That the tragic past had determined his future because the future would merely repeat the past was perhaps Percy's deepest fear. Percy fought to glimpse southern history as divine comedy rather than ineluctable tragedy in order to dodge its seeming decree of personal doom.

Percy's youngest brother, Phin, was in the car with their mother when, in 1932, the Buick she drove leapt off a bridge outside of Greenville, Mississippi, and plunged twenty feet into the bayou below. As the car filled with water, Phin tugged and tugged, trying to pull his mother free from the driver's seat. When her hand went limp, Phin pushed through the open back window toward the surface. The ten-year-old boy swam to shore and ran for help, but by the time he returned, others had already pulled his lifeless mother from the car. "Uncle Will" Percy, Phin and Walker's second cousin and surrogate (and soon adoptive) father, took command at the scene and had Phin taken home. It was Will Percy—poet, memoirist, semi-closeted gay man, lawyer, and paternalistic planter of the old school—who principally cared for Phin in the aftermath of the accident. When the boy woke in the night, "screaming and crying, terrified by strange, almost metaphysical dreams about the nature of time," Uncle Will "would get up and read to Phin, usually from the Greek myths, including the myth about Chronos and the beginning of time" (Tolson 100).

It's not clear from Jay Tolson's account, based on an interview with Phin, what Chronos myth Will read to the boy; there isn't, strictly speaking, a particular "myth about Chronos" in the Greek tradition. The most likely candidate is Hesiod's *Theogony*, in which the father of Zeus, the Titan Cronos or Cronus—often conflated, even by the ancient Greeks, with Chronos, the personification of time—castrates his abusive father, Ouranos, with a scythe and, later, devours his own children (lines 139ff., 453ff.). As a response to questions about the nature and origin of time, the *Theogony*'s account of Cronus is unlikely to allay anyone's nightmares. For Hesiod, domestic violence inaugurates time, which unspools from there in a tragic cycle of escalating damage.[13]

If Walker Percy was less outwardly affected than Phin at the time of their mother's death, as an adult, the novelist wrestled with the same questions about the nature of time that haunted his brother's boyhood nightmares. The traumatic deformation of time into an inescapable cycle of familial violence marks the narrative technique of *The Last Gentleman*, especially the section in which Will Barrett returns to Ithaca. What's particularly interesting about this sequence is that it also contains the 1966 novel's only explicit treatment of civil rights activism, when Will helps to spring a small interracial group of "outside agitators" free from trouble with the Ithaca police. I read this concatenation of comic plot, political theme, and time-bending technique as Percy's argument for what a novelist such as himself—white, southern, and Christian—could do in the mid-1960s on behalf of the struggle for Black rights: foster a true and healthy reckoning with the violent southern past on behalf of educated white moderates like his protagonist.

When *The Last Gentleman* rewrites as comedy a historical narrative handed down by white fathers as tragedy, it moves toward solidarity across the lines of race and class. Working in a tragic literary tradition that exalted particular great souls and licensed the paternalistic performance of aristocratic virtues in the face of certain defeat, Percy turned to comedy to encourage the recognition of common humanity, a democracy of faults and foibles, with an expectation of ultimate reconciliation. In this, he echoes Campbell's credo: we're all bastards, but God loves us anyway. For Percy, the distinction between tragedy and comedy maps onto the distinction between Stoic and Christian morality. Percy's divinely comic approach to history counsels neither wholesale embrace nor total disavowal of the past. Instead, he balances partial embrace against partial disavowal, selectively plundering the southern heritage for equipment for reconciliation.

In *The Last Gentleman*'s Ithaca episode,[14] Percy merges past and present events to emphasize Will Barret's anxious relationship to his heritage. At some points, this temporal conflation is presented as an effect of Will's dysfunctional psyche. When Barrett arrives in the town at evening, his memory has begun to return after his accident at the State University, but this state of postamnesia only renders him more unstable. Heading into town from his Trav-1-Aire the next morning, Will remembers how he would walk the levee "with his father and speak of the galaxies and of the expanding universe and take pleasure in the insignificance of man in the great lonely universe," while his father, Ed Barrett, recited the doleful poetry of Matthew Arnold or told great tales about Will's grandfather (309). The memory provokes "a little fit" during which Will has a vision of "old men ... in a circle around him, looking at him from the corners of their eyes" (310). All of Will's transactions in Ithaca are carried out under the sidelong looks of his fathers, looks that seem both to acknowledge and to deny Will's family resemblance.

Barrett's forebears, whether attorneys, sheriffs, or politicians, are men devoted to law, aristocratic opponents of the lawless Ku Klux Klan, and defenders of "Negroes"—provided that the latter intend to keep their place. The Barrett men's moral rectitude—like that of gun-toting Atticus Finches—is premised on their aristocratic sense of themselves as a cut above the rabble, whether Black or white. And they are prepared to back up this supposed superiority with violence: almost every memory Will recalls includes at least the threat of gunfire. In Will's father's case, the assurance of one's own moral superiority, liable as it is to morph into doubt of the same, and the willingness to demonstrate that moral superiority at gunpoint, make for a deadly combination. But even if this heritage damages Will psychically and deprives him of his dad, he still longs in some way to imitate his forefathers.

Will's family history won't stay put in the novel; his past isn't even past. At times, Percy allows events Will only knows as family legends to careen into the narrative present without presenting this as an effect of Will's conscious-ness. This technique marks a kind of disorder in the novel's form rather than a psychological difficulty peculiar to Barrett. After he retrieves his money from the Ithaca bank, Will stops in "a Negro district" to call his fiancée on a pay phone: "The telephone was ringing in the purple castle beside the golf links and under the rosy temple of Juno" (313). Will's betrothed, Kitty Vaught, lives in this faux castle on a golf course overlooked by a pastiche Roman tem-ple—a comfily commodified Old South fantasy actually located in the subur-ban New South. In the space between the phone's ringing and its being picked up, Will's dead great-uncle walks onto the scene:

> The sheriff put his hands in his back pockets so that the skirt of his coat cleared his pistol butt. "I respectfully ask yall to go on back to your homes and your families. There will be no violence here tonight because I'm going to kill the first sapsucker who puts his foot on that bottom step. Yall go on now. Go ahead on."
>   "Hello." (313–14)

On the other end of line is David, a mixed-race college student who works for the Vaught family, and an embodiment of the future of the South. Just as Will's great-uncle's character was made by standing between Ithaca's Black community and the white rabble, Will's character will be made by his re-sponse to his Black neighbors like David.

But where the sheriff's showdown with an apparent lynch mob is a life-or-death drama of high moral seriousness, Will's resistance to racist power is rife with low physical comedy. In an Ithaca bar, Barrett meets up with Forney Aiken, a northern journalist who artificially darkens his skin in order to write investigative journalism "under the 'cotton curtain,'" a plan which earns him the epithet "the pseudo-Negro" in the novel's free-indirect narration (130–31).[15] Aiken also directs an interracial troupe of actors to perform antiracist morality plays in small towns throughout the South, and they've just finished up a festival in Ithaca. The Ithaca sheriff picked up one of the troupe; the rest—Aiken, a white Hollywood actor, the actor's white mistress, and a gay

Black New York playwright—are hiding out, and they look to Will for help. Will gives the actors the keys to his Trav-l-Aire and sends them out the back door when the deputies barge in. Will sweet-talks one deputy, an old football buddy, out of chasing the actors, convincing him to bring charges against himself instead—a form of nonviolent resistance by sacrificial substitution.

But nonviolence only takes Will so far. With the other deputy, he takes actions that are at once his most radical and his most faithful to his forefathers' violent legacy: Will knocks him unconscious: "For once in his life he had time and position and a good shot, and for once things became as clear as they used to be in the old honorable days. He hit [Deputy] Beans in the root of his neck as hard as he ever hit the sandbag in the West Side Y.M.C.A." (325). Will practices his fathers' violence in the name of justice, but, ironically, rather than violently *enforcing* the law, Will violently *opposes* the law. In his improvisatory imitation of the moral tradition he inherited, Barrett radically revises its politics. For Will, faithfulness to "the old honorable days" requires a sort of genteel anarchism much like the one Dabbs drew from *The Southern Heritage*. Barrett becomes a half-willing radical, not in spite but because of his aristocratic lineage. Importantly, this revision of his inherited moral tradition is vectored through Will's alienating sojourn in Manhattan, signified by reference to his boxing practice at "the West Side Y.M.C.A." Though he bravely stands up to a racist deputy, Will Barrett is no remarkable hero like his great-uncle, the sheriff. Barrett is rather an almost disposable cog in the hijinks machinery of the actors' escape. Aiken and his troupe leave Will stranded in Ithaca, forcing him to find another way to reach their backup rendezvous across the river in Louisiana.

To escape Ithaca, Will must confront the violence of his past and literally take from it the equipment that he needs. When darkness falls—Barrett, laziest of rebels, naps away the afternoon in a clump of willows—Will sneaks up on his old house. A comically large number of Will's aging aunts sit on the wraparound porch, where they watch *The Price Is Right* and read books defending Jim Crow. Here, in an inverse image of Will's creative imitation of his fathers' just violence, all the worst elements of the white southern tradition collude with televisual consumption society. *The Last Gentleman* presents Will's heritage as a politically unstable resource, liable to co-option for a host of competing interests.

At this moment, the violent past once again crashes into the narrative present. Will relives in full a memory the novel has so far replayed only in fragments: his father's death. The boy Will Barrett sits on the porch tending to a Brahms record on a Philco while his father paces under the streetlamp. On the levee before them, white couples park and neck, much to Ed Barrett's chagrin. From the Black neighborhood down the road come music and laughter and the "ham-rich smell of the cottonseed oil mill" (328). "Father, why do you walk in the dark when you know they've sworn to kill you?" the boy Will asks (330). A policeman stops and gives the lawyer a piece of news and leaves; no one comes to kill Ed Barrett. Ed can only imagine a strict repetition of the Barrett tradition of just violence, where grown-up Will enacts a creative improvisation. The showdown's failure to materialize seems to deprive the elder Barrett of his shot at moral selfhood. The father speaks cryptic words of defeat to his son, walks inside the house, and climbs the stairs to his office, where he loads both barrels of a twelve-gauge shotgun and fires them into his chest with his thumbs. At the sound of the blast, Will snaps back to the present. "A young man his own age," Black, stumbles upon Will in the clump of trees and pauses "for a long half second. They looked at each other. There was nothing to say. Their fathers would have had much to say. . . . But the sons had nothing to say" (332).

This is among the saddest passages Percy ever wrote, and not only for the boy Will's plaintive cry to his father—"Don't leave"—and the grisly details of the father's suicide (331). The adult Will's silent failure of communication with the young Black man in the trees adumbrates the tragic failure of educated white southerners to support the Black struggle for civil rights. Percy echoed these themes in a 1965 essay for the the New York Review of Books entitled "The Fire This Time," riffing on James Baldwin to announce that, in the wake of the violence of 1964's Freedom Summer, judgment for the South was now at hand. In the essay, Percy postulates an alliance between southern Blacks and educated whites—between the man in the trees and Will Barrett—as "the only doorway out of the closed society" of the Deep South. For now, Will fails to open that door.

Yet the "nothing" the two young men share in this moment is neither empty nor insignificant, but a freighted absence, a pregnant pause. It is not the "silence" about racial injustice that Percy considered the "peculiar" sin of "the twentieth-century Christian South" ("The Failure and the Hope" 17). On the contrary, having "nothing to say" is always meaningful for Percy. He repeats the phrase twice at this point in The Last Gentleman. In the essay "The Fire This Time," he rings changes on it three times, twice at the beginning—"There is not really a great deal to be said about Mississippi now" and "there is not much to say now"—and, after quoting one African American woman's account of police injustice, in the essay's final line—"It is somewhere along here that it comes over you that there is not really much to say."[16] There's a great difference between not saying anything, and saying, publicly and repeatedly, in your well-read novel and in the *New York Review of Books*, that *there's really not much that can be said right now*. If the former silence is quietistic (and for Percy, sinful), the latter is invested with moral and political meaning. In *The Last Gentleman*, "nothing to say" catches Will at a crisis of moral awakening, a moment where the old Stoic–Jim Crow script for race relations no longer fits, and he is left groping for new words. It is just possible that here, in a small way, the tragedy of race relations in the South might turn toward comedy, toward reconciliation.

But it doesn't—at least not yet. It would be a mistake to think that Barrett, or the educated white moderates he represents, could move toward interracial brotherhood without first coming to grips with the suicidal ethic of whiteness. Will isn't there yet. When he looks at the man in the trees, Will thinks: "You may be in a fix and I know that but what you don't know and won't believe and must find out for yourself is that I'm in a fix too and you got to get where I am before you even know what I'm talking about and I know that and that's why there is nothing to say now" (*The Last Gentleman* 333). Invoking a racist paradigm of cultural development, Will asserts that this Black man has to progress, to get on Will's level, before there can be commerce between them. But what Percy's novel finally shows us is that *Barrett* is the one who has to change before there can be communion between the two young men. Will must go *backward*, must enter into his past, in order to get out of his "fix" and exorcise the demons of his suicidal aristocratic heritage—a heritage founded on the deadly assumption that white people are more advanced than Blacks.

Barrett begins this exorcism by entering his haunted old house. Will climbs to the attic office, breaks the breech of the very shotgun with which Ed Barrett shot himself to make sure it's unloaded, and beds down in his father's World War I–vintage army cot. In the morning, Barrett grabs his father's collapsible duck-hunting boat, sneaks away, and rows across the Mississippi into Louisiana, where he secures safe passage north for Forney Aiken and his actors. In the very sanctum of his father's suicide, Barrett finds the tools that spring him free—both from the Ithaca sheriff's department and from the mental illness that dogs him throughout the previous sections of the novel. Confronting the wound of his history releases him from the fugue states that render him unable to remember his past, and he doesn't undergo another one for the remainder of the book.

In "The Fire This Time," when Percy insisted that nothing could be said about Mississippi right now, he meant that conversations on what the good society of the South might look like could not even begin until white southerners could no longer kill civil rights activists and Black citizens with legal impunity. He invites the northernization and suburbanization of the South in order to save it: "Yankees, don't go home. If a dislocated and depersonalized suburbia can assist a society which is losing its soul through depravity and brutality, it is for us in the South to be grateful. Perhaps some day the favor can be returned" ("The Fire This Time"). The South must become "dislocated and depersonalized" to save it from "depravity and brutality" before it can take hold of its true heritage, a heritage which just might save North and South alike from dislocation and depersonalization. Percy proposes that the entire South follow the way of Will Barrett, journeying through the purgatory of displacement and deracination to a new apprehension of just what aspects of the southern tradition are worthy of creative imitation. As Barrett's example shows, the politics of that tradition could be utterly changed—radicalized, in fact—through this process of alienation and reapprehension. In "The Fire This Time," Percy goes a step further, locating this purified heritage—a southern Christian humanism—primarily in the Black Church.

Yet as Will Barrett's porch-bound aunts, watching game shows and reading Race and Reason, remind us, the white southern tradition could more easily license conservative retrenchment than Will's erstwhile radicalism. That tradition could also lend its mythopoetic powers to something even more politically nefarious than retrenchment. As Will skitters down the Mississippi in the inflatable duck boat toward his uncle's house, he catches a familiar sight on the Louisiana shore: a Confederate fort, captured during the Civil War and converted into a federal prison, and since become a kind of historic site. Will knows intimately the geography of the entire place, its personnel and its history. When he sees the Stars and Bars flying on the battlement and people moving on the grounds, he assumes a reenactment is on. A closer look reveals a new fence and inmates—men and women, Black and white—in sweatsuits. In this startling image, Percy, writing just at the moment of the old Jim Crow's demise, anticipates the mass incarceration regime that the legal scholar Michelle Alexander has recently called "the New Jim Crow"—an arrangement in which North and South collude, with southern segregation meeting Yankee discipline in the worst of institutional combinations. And there flying over it all is a Confederate flag (or, more probably, the Mississippi state flag, which incorporated the Confederate battle flag into its design), giving the prison the imprimatur of that southern heritage Percy, along with Dabbs and Campbell, tried with all their cunning to resignify.

Percy's skill with interpreting the social symbols that Dabbs called "practical poetry" gave him his own opportunity to punch Deputy Beans in the root of the neck, so to speak. Like his doddering, dislocated protagonist Barrett, Percy was never a willing social activist. An intellectual moralist by temperament, he supported the civil rights movement in print, but, unlike Campbell, Percy was not to be found marching or protesting. Nevertheless, Campbell recognized from the beginning that in Percy's Covington, Louisiana, home— just across Lake Pontchartrain from New Orleans—the novelist had founded "a family residence and base of operation and not a permanent retreat from the world" (Letter to Walker Percy, 1). In his semirural place, Percy established an Audenesque suburb of dissent.

Especially after the "long hot summer" of race riots in 1967, Percy felt compelled to step up his on-the-ground actions in support of social justice in his adopted hometown. With several of his neighbors, "Black and white," Percy helped to form the Community Relations Council of Greater Covington "in early 1968" (Tolson 347). Percy discreetly funded some of the Council's projects, and personally spearheaded the founding of a credit union and a Head Start program, for which he also served as a substitute bus driver. Conservative factions in Covington opposed the Council's actions—sometimes through legal channels, sometimes through extralegal violence.

In the summer of 1970, Percy found himself on the receiving end of this conservative ire, including a Klan bomb threat, when he opposed racist power in federal court. As he told his friend, the novelist and historian Shelby Foote, in a letter:

> This summer I reached the nadir of my popularity here in Covington: testified in federal court as an expert witness (an observer of the culture) in a dispute about flying the Confederate flag at the high school. The blacks want it out. I said they were right. So I got threatened by the Klan: bomb the house etc— we slept in the attic for 2 weeks—not that I thought there was one chance in

1000, but didn't want Ann and Bunt [Percy's daughter and wife] to get blown up. Then I accused the local Catholic school of getting rid of the niggers, running a seg school with holy water thrown on it. Now the Catholics (most) are mad at me. And I do believe they're more unpleasant than the Klan. (Foote and Percy 142)

In his testimony, Percy argued that whatever it may once have meant, in 1970 the Confederate flag symbolized none other than "segregation, white supremacy, and racism," and for that reason had no place in Covington's integrated school system (qtd. in Tolson 353). The flag that Barrett saw flying over the prison just before his escape into Louisiana had to come down. These incidents also demonstrate Percy's leadership from the margins as a churchman, taking his fellow-Catholics to task for capitulating to the world's racist logics.

But in the privacy of his good-ole-boy epistolary exchange with Foote, Percy felt free to use that terrible word to refer to the Black neighbors for whose good he was ostensibly working. As used here, the word is part and parcel of Percy's satirical provocation to his coreligionists—which is to say that in the moment sheer provocation eclipses human concern for his Black neighbors as people; it even eclipses plain good manners. Percy's irascibility—"sometimes I think the creative urge comes from malice," he confided to Foote in another letter—gives his art much of its charm and its moral force (Foote and Percy 128). But his blithe dropping of a word weighty with the bodily and spiritual sufferings of Black people raises the question of whether, when applied to southern history, the lightness of this sort of comedy becomes truly unbearable.[17]

Events in the recent past would seem to show that the efforts of Percy and the Committee of Southern Churchmen to make the southern heritage a help rather than a hindrance to social justice were for naught. In Dabbs's South Carolina in April 2015, a white policeman murdered the Black Charlestonian Walter Scott during a routine traffic stop; in June, a young white supremacist terrorist killed nine parishioners of Charleston's Emanuel African Methodist Episcopal Church after sitting in on their prayer meeting. The most prominent media image of the perpetrator of the latter crime showed him brandishing a gun and several Confederate flags. These two tragedies amplified for many southerners the importance of the nationwide struggle—carried on principally by the Black Lives Matter movement in the wake of the

2014 shooting of Michael Brown in Ferguson, Missouri—against persistent racism, inequality, and threats of violence (in particular, from police) faced by Black people in the United States today. Subsequent calls for the Confederate flag to be removed from the Civil War monument on the grounds of the South Carolina Capitol were met with anxious protests from some white southerners that the flag represented "pride and heritage, not hatred" (Jones). In response, several journalists questioned whether the two could be separated—whether the southern heritage was anything else but hate.[18]

In this light, the efforts of Percy and the Churchmen to redeem southern tragedy seem woefully misguided. How can anyone these days imagine the southern heritage as a resource for a solidaristic, democratic, antiracist politics? Perhaps the idea of a southern heritage ought to be retired rather than redeemed, taken down like the bankrupt symbol that Percy helped remove from Covington schools in 1970 and that the activist Bree Newsome, acting "in the name of Jesus," snatched from the grounds of the South Carolina state house in 2015 (Cep).

These and similar events have prompted a wider conversation among journalists and historians about whether it is legitimate to look to history for any sort of political inspiration.[19] In the essay "Letter to My Son," later included in the National Book Award–winning *Between the World and Me* (2015), the journalist Ta-Nehisi Coates levels a tragic-atheistic critique of any narrative—especially the religious kind—that attempts to redeem a history of suffering. Coates counsels:

> You must struggle to truly remember this past. You must resist the common urge toward the comforting narrative of divine law, toward fairy tales that imply some irrepressible justice. The enslaved were not bricks in your road, and their lives were not chapters in your redemptive history. They were people turned to fuel for the American machine. Enslavement was not destined to end, and it is wrong to claim our present circumstance—no matter how improved—as the redemption for the lives of people who never asked for the posthumous, untouchable glory of dying for their children. Our triumphs can never redeem this. Perhaps our triumphs are not even the point. Perhaps struggle is all we have. ("Letter to My Son")

Elsewhere, Coates has written that a historian "wedded to 'hope' is divorced from 'truth'" ("Hope and the Historian"). The proximate targets of Coates's critique of hope are the civil rights movement–inspired liberal tradition embodied by President Barack Obama and the Black Nationalist tradition in which he was raised. But Coates's arguments react all the more strongly against the comic vision of a white southern Calvinist like Dabbs.

I won't dispute Coates's claims that history *is* tragedy, and that to narrate it otherwise is to falsify the facts. Such claims, as bracingly put as they are by Coates, seem to me by nature unknowable and unchallengeable. But I would contend that *either* tragic or comic histories can license struggle *or* acquiescence, and that particular historical narratives take on their political meanings in the historical contexts of their own production. After all, the tragic paradigm has been invoked for very different political ends by Coates in 2015 and by Ransom in 1930. Percy and Dabbs worked in a white southern literary tradition that had narrated the southern past tragically in order to own the evil of slavery and its legacy without rousing opposition to the injustices Black southerners faced. The tragic sensibility of the Southern Renascence thus underwrote the same melancholically conservative implied politics that Empson ascribed to the pastoral form. When the Churchmen reframed the southern heritage as divine comedy, the shift was politically momentous because it "corrected" the tragic view of a previous generation of southern writers. This comic history motivated civil rights activism, but it came at the peril of redeeming the sufferings of Black southerners too lightly—a charge to which Dabbs's "fortunate fall" narrative is particularly vulnerable. It may be that Coates is right and that today is a time for tragedy, not comedy.

Or we might a find a more measured expression of southern political hope in the work of the contemporary neo-agrarian Kentucky writer and farmer Wendell Berry (1934–). An ally but not a member of the Committee of Southern Churchmen who began his career in the 1960s,[20] Berry synthesizes the tragic and comic perspectives of the two preceding generations of white southern writers I've outlined here. Berry's oeuvre as an essayist, poet, and novelist is vast, and I won't pretend to give a full or adequate account of his significance in this space. But as a coda to my reflections on the Churchmen, I want to suggest that Berry's "Mad Farmer" poems might offer a tragicomic take on southern agrarianism better suited to Coates's skepticism toward redemption.[21]

The comedic, self-mythifying figure of the Mad Farmer first appears in Berry's 1970 collection *Farming: A Hand Book*. These poems—some narrated in the first person, some in the third—recount the legend of a persona that is part Piers Plowman, part Jeffersonian revolutionary, part Southern Agrarian, and part anarchist saboteur. "The Mad Farmer Revolution," subtitled "a fragment of the natural history of New Eden," shows Berry at his most mythic and humorous (*New Collected Poems* 137–38). The Mad Farmer "threw a visionary high / lonesome on the holy communion wine" and went on a drunken spree of plowing and planting (lines 3–4):

> He plowed the churchyard, the
> minister's wife, three graveyards
> and a golf course. In a parking lot
> he planted a forest of little pines. (lines 9–12)

Filled up with "the blood of a god" from the Eucharistic table, the Mad Farmer disestablishes, as it were, the church and liberates the minister's wife, even as he rolls back the ugly and unproductive suburban developments of the golf course and the parking lot (line 7). Berry presents the Mad Farmer, and not the bloodless institutional church or its ministers, as the true bearer of divine prophetic vision. This vision is of a reenchanted world of "goddesses" and "spirits," one where "flowers sprang up in his tracks / everywhere he stepped" (lines 15, 37, 22–23).

To represent this reenchanted world, Berry employs a medievalist temporal drag akin to Scudder and Converse's. His farming rampage quieted, the Mad Farmer turns once more to the minister's wife, who claims him as her true husband:

> [H]is planter's eye fell on
> that parson's fair fine lady
> again. "O holy plowman," cried she
> "I am all grown up in weeds.
> Pray, bring me back into good tilth." (lines 24–28)

If the alliteration on "p" and "f" in these lines recall Middle English prosody, the diction is even more emphatically medievalist. The minister is renamed as a Chaucerian "parson," while the Mad Farmer is dignified as a "holy plowman," a latter-day avatar of William Langland's farmer-Christ. "Tilth" is the poem's most important word; it gathers the whole meaning of the poem into itself. According to the *OED*, the word carries senses of "labor, work, or effort directed to useful or profitable ends"; "agricultural work, husbandry"; "the cultivation of knowledge, morality, religion, the mind, etc."; and "plowing"—and Berry exploits this last sense for its sexual pun ("tilth, n."). "Tilth" resonates with economic, agricultural, cultural, and sexual meaning; it binds all these domains of meaning together in ways that can only seem strangely anachronistic to modern readers. It is a fragment of wholeness, a shard of Berry's vision—a poem in itself. The OED references no uses of the word after 1884. Its passage out of common usage in modern English—the very fact that this word presents as archaic—stands as Berry's condemnation of the twentieth century.

In other Mad Farmer poems, Berry welds the rhetoric of the 1960s and 1970s avant-gardes—"Revolution," "Manifesto," and "Liberation Front" all appear in the titles of the poems—to that of southern rebellion. "The Mad Farmer Manifesto: The First Amendment" (1973) begins by quoting that Virginian declarer of independence, Thomas Jefferson (*New Collected Poems* 177). In a 1994 poem, the Mad Farmer "Secedes from the Union" in Maurinesque repetitions:

> From the union of power and money,
> from the union of power and secrecy,
> from the union of government and science,
> from the union of government and art,
> from the union of science and money,
> from the union of ambition and ignorance,
> from the union of genius and war,
> from the union of outer space and inner vacuity,
> the Mad Farmer walks quietly away. (*New Collected Poems* 326, lines 1–9)

Midway through, the poem shifts into first person, and the Mad Farmer cries out to his neighbors: "From the union of self-gratification and self-annihilation, / secede into care for one another / and for the good gifts of Heaven and Earth" (lines 35–37). Like Campbell, Dabbs, and Percy, Berry radically resignifies the practical poetry of southern cultural history—in this case, the notion of secession. Instead of a Confederate flag, the Mad Farmer flies "the Flag of Rough Branch," his own local place (326). The idea of "The South," to the Mad Farmer, is just another abstraction, and a distraction from the real bonds of neighborliness that neighbors must either recognize or culpably neglect.

Another name in Berry's poetry for the space into which the Mad Farmer quietly secedes, the neighborly place where "the good gifts of Heaven and Earth" are given and received, is the Sabbath. The practice of regularly observing a day of rest within the rhythms of work opens a space within time that escapes the demands of workweek productivity. For Berry, this is a favorite space of poetic composition, and he marks its sanctification by collecting his Sabbath poems in a different volume from the rest of his work. If this poetic Sabbath-keeping is a form of sacred time, a "poetic rest [which] is modeled on and participates in the Creator's rest," as the Berry scholar Jeffrey Bilbro puts it, it is also a time in communion with creation (50). The cyclical temporality of the Sabbath, Berry writes in his introduction to the Sabbath poem collection, echoes the cyclical but not repetitive time of the natural world, its seasons of growth and decay. Nature's "ways are cyclic, but she is absolutely original. She never exactly repeats herself, and this is the source equally of our grief and our delight. But Nature's damages are followed by her healings, though not necessarily on a human schedule or in human time" (Berry, *This Day* xxiii). This natural time serves as a limit to the all-too-human reckoning of time in terms of capitalist development; as Dabbs might put, it brings the diesel home at sundown. In Berry's eyes, "the 'creative destruction' of industrialism, by contrast, implies no repayment of what we have taken, no healing, but is in effect a repudiation of our membership in the land-community" (xxiii). "The fundamental conflict of our time," he concludes, strangely echoing the culture-war visions of Lytle and Ransom, "is that between the creaturely life of Nature's world and the increasingly mechanical life of modern humans" (xxiii).

Berry likewise revises the Twelve Southerners' tragic agrarian commitment to limits or margins. "My work as a writer . . . is intimately related to my work as a marginal farmer," Berry affirms (*This Day* xxiv). By "marginal," he means equally that he is a small landholder, a farmer off to the side and out of the way of the industrialist mainstream, and one who intentionally preserves margins of land against ecological depletion. Keeping the Sabbath is, for Berry, protecting a temporal margin, the analogue in time of the way he farms in space. "The idea of endless economic 'growth'" is inimical to Sabbath because "to rest, we must accept Nature's limits and our own. When we come to our limit, we must be still" (xxiii). By uniting natural with supernatural rest, Berry's poems of Sabbath stillness record his perceptions of a material world saturated with spiritual meaning. They argue for the indissolubility of matter and spirit, carrying forward Dabbs's efforts not so much to defend spiritual values against materialism as to reinvest the material itself with spiritual significance. Even the anarchic Mad Farmer, who rails against all invidious human-created boundaries, comes to rest at the life-giving limit of the Sabbath.

But for Berry, this Sabbath peace is only ever enjoyed as a fragment of a promised whole that remains beyond our limited human experience. Margins—even wide ones, carefully guarded—are but a fraction of the page, the field, the time of one's life. His political ambitions, too, are limited: unlike the Churchmen, Berry's writings reveal no conviction that the South has some special cultural mission to share with the rest of the nation or the West or the world. His agrarianism rejects regionalism in favor of a more particular sense of place. The small farm, at once more specific than a regional culture and more universal, *does* have something to teach the world under its current dispensation of international capitalism. One of the most important lessons that the ecosystem of a small farm can teach, though, is that the work of a person responsive to her place is inimitable just because it is particular; no two well-run farms, and no two well-lived lives, look precisely alike.

Berry's hopes are slower and smaller than Dabbs's or even Percy's, but they are firmly rooted in specific soil.[22] His prophetic voice is one of the best examples of the enduring political genius of agrarianism, which is not only the idealized refuge of conservative nostalgia. For the literary Christian Left from the Depression to today, agrarianism has been a dynamo of ideas about how to reorganize our economic livelihood in ways attentive to the human-scale geographies of the places we inhabit.

6

NEW ENGLAND'S "PERMANENT OF REBELLION"

Catholic Socialism in the American Grain

Rebelling against New England is an old New England tradition. Indeed, this heritage of dissent extends back almost to the founding of the Massachusetts Bay Colony. In 1637, Anne Hutchinson (1591–1643) and her brother-in-law John Wheelwright (1592–1679) were exiled from Massachusetts Bay for proclaiming a radical doctrine of Christian liberty dubbed "antinomianism." For the antinomians, no good works, no obedience to God's laws, could offer assurance of one's salvation—only Christ himself could do that. Further, those who sought assurance in their good deeds and taught others to do the same corrupted true Protestant Christianity, bringing New England closer to Roman Catholicism and, thus, to Satan.

This conflict was more than theological hairsplitting. In the infamous Fast Day Sermon that provoked his banishment, Wheelwright leveled the antinomians' protest at the governing authority of the Massachusetts Bay theocracy. Considering the objection that "this will cause a combustion in the church and comon wealth," Wheelwright responded: *Let it burn.* "Did not Christ come to send fire on the earth? and what is it that it were already kindled?" (169–70). Such a fire would only hasten the burning of Antichrist and the whore of Babylon (the pope and the Roman Catholic Church, respectively), drawing nearer the conversion of the Jews and the Second Coming of Jesus. "Therefore," Wheelwright admonished, "never feare combustions & burnings" (170).

Three hundred years after this sermon, John Brooks Wheelwright, the antinomian preacher's remarkable descendant, hymned his seventeenth-century namesake in a poem entitled "Bread-Word Giver," published in his 1940 collection *Political Self-Portrait*:

> John, founder of towns,—dweller in none;
> Wheelwright, schismatic,—schismatic from schismatics;
> friend of great men whom these great feared greatly (115, lines 1–3)

Despite his friendship with Puritan eminences such as Governor John Winthrop, Wheelwright was forced to dwell in exile, founding Exeter, New Hampshire, and Wells, Maine, during his years of sojourn. John Brooks Wheelwright lived his own kind of twentieth-century exile as a Trotskyist radical and a devout Anglo-Catholic Christian preoccupied with various heresies. Though he published three books during his lifetime—1933's *Rock and Shell* and 1938's *Mirrors of Venus* alongside *Political Self-Portrait*—and was at work on a fourth, under the title *Dusk to Dusk*, at the time of his death, Wheelwright has flown under the radar of most poets and critics in the intervening decades.[1] "Bread-Word Giver" shows that he felt bound to his ancestor by more than the accident of blood: "Saint, whose name and business I bear with me; / rebel New England's rebel against dominion" (lines 4–5). These paradoxical epithets bring an intriguing question into relief: if you rebel against rebellion, if you protest Protestantism, if you, to borrow a phrase from Milton, "reform Reformation itself"—in what direction do you go?

Let two representative men of nineteenth-century New England stand for two possible trajectories of rebellion against rebellion: first, Ralph Waldo Emerson, to whom "the fertile forms of antinomianism among the elder puritans, seemed to have their match in the plenty of the new harvest of reform." In his 1844 lecture "New England Reformers," Emerson argued "that the Church [capital-C], or religious party, is falling from the church nominal [that is, small-c], and is appearing in temperance and non-resistance societies, in movements of abolitionists and of socialists" and other idealists. The seventeenth-century root of antinomianism bore the nineteenth-century fruit of activist combustion in the commonwealth, and the true Church, divested of its sacramental trappings, could be found in places like the Brook Farm utopian commune.

On the other hand, consider Emerson's sometime Brook Farm comrade, the ex-Transcendentalist Orestes Brownson. In 1844, the same year Emerson delivered "New England Reformers," Brownson, having migrated through atheism, Universalism, Unitarianism, and orthodox Protestantism, was received into the Roman Catholic Church (Grocholski). He too was looking for the capital-C Church, but he found it in a very different place than Emerson did. Soon after his conversion, Brownson began to publish his *Quarterly Review,* the journalistic vantage from which he launched salvo after salvo of conservative critique against American culture and society. For the critical daughter or son of New England, then, rebellion against rebellion could go in at least two different directions typified by Emerson and Brownson, respectively: progressive or reactionary, post-Protestant or Catholic, the "party of the future" or of the past.

With these two possibilities in mind, consider the imagery with which Jack Wheelwright rounds out the opening stanza of "Bread-Word Giver":

> Saint, whose name and business I bear with me;
> rebel New England's rebel against dominion;
> who made bread-giving words for bread makers;
> whose blood floods me with purgatorial fire;
> I, and my unliving son, adjure you:
> keep us alive with your ghostly disputation
> make our renunciation of dominion
> mark not the escape, but the permanent of rebellion. (lines 4–11)

Wheelwright refers to his antinomian ancestor as a "Saint"—not in the Calvinist sense of being counted among the elect of God, but in the Catholic sense, as a patron whose name you take, invoking blessing on your particular vocation. This saint "made bread-giving words for bread makers"—an image that transforms John Wheelwright's Fast Day Sermon into a Eucharist for bakers—that is, for workers. The next line moves from Eucharistic bread to wine, in a sanguinary communion of saints "whose blood fills me with purgatorial fire," a most un-Protestant locution. The Purgatory imagery is all the more remarkable considering the elder Wheelwright's virulent anti-Catholicism—after all, for him, Rome was a Satanic power.

Wheelwright dedicates the poem *"To John, unborn"*—a son never to be born, as Wheelwright died the year this poem was published when a truck struck and killed him on the streets of his native Boston, silencing prematurely one of the strangest and most compelling voices in modernist American poetry. Wheelwright's hypothetical son would carry on this radical name and business for the next generation. The line "I, and my unliving son, adjure you" reveals the grammatical subject and predicate of the long sentence comprising the poem's first stanza: a speaker who pleads for help from the revolutionary past on behalf of an unrealized revolutionary future. This position of barrenness and expectation is a fatherly analogy to that of biblical mothers such as Sarah, Rachel, Hannah, and Elizabeth—a lineage typologically fulfilled by the Virgin Mary and her impossible conception of the Christ-child. The unborn John, then, symbolizes the Messianic expectation—always coming, but perhaps never to arrive—of revolution.

Through the imagery of saints' prayers and patronage, a bloody Eucharist, purgatorial discipline, and virgin birth, Wheelwright deploys Catholic rhetoric in the mold of Brownson to argue for a social vision closer to Emerson's. When the stanza ends, "make our renunciation of dominion / mark not the escape but the permanent of rebellion," it marks the two alternatives of rebellion against a rebel dominion: "the escape" from rebellion—the conservative, Brownsonian option—or "the permanent of rebellion"—the progressive option, expressed here in language that outstrips Emerson at his most vehement. "The permanent of rebellion" is a synonym for Trotsky's doctrine of permanent revolution—by 1940, Wheelwright had become a leading figure in the Trotskyist Socialist Workers Party. In "Bread-Word Giver," Wheelwright reconciles two genealogies of New England dissent, and the resulting fusion of Brownson and Emerson is something like *Catholic Socialism*.

This hybrid perspective of Catholic Socialism unites three important intellectuals of Boston's Literary Left in the 1930s and 1940s: the poets Wheelwright and Robert Lowell and critic F. O. Matthiessen. Children of privilege who turned their cultural and monetary wealth to fund radical endeavors, Wheelwright, Lowell, and Matthiessen were, in the estimation of Alan Wald, "rebels" who "grapple[d] with the cultural legacy of New England" (*The Revolutionary Imagination* 36). They also represent some of the highest poetic and critical achievements of the literary Christian Left in the twentieth century. These writers constitute a sort of New England delta in which the three streams of tradition I've examined so far—Anglo-Catholic Socialism, Roman Catholic personalism, and Southern Agrarianism—meet and mingle with the native waters of New England history.

Wheelwright's architect father, Ned Wheelwright, was a professional friend of Ralph Adams Cram, while the critic and novelist Vida Scudder anticipated his radical alignments most closely as an Anglo-Catholic churchwoman and, from 1912, a member in good standing of the Socialist Party. From the time of his political awakening in the early 1930s until his death, Wheelwright belonged to the Socialist Party and the Socialist Workers Party; he was one of the few members of the period's Literary Left to have no truck with the American Communist Party. For his part, Matthiessen took up Scudder's mantle as gay Socialist literary critic. But where Scudder focused on British and Italian archives, Matthiessen helped to found the discipline of American studies by his close, historically informed attention to nineteenth- and twentieth-century U.S. literature. Matthiessen's critical and religious sensibilities alike were forged by his encounter with the Anglo-Catholic T. S. Eliot, who was the subject of his second book, *The Achievement of T. S. Eliot: An Essay on the Nature of Poetry* (1935). This was the first major monograph by an American scholar on Eliot.

Much like his contemporary Eliot, Wheelwright's style defines the fractured density of modernist poetics. He tackled his religious and political themes in experimental forms: a "novel in sonnets," closet dramas, allegorical epigrams, and sprawling prose-poems, exemplifying a stylistic range from agitprop sloganeering to surreal esoterica. This technical exuberance made Wheelwright an appealing artistic elder for the young Lowell when they met in 1940; however, their acquaintance seems to have been rather slight (Wald, *The Revolutionary Imagination* 174). In a 1973 letter to the critic and editor Robert Boyers, Lowell refers to Wheelwright as "the sort of true eccentric I somehow dreaded coming also from Boston and almost the same family. He seemed like a knotted Cummings, so knotted it stopped reading, though not admiration" (*Letters* 602). One notices certain affinities of style and intellectual temperament here—"so knotted it stopped reading, though not admiration" pretty accurately reflects my own first impression of *Lord Weary's Castle*, for instance, though I've since acclimated better to its granitic verses.[2]

Reading Wheelwright and Lowell together helps us see the early portion of Lowell's career as a "fire-breathing Catholic C. O."—that is, a Conscientious Objector—as more than "seedtime" preparing him for future blossoming, as Lowell himself put it in 1959's *Life Studies* (*Collected Poems* 187). Kay Redfield Jamison helpfully glosses this phase as an early eruption of the mania that ravaged Lowell, tempered at this point by the logic and practice of religious discipline. But placing Lowell alongside Wheelwright and Matthiessen suggests a slightly different frame, one larger than the personal: together, these three writers comprise a Catholic Socialist chapter in the literary history of New England rebellion.

Wheelwright, Lowell, and Matthiessen also bring this book's narrative to completion, serving as a lynchpin binding the largely Anglo-Catholic Christian Socialists of early twentieth-century Boston to Dorothy Day's Roman Catholic Workers in New York City, as well as the Southern Agrarians. Wheelwright dedicated a late poem to Day, and Lowell moved in the orbit of the Catholic Worker while living in New York. Lowell likewise studied a long apprenticeship with the Southern Agrarians, following John Crowe Ransom from Vanderbilt in Nashville to Ohio's Kenyon College, where Lowell completed his bachelor's degree. He spent two summers living with Allen Tate and Caroline Gordon in Tennessee—one in a tent in the couple's front yard. Lowell converted to Catholicism while studying with another of the Twelve Southerners, Robert Penn Warren (not himself a Catholic), at Louisiana State University in Baton Rouge.

Wheelwright, Lowell, and Matthiessen don't just bring my story together, however; they also advance it. The Catholic Socialisms these three writers articulate differ from the main tendencies of the writers I've explored so far in their emphatic and self-conscious *Americanness*. Scudder, Cram, Day, Eliot, and Ransom are all marked by a reflexive anti-Americanism, and anti–New England or anti-Boston sentiments in particular, in favor of Anglophile, medievalist, and southern regionalist perspectives. Wheelwright, too, began his poetic rebellion by blasting his birthplace. The penultimate poem of his first collection, 1933's *Rock and Shell*, is particularly vehement. "Come over and Help Us" personifies the spirit of Boston as "a Castrate who, with tongue plucked out; arms, legs sawed off; / eyes and ears, pierced through; still thinks thinks," consumed by a hatred "fierce as the love of God" (*Collected Poems* 47). In his notes at the end of the volume, Wheelwright says that the poem's titular plea, "Come over and Help Us"—taken from the summons delivered to Saint Paul in a dream by a Macedonian in the book of Acts—addresses, in this case, "the world that is not Boston" (60). Help for New England could only come from without. But his epithet for his ancestor in "Bread-Word Giver"—"rebel New England's rebel against dominion"—shows how, by 1940, his disposition toward his homeland had changed. The possessive construction is key: John Wheelwright, the rebel preacher, *belongs* to New England; he, too, is part of the region's heritage, among the most usable figures of its past. Lowell and Matthiessen likewise wrestle with their New England heritage, eventually coming to find in its nineteenth-century rebels—Henry David Thoreau in particular—rich equipment for living and writing as Christian radicals.

"TO BUILD A CHRISTIAN SOCIETY": ROBERT LOWELL'S
CATHOLIC QUARREL WITH NEW ENGLAND

Though Boston boasts a deep well of Anglo-Catholic radicalism, becoming Anglo-Catholic was likely never on the table for Robert Lowell. Whereas Wheelwright, like fellow Anglican converts Eliot and Cram, hailed from a Unitarian family, Lowell was a cradle Episcopalian, unmoved by that denomination's High Church party. In an early letter to Ezra Pound, Lowell rails against what he calls the "insipid blackness" of the Protestant Episcopal Church (*Letters* 4). Later, in 1941, while on fellowship at Louisiana State University, Lowell took instruction and was received into the Roman Catholic Church. Soon after, he went to work for the Catholic publishers Sheed and Ward in New York City. There, his first wife, the novelist Jean Stafford, volunteered (somewhat unwillingly) at Dorothy Day's Catholic Worker house in the Bowery. Her descriptions of its squalor entranced Lowell, and he wanted the couple to move in with Day and her community of bums and mystics. With the help of their priest, however, Stafford dissuaded Lowell from this plan. For the rest of their time in New York, Stafford offered her services to the slightly more palatable Harlem Friendship House, run by the Russian émigré Catherine de Hueck (Hamilton 81–82). Friendship House would soon nurse an ailing Claude McKay back to health and help to facilitate his Catholic conversion in 1943.

Lowell and Stafford were back in New York, and Sheed and Ward was still Lowell's mailing address, though no longer his employer, when he sent his infamous 1943 letter to President Roosevelt objecting to military service in World War II. After volunteering for service twice early in the conflict and receiving medical rejections, Lowell was finally called up just after the firebombing of Hamburg, news of which had seared the young poet's conscience. His letter to FDR argued that the mass aerial bombardment of German civilians violated Catholic principles of just warfare.

Lowell's rejection of Allied strategy in World War II wasn't simply a matter of individual ethical scruples; it stemmed from his deep immersion in Catholic Social Teaching. A fellow C.O. and inmate of the Federal Correctional Center in Danbury, Connecticut, recalled Lowell's single-minded obsession with what he called "Catholic communities" during his imprisonment (Hamilton 93). The poems in 1944's *Land of Unlikeness*, printed in a small run while Lowell was in prison and featuring an introduction by Allen Tate, reflect this social vision. Lowell wrote to his mother that the poems in this first volume were "all cries to recover our ancient freedom and dignity, to be Christians and build a Christian society" (*Letters* 36–37). Though no Trotskyist like Wheelwright, Lowell's poetic vision of a Christian society was antiwar and anticapitalist, emphases that persisted into the more substantial book *Lord Weary's Castle* of 1946. For Randall Jarrell, this latter volume exemplified the spirit of "the perfect liberator whom the poet calls Christ" (189). Likewise, Alan Williamson, in his perceptive study of Lowell's political vision, detects "at least a vague hint of Christian socialism" among the book's images of "apocalyptic liberation" (17). I see here more than vague hints. The early Lowell's perspective aligns with what, in light of the long history of New England radicalism, I identify in this chapter as Catholic Socialism.

The call "to build a Christian society" in Lowell's *Land of Unlikeness* echoes, in many ways, the Puritan ambition to create a Christian commonwealth in Massachusetts Bay. Nevertheless, the poems in Lowell's first book visit divine destruction upon much of the New England heritage. Like the elder John Wheelwright in the seventeenth century, Lowell invites "combustions and burnings" upon his homeland without fear, though he swaps Wheelwright's anti-Catholicism for anti-Protestantism. Here is a brief list of the cataclysms that hit New England in *Land of Unlikeness*: The *Mayflower* rots. Concord's "shot heard round the world" transforms into a suicidal "boomerang." A tornado tears up Emerson's grave. "Sewage," not pillaged tea, fills Boston's "rebellious seas." New England murders Indians, enslaves Africans, and pillages the American West for gold. Its dead are reduced from myths to facts, on the cusp of being forgotten. Its divine light, instead of gleaming on a hill, dims to Satanic darkness.

In the period leading up to the publication of *Lord Weary's Castle*, Lowell's stance on New England shifts. His criticisms of the culture that nurtured him wax profound; they lose their quality of mere adolescent vindictiveness and pierce to the roots of modern Bostonian soul-sickness. Even as he questions more deeply New England's distempered part, though, Lowell emerges as a wounded surgeon. *Land of Unlikeness* attempts to stand outside the culture it condemns. But in *Lord Weary's Castle*, Lowell identifies with figures of New England's cultural history, both for good and ill. The poems of *Lord Weary's Castle* are like the spiritual weapons of Jack Wheelwright's "Bread-Word Giver": "two-edged" swords that "cut their / wielders' hearts" (lines 35–36). We can see this transition in the poems published in *Land of Unlikeness* that also appeared, in revised form, in *Lord Weary's Castle*. The poem best known as "Christmas Eve under Hooker's Statue" in *Lord Weary's Castle* was first published in *Partisan Review* in 1943 as "The Capitalist's Meditation by the Civil War Monument, Christmas, 1942" (*Collected Poems* 1153–54). The first stanza describes the monument's "Union generals / Perching upon a pillar of dead snow, / Two cannon and a turdlike cairn of balls" (1153, lines 4–6). For *Land of Unlikeness*, Lowell wisely removed the scatological descriptor and reworked the title to "Christmas Eve in the Time of War" with "(A Capitalist Meditates by a Civil War Monument)" demoted to a parenthetical subtitle (887). This version gives the war-profiteering capitalist a son killed in combat, introducing a note of pity to his plight. In the final version, Lowell gets rid of the distancing device of naming the speaker a "capitalist" in the title, inviting us to read the poem's "I" in closer relation to the book's other speakers. The final lines of "Christmas Eve under Hooker's Statue" read: "'All wars are boyish,' Herman Melville said; / But we are old, our fields are running wild: / Till Christ again turn wanderer and child" (21, lines 25–27). Lowell renders his speaker a flawed figure of tragic wisdom rather than a merely disgraceful or pitiable object of scorn. In fact, this speaker sounds like Lowell himself, ruefully quoting Melville and speculating on Christ's apocalyptic return.

"The Park Street Cemetery," the opening poem of *Land of Unlikeness*, becomes "At the Indian Killer's Grave" in *Lord Weary's Castle*, raising the specter of the gratuitous violence wreaked by Anglo-American colonists on the Wampanoags and Narragansetts in the conflict known as King Philip's War of 1675–78 (*Collected Poems* 56; 861). But here again, a new ending brings sympathy and insight in lines soldered on from the ending of a different poem, called "Cistercians in Germany" in *Land of Unlikeness* (889–90). Lowell transforms the King's Chapel cemetery into the garden of Christ's tomb as Mary Magdalene, "her whole body an ecstatic womb," gives birth to faith, glimpsing the risen Savior through a trellis (58).

Most telling are the revisions to the sonnet "Concord," Lowell's sardonic riff on Emerson's "Concord Hymn" (1837). In its initial form, "Concord" dismissed the Emersonian tradition of New England radicalism as ultimately fireless. This first published version of the poem, which appeared alongside "The Capitalist's Meditation" in *Partisan Review* in 1943, accuses Thoreau and Emerson of "fleec[ing] Heaven of Christ's robe," while Concord's eponymous "peace" becomes a tourist trap, "for hire or show" (*Collected Poems* 1152). In its *Land of Unlikeness* iteration, Thoreau gets off a bit easier, while "the Emersons

/ Washed out the blood-clots on my Master's robe" (874)—a powerful condemnation from the Catholic Lowell, especially if you recall that it was Emerson's refusal to celebrate the Eucharist that forced him to step down from
his post as a Unitarian minister and take up freelance literary sagery. Emerson's tepid spiritual moralizing constitutes, for Lowell, an ironic betrayal of
the Revolutionary tradition Emerson immortalized in the verses of his "Concord Hymn." The last words of Lowell's "Concord"—"the imperfect globe"—
place the blame for this betrayal at the feet of Emerson's belief in human perfectibility, or conversely, his abandonment of the doctrine of original sin.

In the final, *Lord Weary's Castle* version of "Concord," Emerson's name dis-
appears; his presence is invoked only by geographical and linguistic echoes.
But a still greater alteration to the poem comes when Lowell exchanges the
"embattled scream" of the Concord farmers in the Revolutionary War for the
"death-dance of King Philip and his scream" (*Collected Poems* 30). Here, it is
the sound of war crimes perpetrated by the colonists against Native Americans, rather than their brave resistance to English tyranny a century later, that
"girdles this imperfect globe."

Thoreau, however, comes off looking much better in this version of the
poem. Lowell alludes to the "Higher Laws" chapter of *Walden*, in which Thoreau meditates on his own penchant for savagery and violence in the activities
of hunting and fishing. While living at the pond, Thoreau says, "I did not pity
the fishes nor the worms" (259). Yet he confesses, "I have found repeatedly, of
late years, that I cannot fish without falling a little in self-respect" (261). By
Lowell's time, New England is home to no such sensitive conscience; Walden
Pond is all "fished-out" ("Concord," line 4). All that remains is the memory of
Thoreau, who

> Named all the birds without a gun to probe
> Through darkness to the painted man and bow:
> The death-dance of King Philip and his scream
> Whose echo girdled this imperfect globe. (lines 11–14)

In light of Lowell's conscientious objection, the phrase "without a gun" leaps
out at me here. "I . . . sold my gun before I went to the woods," Thoreau writes
in "Higher Laws" (*Walden* 259). "There is a finer way of studying ornithology
than" by hunting birds, he claims. Birding without a gun requires stricter "attention to the habits of the birds" and so proves more scientifically rewarding
(259). The solitary writer likewise applied his keen attention to the history

of Native Americans in New England. According to Matthiessen, Thoreau "left at his death eleven manuscript notebooks, running to over half a million words, in which he had recorded what he had learned of the Indians, their customs and lore, and their enduring struggle with the elements" (*American Renaissance* 163). By 1946, Lowell found in Thoreau's civil disobedience and concern for Native American history a model of the writer as the unarmed but incisive conscience of New England, uncovering the region's history of violence.

"LITERATURE FOR OUR DEMOCRACY": F. O. MATTHIESSEN'S QUEER CHRISTIAN SOCIALIST CRITICISM

In the late 1960s, the older, ex-Catholic Lowell wrote a sonnet elegy for Matthiessen, depicting the scholar as a fellow sufferer of bipolar disorder whose death broke "his mania barrier to despair" (Lowell, *Notebook* 172, line 2).[3] When Matthiessen jumped from a twelfth-floor window at Boston's Hotel Manger, just after midnight on April 1, 1950, he left behind a note acknowledging the many "severe depressions" from which he had suffered (Sweezy and Huberman 91).[4] "How much the state of the world has to do with my state of mind I do not know," Matthiessen confessed. "But as a Christian and a socialist believing in international peace, I find myself terribly oppressed by the present tensions" (92). The "present tensions" to which he refers are those of the rapidly thawing Cold War—three months after Matthiessen's death, the United Nations would send troops, principally Americans, to the Korean peninsula to contain the spread of Communism.

Lowell's sonnet draws on the two writers' common devotion to Thoreau to reject the violence of Matthiessen's suicide. The critic failed to reckon the potential collateral damage of his fall: "Who knows whom he might have killed? / falling bald there like a shell" (lines 4–5). For Lowell, Matthiessen's self-harm is an act of war, his body an artillery shell that could have struck some unwitting pedestrian. Such violence betrays their common Thoreauvian ethos. Lowell risked and suffered prison during World War II, refusing to serve because he objected to the bombing of civilians; in 1967, he marched on the Pentagon to protest the war in Vietnam. Both acts of civil disobedience followed the example of the model he and Matthiessen held in common: Thoreau, probing New England history and the Massachusetts woods "without a gun." With self-deprecating irony, Lowell steels himself against the temptation to suicide by drawing on these antiwar commitments: "I wouldn't / be murdered, or even murder, for my soul; / no one has a good face to die in war" (lines 7–9). Ultimately, his elegy laments Matthiessen's death as a kindred spirit's tragic break with Thoreau's legacy of nonviolence.

Matthiessen's demise can't escape our attention, if only because so much previous commentary, including Lowell's, has focused on it. But if we let Matthiessen's end overshadow his life and work, we can miss the ways in which he carried forward the labor of others. A politically active Socialist and an Ivy League professor, Matthiessen was also a committed Christian and an equally committed romantic and sexual partner to another man, the painter Russell Cheney, who preceded him in death in 1945. Matthiessen's career advanced the late nineteenth- and early twentieth-century New England literary tradition braiding together radical religion, politics, and sexuality—the queer Anglo-Catholic Socialist stream of Cram, Scudder, Wheelwright, and Auden. Matthiessen's field-defining 1941 study *American Renaissance: Art and Expression in the Age of Emerson and Whitman* brings that tradition's vision of the political vocation of literature, its capacity to catalyze a spiritually vital democracy, to its fullest critical expression. By reading his work in light of this tradition, I hope to join with the critic Jay Grossman's efforts to uncover "a Matthiessen who is more than a suicide" ("Autobiography" 51).

Grossman sets out to correct two oversimplified portraits of Matthiessen painted by previous scholars. On the one hand, we have Matthiessen as heroic gay critic, covertly inscribing his love for Cheney into the pages of *American Renaissance*. On the other, we have a tragically repressed Matthiessen who throws Walt Whitman (and Cheney and himself) under the bus by calling "the passivity of the poet's body" in *Leaves of Grass* "vaguely pathological and homosexual" (*American Renaissance* 535). Grossman, by contrast, gives us a Matthiessen culturally constrained by "the discipline of heteronormativity," whatever his personal heroism or cowardice ("Canon" 828n5). For Grossman, Matthiessen's public performance of professional dispassion and genteel homophobia was the very strategy by which he secured a private, domestic space of same-sex love with Cheney. This was analogous to their living arrangement: Matthiessen and Cheney lived in a cottage in Kittery Point, Maine, on weekends and in the summers, while Matthiessen spent his working weeks in Cambridge as the resident tutor of Harvard's Eliot house and, later, in a Pinckney Street apartment on Boston's Beacon Hill, perched just at the edge of Brahmin respectability. (Cram lived on the same street in the late 1880s and early 1890s, and Lowell grew up around the corner at 91 Revere Street, the house immortalized in *Life Studies'* prose sketch of the same name.)

Grossman sees these cultural constraints at work principally in Matthiessen's treatment of Whitman. He notes that *American Renaissance* ignores completely Whitman's "Calamus" sequence of homoerotic lyrics, despite the importance of those very poems to Matthiessen's literary courtship with Cheney. Further, at several key points in his study, Matthiessen suggests the continence of Thoreau as a better alternative to the promiscuity of Whitman, "replacing the poet who in the first edition of *Leaves of Grass* proclaimed the equivalence of the demands of the body and the soul with a writer who, Matthiessen insists, demonstrated a more coherent and controlled relation to these demands" (Grossman, "Canon" 823). I want to take a closer look at the end of Matthiessen's *Walden* chapter in *American Renaissance*, which confirms just how important the notions of order, discipline—and indeed "chastity," as Thoreau himself puts it—are to Matthiessen's interpretation and valorization of Thoreau. But I'll go on to suggest that concepts like "order," "authority," "discipline," and "chastity" take on new dimensions of significance besides sexual repression or social interpellation when we read Matthiessen alongside Boston's other queer Christian Socialist literary intellectuals.[5]

Matthiessen's summary statement of Thoreau's importance begins by praising not his control but his recklessness, "his full discovery that the uneradicated wildness of man is the anarchical basis both of all that is most dangerous and most valuable in him" (*American Renaissance* 175). Yet by the end of the paragraph, Matthiessen's approbation shifts from anarchy to order. Thoreau's theory and practice of artistic expression involved "a man's whole being, and his natural and social background as well, function[ing] organically together." In this way, Thoreau, according to Matthiessen, "had mastered a definition of art akin to what Maritain has extracted from scholasticism: *Recta ratio factibilium*, the right ordering of the thing to be made, the right revelation of the material" (175). It's fascinating to me that Matthiessen concludes his Thoreau chapter by quoting the French Catholic neomedievalist philosopher Jacques Maritain. Earlier in the chapter, Matthiessen cautions his readers that we misunderstand Thoreau by "thinking of him only as the extreme protestant" (173). But here Matthiessen goes even further by suggesting that Thoreau inherits the aesthetics of Roman Catholic medieval scholasticism!

When he cites Maritain, Matthiessen isn't invoking a conservative European counterweight to balance Thoreau's American anarchy. As noted in chapter 3, Maritain was an important friend to and influence on the medievalist radicalism of Dorothy Day and Peter Maurin in the Catholic Worker movement. Maritain was a fierce antifascist, and later a theorist of European "Christian democracy."[6] Matthiessen's appeal to Maritain enlists a political ally, a cobelligerent on the Christian left. Further, in revealing Matthiessen's desire for a "Catholic Thoreau," this passage crystallizes one of the central ambitions of *American Renaissance:* to baptize American literature in the deep waters of Christian tradition. In agreement with the Lowell of *Lord Weary's Castle,* Matthiessen counterintuitively appropriates Thoreau as a homegrown resource for a nonviolent Catholic Socialism.

Matthiessen anticipates the fusion of transcendentalist and medievalist he proposes at the end of *American Renaissance's Walden* chapter in a wonderful letter he wrote to Cheney in 1925. At the time, Matthiessen was studying at Oxford, soon after the two men met on an Atlantic passage. The letter records Matthiessen's visit to Wells Cathedral, a Gothic church in Somerset, England: "Going into the cathedral this morning we passed a workman— husky, broad-shouldered, 40, the perfect Chaucerian yeoman. He caught my eye—both as a magnificently built feller, and as fitting in so perfectly to the type of fourteenth century work man [*sic*]. He might just as well have been building the original cathedral, as repairing it centuries later" (Matthiessen and Cheney 124). Matthiessen freely blends the aesthetic attractions of the "fine old building" and the charms of this older man with his "unusually gentle" voice and "dark full brown" eyes. (Matthiessen's "type" was an older but still energetic man, like Cheney himself.) The class position of the "workman" is crucial here as well: the filaments of homoeroticism bind the wealthy college student and the working-class artisan into an organic social whole.

As the letter goes on, these erotic filaments become incarnate in a brief touch:

> I deliberately let my elbow rub against his belly. That was all: there couldn't have been anything more. I didn't want anything more. I was simply attracted by him as a simple open-hearted feller, and wanted to feel the touch of his body as a passing gesture. I had a hard on, but there was no question of not wanting to keep myself for you. For a passing gesture is one thing, but you can give the deepest spring of your life *with its full significance*—the passionate uncontrolled offering of your body—only to the man you love. (124, emphasis in original)

This gesture of cross-class attraction under the roof of an Anglican cathedral embodies eros with another telos: not sexual consummation, "the passionate uncontrolled offering of your body," but solidarity and friendship. Matthiessen doesn't deny the erotic, embodied nature of his connection to the workman. "[I]t thrilled me: not only with sex, but with friendliness," he writes (124). Friendship and sexual love, philia and eros, are distinct but commingled for Matthiessen. Nevertheless, his devotion to Cheney acts as a form of ascetic discipline which, even as it constrains some erotic possibilities, makes others possible. Holding in abeyance the possibility of sexual consummation enables Matthiessen to enjoy a sociable erotic connection with the workman that feels deeply significant, though he struggles to put it into words. I want to name this erotic economy of incarnate friendship Matthiessen's *queer Christian Socialism*.

For complicated reasons, Matthiessen resisted referring to his relationship with Cheney as a "marriage," but in this cathedral encounter, his devotion to Cheney works much like Christian marriage (as it is pictured in moral theology, at any rate), governing his erotic life according the virtue of chastity, which is supposed to pertain to the married vocation as well as to the celibate. Crucially, as with the playful chastity Cram displayed at the Caldey monastery, Matthiessen's chastity doesn't entail the denial of the body or of eros. Matthiessen reserves sexual consummation for Cheney, but he doesn't anxiously police his desires outside their bond. Rather, his desire undergoes transformation at once embodied, spiritual, and political as it reaches toward objects other than his avowed beloved. And Matthiessen doesn't feel this discipline as imposed but as natural: "I didn't want anything more," he writes. He finally correlates the naturalness of this disciplined desire with Whitman's poetry. "[I]t was so natural, so like Walt Whitman," Matthiessen concludes his account to Cheney, giving a modern gloss to his encounter with the temporally displaced workman (124). It's important that Matthiessen identifies Whitman with this constrained, yet liberating, expression of desire. At this point, fifteen years before the publication of *American Renaissance*, Matthiessen's categories hadn't yet hardened into the binary identified by Grossman: Thoreau = good bodily restraint, Whitman = bad unbridled sensuality. Or perhaps we can read the tortuous displacement of Thoreau and Whitman in *American Renaissance* as a struggle to make publicly representable the paradoxical erotics of Matthiessen's queer Christian Socialism, privately displayed in this letter to his lover.

American Renaissance's treatment of Thoreau's relationship with the burly French Canadian woodchopper in *Walden* echoes the young Matthiessen's attraction to the rough-hewn, medieval-ish workman at Wells Cathedral. In the same summary paragraph at the end of his chapter on *Walden* I've been focusing on, Matthiessen ties Thoreau's affection for the woodchopper to his love of "uneradicated wildness" (*American Renaissance* 175). Thoreau himself makes this connection at the opening of the "Higher Laws" chapter of *Walden* (the same one Lowell references in his sonnet "Concord"). Thoreau begins the chapter by expressing his desire to grab a live woodchuck and "devour him raw; not that I was hungry then, except for that wildness which he represented" (257). A few sentences later, he claims that "fishermen, hunters, woodchoppers," and other outdoorsy types are "in a peculiar sense a part of Nature themselves" (257–58). Woodchoppers and woodchucks both embody Nature's wildness. This connection—not to mention the Freudian slippage between "woodchuck" and "woodchopper," and the sonic and semantic resonance of "uck" and "wood"—suggests Thoreau may have been *hungry*, in an erotic sense, for the wild woodchopper himself. Henry Abelove explores this possibility at length in his essay "From Thoreau to Queer Politics," reminding us that Thoreau devotes more ink to the physical description of the woodchopper than any other person in the book. The scene in which Thoreau and the woodchopper read together a conversation between Achilles and Patroclus in the *Iliad*, Abelove describes as "a representation of seduction" (36).

In *Walden*, the Greek epics, the woodchuck, and the woodchopper are all figures for the wild, which is the acknowledged object of Thoreau's attraction. "In literature it is only the wild that attracts us," as he puts it in his posthumously published essay "Walking." "Dullness is but another name for tameness. It is the uncivilized free and wild thinking in *Hamlet* and the *Iliad*, in all the scriptures and mythologies, not learned in schools, that delights us." According to Matthiessen, it was this abiding attraction to the wild that enabled Thoreau "to create," in *Walden's* pages, "a true Homeric . . . man' in the likeness of the French woodchopper" (*American Renaissance* 175). Here we might see in Matthiessen what Jack Halberstam calls an "epistemology of the *ferox*."[7] According to Halberstam, desire for the wild might be understood not just as a screen for desires we would now identify as gay, but as the desire to break out of systems for classifying desire. Halberstam's argument about desire for wildness and Benjamin Kahan's argument about celibacy—crucial to my analysis of Cram and Scudder's queer Socialism in chapter 1—share a similar structure: both want to get beyond paranoid ways of reading that see feralness and celibacy as simply coded ways of talking about homosexual desire. Both critics want to lend these underexplored forms of eros their own ontology. Desire for the wild and celibacy—or more precisely, "chastity"—collide in a remarkable fashion in the "Higher Laws" chapter of *Walden*.

When Matthiessen's praise of Thoreau moves in one paragraph from anarchy to order, from wildness to scholasticism, he mirrors Thoreau's own process of thought in "Higher Laws." Thoreau begins the chapter willing to tear into the blood-warm body of a woodchuck with his teeth, but he ends it preaching vegetarianism, even if that choice causes him to starve. Like Whitman, he contains multitudes: "I found in myself, and still find, an instinct toward a higher, or, as it is named, spiritual life, as do most men, and another toward a primitive rank and savage one, and I reverence them both. I love the wild not less than the good" (Thoreau 257). The "good" and the "spiritual life" find their culmination in the virtue of chastity, to which Thoreau sings a paean: "Chastity is the flowering of man; and what are called Genius, Heroism, Holiness, and the like, are but various fruits which succeed it. Man flows at once to God when the channel of purity is open. By turns our purity inspires and our impurity casts us down. He is blessed who is assured that the animal is dying out in him day by day, and the divine being established" (267). The image of chastity as a "channel" that "flows . . . to God," rather than a cork in the bottle of eros, resonates with Kahan's suggestion that we read celibacy as an "elegant formation" instead of a "blockage . . . obstructing a flow elsewhere" (5). Thoreau's source for his teaching is the ancient Hindu Vedic texts. It also recalls Christian theories of chastity as the intensification rather than the denial of desire, like that recounted in Saint Gregory of Nyssa's fourth-century treatise *On Virginity*.

Yet Thoreau's redemption of desire remains incomplete. In the closing passages of "Higher Laws," he figures "appetite" as a Satanic, burrowing "reptile," concluding: "Nature is hard to be overcome, but she must be overcome" (268). Nature, so often the measure of goodness in *Walden* as well as the object of its author's guiltless craving, here takes on a Calvinistic taint of depravity. The only way Thoreau can figure to resolve the double-bind of his simultaneous attraction to the spiritualistic and the animalistic is "to let his mind descend into his body and redeem it, and treat himself with ever increasing respect"— which sounds like a neat solution until you realize that what Thoreau means by respecting his body is "to practise some new austerity" (269).

That practicing austerity could be a way of respecting rather than denigrating the body, that chastity could channel rather than suppress desire: these interpretive possibilities are difficult for contemporary readers to countenance because of what Kahan, riffing on Foucault, calls "the expressive hypothesis," which "posits that regimes of censorship [such as what Grossman calls 'the discipline of heteronormativity'] create . . . a proliferation of perceived sexual activity" in response (5). Kahan argues that in the face of political threats like the homophobic Religious Right and existential threats like the AIDS crisis, having queer sex—and reading for queer sex—acquire a double force of necessity. Yet Kahan points out that one unfortunate by-product of this necessity is the erasure of celibate and asexual persons.

What to make, for instance, of someone like Scudder, Matthiessen's most important forebear as a queer Christian Socialist literary critic in New England. Tragically, she outlived him by a few years, though her writing career was all but concluded by the time Matthiessen published *American Renaissance* in 1941. (If Matthiessen knew of Scudder, I haven't seen anywhere in print that he acknowledges her.) Scudder's most ambitious work of literary criticism, *Social Ideals in English Letters*, was published in 1898 and reissued with a new conclusion in 1923. Her method in the book is Yankee Anglophile Hegelian, tracing the emergence of a kind of Socialist world-spirit in English literature from *Piers Plowman* to the Victorian sages and giving special attention to relatively extraliterary matters such as the rise of women's colleges, settlement houses, the Oxford movement, and the career of the Victorian Socialist divine F. D. Maurice. After this book, she turned principally to writing fiction, social theory, theology, and a wonderful memoir, *On Journey*, published in 1937.

Scudder, as discussed in chapter 1, lived in a "Boston marriage" with her "Comrade and Companion," the Socialist novelist and poet Florence Converse, also her former student at Wellesley College. Yet in *On Journey*, Scudder professes lifelong celibacy without a hint of shame or secrecy—indeed, with a kind of erotic playfulness: "At this point the reader—if I have any— will immediately become less languid. He knows what to expect. He is now going—yes, you anticipate—he is going to hear about my Sex Life" (*On Journey* 210). After a sly paragraph break, she continues: "I am sorry to disappoint." She insists that she isn't "squeamish" or priggish—after all, she's read Freud and even Proust! "My imagination is immune from shock; but I do not see why one should pay so much attention to one type of experience in this marvelous, this varied, this exciting world" (211–12). By her account, Scudder's celibacy allowed her to focus her desires on her intense female friendships with Converse and her sisters in the Society of the Companions of the Holy Cross, and ultimately on the coming of world Socialism. Scudder's 1903 autobiographical novel *A Listener in Babel* identifies this dispersed, sociable eros as something akin to her authentic orientation: "Not . . . the presence of one exclusively beloved, but the presence of all men, had ever been, so she believed, the substance of her unconscious desires," as "the craving for joy of a whole race sorrowing and dispossessed throbbed . . . in her heart" (4).

Early in his relationship with Matthiessen, Cheney, fearing his intermittent alcoholism would pollute their relationship, insisted that the pair give up on sex and live together in a chaste spiritual friendship along the lines of that enjoyed by Scudder and Converse. But Matthiessen, gently and with great compassion for Cheney, sensing that his motivations lay in his shame, remonstrated, though he was willing to try it. "You will say that the body is not necessary to a full love. Perhaps, but I very much doubt it," Matthiessen wrote in a letter of February 7, 1925 (Matthiessen and Cheney 88). Acknowledging the example of Christ's celibacy, Matthiessen questioned its literal applicability to his case: "I worship Christ, but I follow him in the spirit, not in the letter. And in our union . . . I feel that I have followed the deepest voice of my nature. I have loved, and I have given everything for love. I have accepted my deepest instincts and have acted upon them. I felt myself a full and abundant personality for the first time in my life" (88).

During this period of discernment, the couple considered only celibate spiritual partnership and exclusive monogamy as options. As Matthiessen wrote on February 9: "What you want is no further sexual expression. (For it is obvious that the only conceivable sexual expression for either of us is with the other.) For it is (as we both are sure) pure and beautiful. Promiscuity and self-abuse are impure and ugly. So if, for the sake of achieving a full personality, we decide that it is necessary to stop our intercourse since the world cannot understand it, it is clear that we definitely adopt the course of sublimating our entire sex lives" (Matthiessen and Cheney 93). Matthiessen uneasily juxtaposes heteronormative social discipline ("since the world cannot understand it") and self-realization ("for the sake of achieving a full personality") as possible reasons for adopting sexual abstinence. The former likely makes sense to us, but we should consider how a liberated intellect such as Matthiessen's was able to take the latter so seriously as well. Two months later, after they had come back together in a sexual relationship by mutual consent, Matthiessen wrote to Cheney: "I realize that in the last months I am a whole man for the first time: no more dodging or repressing for we gladly accept what we are. And sex now instead of being a nightmare is the most sacred, all-embracing gift we have" (Matthiessen and Cheney 116). The important thing to see here is that both Scudder's celibate spiritual friendship and Matthiessen's spiritually dedicated exclusive monogamy—basically, his "marriage" to Cheney—are ascetic vocations, disciplines of desire which transform eros, enabling some forms of fulfillment just because others are proscribed. In this sense, Matthiessen and Cheney's letters present one of the most eloquent arguments I know of for gay marriage not only as a civil right but as a sacrament.

Matthiessen's blossoming romance with Cheney coincided with his belated discovery of American literature. It was only in England, while studying at Oxford, that Matthiessen read American authors seriously for the first time, beginning with Whitman. "Whitman was my first big experience, particularly *The Children of Adam* and *Calamus* poems, which helped me begin to trust the body," he recalled in *From the Heart of Europe* (1948), giving the homoerotic lyrics that Grossman notes are conspicuously absent from *American Renaissance* something of their due in this later, more personal work (*From the Heart of Europe* 23). *From the Heart of Europe* is a travel journal documenting Matthiessen's experiences in Europe in 1947 as a visiting lecturer at Charles University in Prague and as a member of the Salzburg Seminar in American Civilization. Matthiessen's journeys among writers, intellectuals, and academics in de-Nazifying Austria, National Front–era Czechoslovakia (Communist-led, but not yet fully under the thumb of Stalin's USSR), and other European destinations capture a moment just before the iron divisions of the nascent Cold War had fully set. As he lectures to war-scarred Europeans on Whitman and Thoreau, Melville and Hawthorne, revisiting the canon he had defined in *American Renaissance*, Matthiessen articulates with fresh urgency the political-religious-erotic vision he divined through these authors. What he ultimately calls "a democratic socialism" could, he hoped, thread the needle between the two increasingly antagonistic emerging superpowers (194).

This book contains Matthiessen's most personal published confession of his political and religious beliefs: "It is as a Christian that I find my strongest propulsion to being a socialist. I would call myself a Christian Socialist, except for the stale and reactionary connotations that the term has acquired"

(82). His Christian convictions, Matthiessen acknowledges, "separate me from most of my radical friends. They are the grounds that keep me from being a Marxist in any sense, no matter how much my thought has been influenced by Marx. I am a Christian, not through upbringing but by conviction, and I find any materialism inadequate." Joining with Lowell to critique Emerson's notion of human perfectibility—and "influenced by . . . Reinhold Niebuhr"— Matthiessen invoked "the doctrine of original sin, in the sense that man is fallible and limited, no matter what his social system, and is capable of finding completion only through humility before the love of God" (*From the Heart of Europe* 82). If his Christianity divided him from his radical comrades, though, his Socialism divided him just as firmly from his coreligionists, including his literary hero Eliot. "I would differ from most orthodox Christians today, and particularly from the tradition represented by T. S. Eliot, in that, whatever the imperfections of man, the second of the two great commandments, to love thy neighbor as thyself, seems to me an imperative to social action"—which for Matthiessen means working to bring about democratic Socialism, not just the resigned ameliorative efforts that Eliot also approved (82).

A further confession shows why reviewers on the anti-Stalinist left skewered the book on its publication:[8] "unlike most Christian Socialists, I accept the Russian Revolution as the most progressive event of our century, the necessary successor to the French Revolution and the American Revolution and to England's seventeenth-century Civil War" (82–83). Matthiessen's reasoning here, seeking a backward historical resonance that can direct one's present action, resembles the figural methods deployed by Dabbs, Auden, Maurin, and McKay, among others: "The discipline of history seems valuable only if it can enable you to perceive and to hold fast to such broad analogies" (83). Matthiessen walks a fine line, one pro-Lenin but anti-Stalin. To accept the Russian Revolution, for him, means to accept "the reasons why it had become necessary and the goals it had aimed at," not the "aberrations from or distortions of . . . Lenin's aims" carried out under "the grim pressures of dictatorship" (83). Matthiessen knew the anti-Communist ire such statements would arouse upon publication, and he tried to show that his ideas were not at all un-American, but rather firmly in the American grain. "The right of all to share in the common wealth" was "insisted upon by Walt Whitman and Henry George no less than by Marx and Lenin" (83–84). But his contemporaries didn't buy it. "The anticommunist argument prevailed in the United States, and Matthiessen became more and more alienated from colleagues and from the American political mainstream" after the book's publication (Blaustein 223).

Like *American Renaissance, From the Heart of Europe* envisions Christian democratic Socialism as a fusion of Transcendentalist and medievalist—though here refracted through the early modern irony of Rabelais. As "a group of the poor scholars for whom Thoreau wrote especially," living on "*ersatz* coffee and the dwindling rations of cigarettes," the Salzburg seminar embodied "the possibility of communication" between East and West, a suburb of dissent against world-ending atomic rivalry (65–66).[9] "We had a sense of creating a new Abbey of Theleme," Matthiessen writes, citing Rabelais's decidedly unmonastic imaginary abbey whose only rule of life is, *Do what you want.* "Or, to stick to the New England analogy, here was our Brook Farm, here was our ideal communistic experiment, where each . . . gave according to his abilities, and received according to his needs" (66). On leaving Salzburg, he took with him as souvenir a Hungarian translation of part of *Leaves of Grass* and promised to send "the poems of Robert Lowell" to an Austrian colleague (66). Matthiessen's interleaving of American literary radicalism with European communal imagination extended beyond the nineteenth century to encompass then-contemporary writing as well.

From the Heart of Europe emphasizes that intimate and erotically charged bonds between men—whether fleeting, like his encounter with the workman at Wells Cathedral, or enduring, like his relationship with Cheney—were Matthiessen's most powerful experiences of perceiving the essential equality between persons, his core religious and political conviction. Crucially, he found such intimate bonds in American literary history and sought to convey their power to his European audience when he taught *Moby-Dick* at Salzburg. Rereading Melville's famous review of Hawthorne's tales, "Hawthorne and His Mosses" (1850), "which he wrote in the fervor of composing *Moby Dick*," Matthiessen "found a new clue to [Melville's] own creative intention, in his statement that American literature ought to be most characterized by writers 'who breathe that unshackled, democratic spirit of Christianity in all things'" (*From the Heart of Europe* 35). Melville's review of Hawthorne is a key text for recent queer reappropriations of nineteenth-century American literature because of the intensity of its homoerotic imagery. "Melville's sentences burst with erotic double entendres that only the most willfully tone-deaf modern reader could miss," as Jordan Alexander Stein puts it in an essay wonderfully titled "History's Dick Jokes."

An attentive close reader, Matthiessen surely did not miss these meanings. He finds the strongest evidence of Melville's democratic Christianity in "the relationship between Ishmael and Queequeg," *Moby-Dick*'s queer bedfellows (*From the Heart of Europe* 36). Early in the novel, after spending the night together in the innkeeper Peter Coffin's marriage bed, Ishmael and Queequeg are "married" as "bosom-friends" in a brief ceremony at the Spouter-Inn (*Moby-Dick* 81). The procedure recalls strikingly the medieval Christian rituals of wedded brotherhood analyzed by Boswell and Bray and poetically reimagined by Scudder and Converse—though here binding the erstwhile Presbyterian Ishmael to his pagan companion. The sailors' wedded brotherhood demonstrates for Matthiessen that "Melville's sense of Christianity is most living at the point where Christianity and democracy fuse, in his belief in the equality of man with man," regardless of race or creed (*From the Heart of Europe* 36). The tragedy of Melville's novel is that "the friendship between Queequeg and Ishmael was dwarfed and finally lost sight of in the portrayal of Captain Ahab's indomitable will" (36). In terms of Matthiessen's half-hidden allegory, this means that capitalist individualism crushes queer Christian solidarity.[10]

Before leaving Prague, Matthiessen gave his final lecture on Lowell, among other recent American poets. He spoke admiringly of Lowell's conscientious objection and imprisonment, as well as the "opulent and . . . stark grandeur" of *Lord Weary's Castle* (180). Matthiessen's lecture underlined Lowell's "break with earlier New England," his Boston no shining city on a hill but "a city burning itself out in heavy corruption" (181). It was almost Christmas when Matthiessen spoke, and he left his audience with Lowell's "Christmas Eve under Hooker's Statue." The poem invokes Melville, but its last line turns away from Melville's tragedy to a note of tragic optimism: "Till Christ again turn wanderer and child" (line 27). In this vision, the coming Christ brings with him Thoreau's anarchic, "uneradicated wildness."

Matthiessen praised Thoreau for his demand that human wildness remain undomesticated. Similarly, in love, Matthiessen sought a discipline that would not stifle his desire; in religion, he sought a devotion that would not constrain his development. In politics, he envisioned a social order that would channel the anarchistic impulse of personal liberty toward the common good. Together, these constitute his queer Christian Socialism. In his elegy for Matthiessen, Lowell puts his finger on the particular relevance of Matthiessen's sexuality to his struggle with reconciling anarchy and order. He imagines Matthiessen "torn / between the homosexual's terrible love / for forms, and his anarchic love of man . . ." (lines 10–12, ellipsis in original). Lowell's language essentializes the psychic condition of gay men, but at the same time this is a moment of deep personal identification with Matthiessen for the straight poet. Lowell himself was riven by his anarchic and formal loves—between unsparing personal confession and rigorous poetic craft, his impulses toward "the raw and the cooked," as he once memorably put it. Lowell pingponged between elevated formal verse and free, prosy explorations from the mid-1950s until his death, from a heart attack, in 1977. Though he left the Roman Catholic Church for good in 1948 and never returned, the intellectual, aesthetic, and political paradoxes of formal anarchy—or put another way, of Catholic Socialism—remained generative throughout his career.

Like Lowell, both Scudder and Matthiessen found in the conjunction of literature and theological ethics rich conceptual models for finding freedom within form. As Scudder put it in Social Ideals in English Letters: "The search for authority pervades the best social teaching of the Victorian age. Consciously or unconsciously, men have been reverting from the revolutionary idea of freedom, which regards it as the natural birthright of humanity and of each individual, to the Christian ideal, so magnificently set forth in Dante's 'Divina Commedia,' which views it as the great gift, to be won, either by society or by the man, only as the result of long discipline and willing acceptance of righteous law" (263). The tension between law and liberty is fundamental to Christianity for Scudder. Yet she hopes, in her Hegelian way, that out of this tension will arise a new and higher social form: "Will that synthesis be the social democracy of the future?" she asks. "Will it be the socialist state?" (275). The question, for Scudder, is rhetorical.

As a queer Christian Socialist critic, Matthiessen carried forward Scudder's efforts to synthesize democracy and authority. But Matthiessen's great advance over Scudder was to achieve a literary-critical method that refuses to eradicate the wildness of the individual work in its quest for historical understanding. Scudder's method of summary, paraphrase, and grand historical generalization is the weakest part of her legacy. "The common reader . . . does not live by trends alone," Matthiessen admonishes in the introductory note on "Method and Scope" to American Renaissance. "He reads books, whether of the present or past, because they have an immediate life of their own" (x). These words could be targeted at the woman who wrote Social Ideals in En-

glish Letters. For Matthiessen, the only way into the literary work's immanent principle of life is "direct experience . . . again and again," sustained by "close analysis, and plentiful instances from the works themselves" (xi). Such close reading must be joined not only to an understanding of historical context but also an appreciation of contemporary exigencies: "works of art can be best perceived if we do not approach them only through the influences that shaped them, but if we also make use of what we inevitably bring from our own lives" (xiii). He admits that this "is an unorthodox postulate for literary history," at least in his time (xiii). But it's crucial to understanding the full import of Matthiessen's project.

While *American Renaissance* has often been appreciated for combining historical and biographical methods with the close analysis typical of the New Criticism, I think its true significance is more original and profound. In his magnum opus, Matthiessen pioneers a queer Christian Socialist method of literary criticism—one I've taken as a paradigm for my own work in this book. In this sense, though his canon has been disputed and his judgments updated, I believe Matthiessen's work can still serve the purpose he hoped for: offering "literature for our democracy" (*American Renaissance* xv).

WEIRD CHRISTIAN SOCIALISM

The Literary Christian Left between
Liberalism and Antiliberalism

The literary Christian Left is not emerging; it has been active in the United States for a long time, welding spiritual, corporal, and imaginative labor toward realizing the community of equals promised in the Body of Christ. Beginning with Christian Socialists such as Vida Dutton Scudder and Ralph Adams Cram at the end of the nineteenth century, I've shown how Christian leftist writers, including Dorothy Day, Claude McKay, Robert Lowell, W. H. Auden, Walker Percy, and F. O. Matthiessen, leveraged their strong faith in sacred history to imagine surprisingly progressive responses to the social crises of the Gilded Age, the Depression and World Wars, the Cold War, and the civil rights movement. One thing that has changed, though, across the period I survey and after, is the Christian Left's language of self-identification. The adoption of an explicitly "Socialist" label, proudly claimed by Scudder, James Dombrowski, and John Brooks Wheelwright up through the end of the 1930s, proved problematic, to say the least, for Matthiessen at the outset of the Cold War. The generational shift of southern radicals from Dombrowski's Socialist Fellowship of Southern Churchmen in the 1930s to the diffuse, anarchistic contrarianism of Will Campbell's Committee of Southern Churchmen in the 1960s reflected a wider pivot from an "old" to a New Left, which eschewed programmatic Socialism even as it was reshaped by a wide coalition of identarian movements.

But in these latter days, after Occupy Wall Street, the presidential campaigns of Vermont democratic Socialist Bernie Sanders, and the rise of Black Lives Matter, Socialism is riding higher in U.S. political discourse than it has in decades. One perhaps underrecognized voice in this chorus is a new wave of avowed "Christian Socialists." By reputation, the public voice of the current American Left is triumphantly scurrilous, as in *Chapo Trap House*, the foul-mouthed podcast produced by mavens of the "Dirtbag Left."[1] But today's radicals also speak in the voice of prayer. *Chapo's* religious counterpart might be *The Magnificast*, the ecumenical Christian Socialist podcast that takes its name from the Magnificat—echoing the Virgin Mary's revolutionary prayer also taken up by Scudder and the Brotherhood of the Carpenter in the 1890s.[2] Christian writers occupy the recent pages of radical magazines new and old, such as *Jacobin*, *Dissent*, and *In These Times*. Sometimes they even make it into the mainstream, as with Elizabeth Bruenig, the Catholic Socialist, sometime Augustine scholar, and current *New York Times* (and former *Washington Post*) opinion writer.

This Christian Socialist renaissance does not, however, always pray for social justice in the same language. Two manifestos by Christian Socialist groups organized online illustrate a fault line in the current Christian Left that harks back to divisions I trace throughout this study, from the dispute between the Franciscan Scudder and the Benedictine Cram forward: Will a Christian Socialism be liberal or antiliberal?[3] Should Christian leftists join themselves to a Popular Front, or stand apart as a sign of contradiction to all secular constructions of politics?

The 2016 manifesto of the now-defunct Tradinista! collective speaks for a contemporary antiliberal Christian Socialism. (The name is a portmanteau of "traditional" and "Sandinista!"—given the exclamation point, I think the reference for the latter term is the Clash's 1980 triple album, more so than the historical Sandinista Liberation Front of Nicaragua.) It begins with a Latin blessing: "*In nomine Patris et Filii et Spiitus Sancti*."[4] This improbably ties the Tradinistas' Socialism to those so-called "traditionalist" Catholics who continue to favor the Latin Mass over the vernacular. The manifesto ends with "*Amen*," sealing its status as prayer. Its first English words—"we believe"— sound a creedal note, and indeed the first point of the Tradinista program riffs lightly on the affirmations of the Nicene Creed: "Jesus Christ is the way, and the truth, and the life, who became man for the salvation of all." They claim to be "a small party of young Christian socialists committed to traditional orthodoxy." The movement likewise announce their commitment to "virtue" and "the common good"—shout-outs to the antiliberal philosophy of Alasdair MacIntyre—"and to the destruction of capitalism and its replacement by a truly social political economy." The collective's blog ironically appropriates Mao's "Combat Liberalism" for its title. In its language of conflict and destruction, Tradinista! Socialism sounds like it means business; certainly, its antipathy to liberalism is genuine. But the constant rhetorical gestures to a Marxist tradition of revolutionary violence the rest of the manifesto disclaims makes me wonder whether the Tradinistas reduce radicalism to mere style, a serious expression of discontent with the political status quo but nothing more.

On the liberal side, Christians for Socialism begin their 2018 manifesto by quoting the Bible in English, testifying to the group's ecumenical alignment. Where the emphatically Catholic Tradinistas take their theological bearings from the doctrine of incarnation ("Jesus Christ . . . who became man"), Christians for Socialism lead with inspiration, emphasizing God the Holy Spirit rather than the God the Son. Riffing on Marx and Engels, by way of Derrida, Christians for Socialism announce: "A spectre is haunting the world— the Holy Ghost, the Spectre of Liberation." While they call for the "embodied resurrection of a Christian left," Christians for Socialism envisions its hoped-for movement as "neither church nor party." This resurrected body is not quite the Body of Christ or the body politic, but a *tertium quid redivivus*. Taking their name from the *Cristianos por el Socialismo* of 1970s Chile, Christians for Socialism further claim the heritage of Latin American liberation theology without any intervening postpunk irony.

No manifesto would be complete without a little intra-Left sniping, and indeed Christians for Socialism seem to take aim at the Tradinistas toward the end of their document: "Christians for Socialism refuses the insular attitude of a kind of traditionalist 'left' found within many denominations. Some who say they are part of a Christian left, for example, nevertheless attempt to reserve a right of Christian privilege that is strategically invoked to keep them from fully affirming the liberation of certain groups, most notably LGBTQ+liberation. A true Christian left rejects this as a reactionary purity narrative that fears the full self-determination of those who have already been marginalized primarily by Christians." This critique may not be entirely fair to the Tradinistas, however, as point 11 of their manifesto reads, "Racism, misogyny, homophobia, transphobia, and similar forms of oppression must be eradicated." By taking Jesus and Mary primarily as radical exemplars to be followed, emphasizing the wide-ranging activity of the immaterial Holy Spirit over the embodied particularity of the Church, and pitching a Christian Left as one partner in a pluralistic coalition for liberationist struggle, Christians for Socialism embodies a liberal Socialism.

These competing manifestos, and the wider tendencies they represent, highlight the urgency of working out the complex relationship between religion and politics for Christian leftists in this moment. Tradinista! give pride of place to religion, underlining the Christian character of the Socialism they profess. Understood as a "politics of virtue and the common good," which makes it easier to "advance toward the True, Good, and Beautiful" in "quest for holiness," this Socialism comes dressed in the clerical garb of Catholic moral theology ("Tradinista! Manifesto"). You're unlikely to hear such terms thrown around at your local Democratic Socialists of America meeting. This theological vocabulary reflects a Socialism deeply embedded in a particular religious tradition, resistant to secular translation but imaginatively and conceptually rich. In this manner of speech, Tradinistas are faithful to the heritage of the literary Christian Left.

But just as the idioms of medievalism, monasticism, and agrarianism were politically fungible, contested symbols for twentieth-century Christian radicals, this vocabulary of moral theology is also liable to competing construals. Catholic defenders of the free market such as the Acton Institute and former House Speaker Paul Ryan speak the same dialect of the "common good" when they give religious sanction to conservative economics.[5] And *First Things* magazine has deployed the language of Catholic "dissent" from liberal modernity both to praise Tradinista! and back the Trump administration.[6] Because of these associations, Tradinista-type leftists need to be ready to answer the question of just what they mean by their professed Socialism. In the *Manifesto*, Marx and Engels railed against a kind of "Christian Socialism" that was "but the holy water with which the priest consecrates the heart-burnings of the aristocrat." It remains unclear whether Tradinista! represents such antimodernist indigestion or a consuming fire of judgment on the inequities of our capitalist status quo.

The grammatical construction of "Christians *for* Socialism," on the other hand, raises the equally pertinent question of what difference Christianity might make to people or movements or thinking on the left. This amounts to more than nit-picking prepositions; Christians for Socialism's manifesto is explicitly "rooted in a Marxist approach" and names Lenin and Castro as models of leftist leaders open to cooperation with progressive believers ("The

Wind Blows"). Such gestures trade the discredit of Christian conservatism for that of Communist totalitarianism. While the mediating activism they pro-pose as "neither church nor party" keeps faith with the vocation of twentieth-century leftist churchwomen and churchmen, Christians for Socialism seem to envision the Left as primarily an intact entity extrinsic to the Church. They offer Christian *reasons* for embracing a basically secular leftist politics. As a result, they run the risk of trading the clerical robes of Tradinista! for pious window-dressing. Leftists of this conciliatory stripe should be prepared to clarify what's at stake in the *Christianity* of their Christian Socialism, making plain how belief transforms conceptions and practices of equality and com-munity.

The question of what's distinctively Christian about these two visions of Christian Socialism is particularly salient because their rhetorical contest takes place within the internet discursive community of so-called "Weird Christians." These "disillusioned" young believers, according to the religion scholar and journalist (and self-described Weird Christian) Tara Isabella Burton, "see a return to old-school forms of worship as a way of escaping from the crisis of modernity and the liberal-capitalist faith in individualism" ("Christianity Gets Weird"). As Burton points out in the *New York Times*, Weird Christians are as thoroughly modern as generations of antimodernists before them, connected to one another across vast distances by social media platforms like Twitter. I originally found links to both Tradinista! and Chris-tians for Socialism in my own Twitter feed, which is full of posts from Weird Christians of various denominational backgrounds—including those respon-sible, by my best guess, for penning the unsigned manifestos above. I think it's helpful to understand the rhetorical challenge facing contemporary Christian Socialists as articulating a *convincingly weird* Christian Socialism. Neither a compassionate conservatism rebranded as radical chic nor a warmed-over re-ligious progressivism will fit the bill, because they simply aren't weird *enough*.

One of my hopes in writing this book is that revisiting the history of the literary Christian Left in the twentieth century might help contemporary Christian leftists find a way through the divide between antiliberal and lib-eral versions of Christian Socialism. It seems to me that one poet discussed in the previous chapter, John Brooks Wheelwright—Anglo-Catholic convert, Socialist, and eventual Trotskyist, and "author of a weird, technically dazzling mix of modernist dexterity and social realism"—offers perhaps the most suit-ably strange archive of Christian Socialist literature to think with in our time

(Wald, "Wheelwright" 206). By way of conclusion, I want to expand here on my reading of his poetry with an eye toward this contemporary dilemma.

Born out of his response to the extended period of political and economic crisis following World War I, which our current distended moment of crisis echoes in so many ways, Wheelwright's work is weird in at least three senses. First, his full-throated commitment to economic leveling through revolution sets him apart from most of his contemporaries on the religious left. Though a Christian and a Socialist, Wheelwright never claimed the reformist "Christian socialism" of the early Scudder or her nineteenth-century precursors— the ones Marx and Engels mocked in the *Manifesto*. (Neither did he ever join the Communist Party or back Stalin.) Wheelwright's poetry is also weird in the characteristically modernist sense of verbal difficulty. The often-knotty syntax and obscure vocabulary of individual poems, as well as the typographical and structural idiosyncrasies of his published collections, are defamiliarization strategies of beguiling perplexity. Related to the poems' verbal difficulty are the high bars of theological and biblical literacy they impose on their readers. Where Pound or Eliot might invoke ancient Chinese poets or medieval English mystics in their modernist epics, Wheelwright relies on the New Testament and its apocrypha for source material. The esoteric energy of his poems resonates with the spirit of the contemporary cohort of disaffected young believers Burton identifies: both are earnestly rooted in the peculiarities of Christian tradition, even when expressing the doubt and contestation which are necessary to keep tradition alive.

Wheelwright's faith was not a ground of settled conviction but rather a site of struggle and self-revision. Would Christianity be the metaphysical ground of his poetry and his politics, or would championing a popular movement in his religious idiolect be counterproductive? Could religion serve instead to add personal symbolism and emotional heft to an essentially secular public Socialism? In this sense, Wheelwright's poetic wrestling mirrors the dispute between liberal and antiliberal factions of the contemporary Christian Left over whether it's more important to embrace Christian distinctiveness or abjure "Christian privilege" (Christians for Socialism, "The Wind Blows"). The poet's most important readers have seen him moving progressively toward the second option across his career. Alan Wald, in his groundbreaking treatment of the poet in *The Revolutionary Imagination* (1983), argues that Wheelwright abandons Christianity in all but the barest rhetorical sense by his last years. His principal literary evidence for this position concerns Wheelwright's oblique, career-spanning series of dramatic poems about Saint Thomas, the doubting apostle: "This initial attempt to establish a systematized imaginative world was displaced and almost abandoned under the impact of the new conditions of the 1930s. The poetic myth of Doubting Thomas . . . was incapable of providing an adequate imaginative response to the changed situation, if only because it required the kind of reader whose thoughts are totally removed from the issues of daily life and international politics" (*The Revolutionary Imagination* 61–62). Wald argues that Wheelwright came to see the project as a failure as he grew into a more thoroughgoing Marxism.

I read the Thomas poems and their place in Wheelwright's oeuvre differently. They are poems, if not of holding on to faith, then of holding on to doubt, which, as we'll see, is for Wheelwright a way of remaining within the historically extended argument of Christian tradition. Saint Thomas, in the New Testament nicknamed Didymus (The Twin), is Wheelwright's figure of doubleness, of suspension between two seemingly contradictory alternatives. The poems wrestle faith and doubt, radicalism and traditionalism, orthodoxy and heresy, in painful but productive tension. Through them, "Wheels Agonistes" might teach today's Christian leftists, in confrontation with the would-be zero-sum alternatives of antiliberalism and liberalism, not to let go of the contradiction until it gives up a blessing.

Five of Wheelwright's works concerning Saint Thomas are included in his posthumous *Collected Poems*: "Forty Days," "Twilight," "Evening," "Morning," and "The Other: A Theologic Dialogue." Some of their content is drawn from the canonical Gospels, some from apocryphal texts like the Gnostic Gospel of Thomas, and some from more or less canonical legends of Thomas's post–New Testament career. "Forty Days," published in Wheelwright's 1933 collection *Rock and Shell* and narrated by Thomas, records a conversation between the risen Christ and the disciples during the forty days between his resurrection and ascension. What makes this poem particularly difficult is that it recounts this conversation *backward*. The crux arrives when Christ tells the disciples he has come back from the dead to give them the gift of doubt.

> Grasp me between your fingers.
> Break me in twain.
> Suck the honey unprisoned
> from the bee's cracked belly.
> Suck bees' honey.

Fear not the sweetness.

. . . .

Thomas, remember my sting.
It is not questioning, but doubt. (17)

In this Eucharistic feast, incorporation into the Body of Christ doesn't do away with doubt. But Wheelwright's Christ distinguishes doubt from questioning: doubt is the sting without which no sweetness of faith, something deeper and more affective than the mere disputation of facts. Wheelwright's insistence on the mutual necessity of doubt and faith drives through the whole Thomas series.

In "Twilight," also published in *Rock and Shell*, Wheelwright revises the queer Christian Socialist valorization of celibacy (Wheelwright, *Collected Poems* 27–37). The poem finds Thomas in India, in accordance with traditions about his later apostolic career. Thomas presides over a marriage ceremony for a Christian couple. The Devil appears in the married couple's honeymoon suite and persuades them, with slick theological arguments, to forgo consummating the marriage and live celibate. When Thomas checks on the newlyweds in the morning, he's horrified that they've been deluded by Satan into rejecting their bodies. In this, Wheelwright joins his contemporary Matthiessen, turning Christian leftist discourse on sex and politics in a Whitmanian direction.

Wheelwright pursues this theme further in "Evening" and "Morning," included in *Dusk to Dusk*, the volume he was preparing when he died (Wheelwright, *Collected Poems* 183–210). The first of these poems scrambles chronology. Thomas travels in a Victorian carriage through a Great Depression landscape, coming upon the dead body of a young Black man, an agricultural worker, in the road. The Devil shows up again, this time as a many-headed dragon, and disputes with Thomas over the dead man's corpse. The dragon argues that the man was struck dead because he was caught in the act of fornication. Thomas seems to go further than in "Twilight" (and further than Matthiessen), here rejecting sexual stigma regardless of marriage; in any case, he refuses the Devil's simple explanation for the man's death. Then he brings life back to the worker's body, raising him from the dead. The driver of the carriage reveals himself to be Christ—here, Thomas's twin—and the dragon leaves.[7] Thomas and Christ bring the resurrected rural proletarian up into their carriage and send him into the city fired with a revolutionary vision of love.

"Morning" continues redeeming the human body through the Body of Christ by having Thomas celebrate a Socialist Eucharist. In a version of the liturgical "Great Thanksgiving" that precedes the ritual meal, he prays:

> Communal God, our communal meal
> wherein each guest thinks himself chief
> provides no one with common thanksgiving
> . . . .
> Unless your sufferings in sacrifice
> wed communal victory, this mere memorial
> is sterile holocaust and hecatomb. (202)

Wheelwright weds his Socialism to high sacramental theology: unless those who participate in the Eucharist go on to suffer for "communal victory," there is no Real Presence of Christ in the sacrament; it is a "mere memorial," a Zwinglian symbolic performance. But divine presence does fill the bread Thomas consecrates, and it burns the fingers of Teckla, a bedridden woman in the congregation whose body has withered under the possession of demons named Dread and Fear. Thomas has her undressed and baptized by an attending woman, and as he prays over her body it becomes clear that what the virginal Teckla dreads and fears is sex and childbearing. Through her exorcism and baptism, she is born again as physically, emotionally, and sexually whole: "a new born Teckla, gallant and fertile / of womb, of maiden mind, and breast / which fear of soil made sterile" (205).[8] To this newly fearless and guiltless Teckla, Thomas offers a Whitmanesque interpretation of sex as another, higher, Socialist sacrament of equality, the "Bed more holy than the Holy Board," in which "each lover [thinks] the beloved chief" (208). Where Teckla feared sex would soil her soul, Thomas redefines it as a purifying act, a physical way to love one's neighbor as oneself.

If one of Thomas's demonic enemies in these poems is fear of the body and its desires, another is fear of doubt. The final Thomas poem, "The Other," unpublished at the author's death, dramatizes this suspension of belief in a stark dialogue between Thomas and his Doubt, a Yes voice and a No voice. As the poem unfolds, Doubt reveals himself as no enemy to Thomas. Together, they voice the necessary twins of positive and negative theology (kataphasis and apophasis), affirmation and denial, faith and doubt, statement and question. Both are needed to reveal the true Christ. As Thomas puts it at the end of the dialogue, "you / who deny my God point out my Lord to me" (*Collected*

Poems 271). The voice of Doubt, the No voice, answers Thomas in the affirmative for the first time: "Yes, but he [Christ] is your twin. / Go. But look back on me." Just as for Eliot blasphemy could be a means of spiritual awakening, for Wheelwright Doubt's "dispassionate Blasphemy" can "allude the hints of God" (271–72). In the end, Doubt leads Thomas back to Christ. In the final lines, their dialogue opens into an image of "three / Handfast, allied reflections, Face to Face"—Thomas, Christ, and Doubt—recalling Rublev's icon of the Holy Trinity (272).

For Wald, the theological vision of the Thomas series is just *too* weird to succeed as practical poetry that might draw readers into political struggle. While it's true that *Mirrors of Venus* and *Political Self-Portrait*, Wheelwright's most mature published collections, contain no Thomas poems, Wald also applies this analysis to the poems Wheelwright intended to publish in *Dusk to Dusk:* "Poems such as 'Morning' failed to reach an audience because their symbols were unable to affect the reader on any level but that of their own arcane meanings, and the meanings remained too private" (*The Revolutionary Imagination* 66). According to Wald, Wheelwright's experience of the Great Depression "gave birth to more appropriate symbols as his ideas about society were altered" (67).[9] But the history I've recounted in this book helps us see that Wheelwright's Weird Christian Socialism wasn't a solo act; he was one voice in a chorus. If we remember that during the period in which Wheelwright composed the Thomas series, Dorothy Day and Peter Maurin launched an urban Catholic insurgency of the Mystical Body of Christ, and the Fellowship of Southern Churchmen instigated a rural sacramental Socialism among farmworkers, then we may not see the "arcane meanings" of these poems as the sort of political liability that Wald does.[10] It is just their theological density that also makes them useful for imagining a Weird Christian Socialism today.

Wheelwright's Thomas poems reveal a Christian materialism, in many ways akin to those of farmer-poets Dabbs and Berry, though drawn from different sources. Warfare with the powers and principalities of the modern world is, in Wheelwright's incarnational Socialism, only truly spiritual when it is material. This theological vision of politics as the redemption of the body, fueled by Christ's incarnation, passion, resurrection, and ongoing presence in the sacraments, affirms the goodness of embodied sexuality and proclaims the necessity of economic struggle. And it is particularly attuned to the unequal distribution of the need for bodily redemption under a capitalism demonically entangled with white supremacy, patriarchy, and ableism, evidenced by Thomas's resurrection of a Black man and exorcism of a disabled woman. Wheelwright's religious vocabulary is rich and strange and capacious, comprehending both class struggle and identity politics.

Yet if such a theopolitical vision is large enough to contain many of the multitudes struggling for liberation in our contemporary pluralistic democracy, it is also irreducibly, strangely Christian. It cannot be trimmed to fit what Matthew Sitman calls the "moral austerity" of "mainstream liberals" suspicious of "robust moral critiques of the status quo, whether connected to religion or angry progressive populism." But as Sitman also argues, this doesn't have to preclude political collaboration across religious and secular borders on the left: "There is no view from nowhere; when it comes to moral argument, there is no universal language. And the hope of democratic politics is that deliberation and persuasion can happen among people who actually engage each other, even if they don't start from the same place. Even more: that political struggle can itself be morally transformative." A Christian Left either too quick to abandon its theological resources or too insulated to be part of progressive coalitions will sacrifice the chance to change and be changed through the necessarily contentious work of politics.

Wheelwright's example counsels holding onto both horns of the liberal-antiliberal dilemma, hoping against hope for such transformation. In the final lines of "The Other," Thomas, Doubt, and Christ, hand in hand, see their own faces reflected back to them in the others'. This is an image of Thomas's human life transfigured though struggle into the trinitarian image of the divine. The poem envisions this spiritual transformation through something like democratic deliberation, the outworking of patient and difficult solidarity between two equals and allies—Thomas and Doubt—who at first blush seem to be at cross-purposes. But they persevere in disagreement until Christ arrives in the unresolved place between them.

NOTES

INTRODUCTION

1. Here's a CNN take from the first Obama campaign: www.cnn.com/2008/POLITICS/ 07/01/obama.evangelicals/index.html. And here's a similar piece from the 2020 election cycle, focused on Pete Buttigieg: www.cnn.com/2019/04/09/opinions/pete-buttigieg-mike-pence-erick-erickson-christian-progressives-graves-fitzsimmons/index.html.

2. In *American Dreamers* (2001), Michael Kazin offers a subtle revision to this position, insisting that liberals' and leftists' "opposing views on U.S. foreign policy, and a good many other subjects" are consequential and stem from the latter's dedication "to a radically egalitarian transformation of society" (xii–xiv). Nevertheless, Kazin also concludes that the Left's most enduring cultural achievement is to have advanced the goal of personal liberty shared by both liberals and leftists, rather than the distinctively leftist aim of equality: "By the early twenty-first century, most ordinary Americans enjoyed a degree of personal freedom that would have been considered ultra-radical in the 1960s" (253).

3. Scudder to Rauschenbusch, March 27, 1918, quoted in Hinson-Hasty 30.

4. Compare the rousing conclusion of Rauschenbusch's *A Theology for the Social Gospel*, which takes the death of Christ as the ultimate example of "the value of the prophets for the progress of humanity" (278). Scudder would not have disagreed, but she insisted that the death of Christ was more than the highest inspirational example for efforts of social reform. As I explore in chapter 1, Scudder believed that when the formerly comfortable suffered with or for the oppressed, they did not only follow Christ's example but actually participated sacramentally *in* his suffering.

5. Alan Wald's criticism, including the "Literary Left" trilogy on which I expand below, is most crucial to my own analysis but see also equally important works including Barbara Foley's *Radical Representations: Politics and Form in U.S. Proletarian Literature, 1929–1941* (Durham, NC: Duke University Press, 1993); and William J. Maxwell's *New Negro, Old Left: African-American Writing and Communism between the Wars* (New York: Columbia University Press, 1999).

6. Auden borrowed this favorite expression from the eighteenth-century German scientist and aphorist G. C. Lichtenberg.

7. See chapter 3.

8. See chapter 5 and Dabbs, "Beyond Tragedy."

9. See chapter 3.

10. See chapter 5 and Percy, "The Failure and the Hope."

11. See chapter 5

12. See chapters 4 and 5.

13. These are certainly not the only traditions important to a literary Christian Left, and I look forward to other books that might shape up differently—particularly studies whose narrative takes off from the Black radical tradition in the United States, which my treatment of Claude McKay, while crucial to *Communion of Radicals*, only begins to address. Tracing patterns of affiliation outward from the Christian Socialist and Catholic Worker movements, these are the groupings that make sense for the story I'm telling.

14. I'm drawing here on the language of "traditioned innovation" developed by the theologian L. Gregory Jones (see faithandleadership.com/content/traditioned-innovation).

15. Under the rubric of "queer temporality," queer studies practitioners have formulated a productive theoretical discourse devoted to unsettling many forms of linearity—including the linear progress narrative of economic development shared by many varieties of capitalism and Socialism. As the theorist Annamarie Jagose succinctly defines it, queer temporality is "a mode of inhabiting time that is attentive to the recursive eddies and back-to-the-future loops that often pass undetected or uncherished beneath the official narrations of the linear sequence that is taken to structure normative life" (Jagose 158).

16. See Coviello; McGarry; Freeman, "Sacramentality and the Lesbian Premodern"; Freeman, "Sacra/mentality in Djuna Barnes' *Nightwood*"; and Kahan.

17. In contemporary scholarly debates, the postsecular commonly names a widespread turn in critical practice away from long-standing narratives of religion's decline and replacement—usually by art or science—that previously grounded both the professional identities of literary scholars and their interpretations of literary texts (Fessenden 154; Kaufmann 607). On this understanding, recent historical developments spurred literary scholars to count religion as culturally forceful rather than inevitably fading. In neighboring halls of academe, social scientists grew disenchanted with secularization theory, while Continental philosophers embraced theology; it was from these two fields that literary scholars first imported the term "postsecular" (Fessenden 156). Meanwhile, "9/11 and the political revival of the religious right" gave students of American culture particularly pressing reasons to renew their inquiries into religion (Rivett 989).

18. Though Hungerford gives prominent place to the liberal Christian novelist Marilynne Robinson in her account, she pairs Robinson up with the popular Evangelical *Left Behind* novels—the literary rise of the Christian Right forms the interpretive context, and Hungerford ultimately uncovers surprising overlap between the *Left Behind* series and Robinson's treatment of belief (131).

19. I take this phrase from Vaneesa Cook's *Spiritual Socialists: Religion and the American Left* (2019). When Cook writes that "the tradition of spiritual socialism provided the American Left with a moral foundation and language that made religion and radicalism congruent, not antithetical," the complementary aims of our respective studies are obvious (9). For Cook, "spiri-

tual socialism" provided an alternative moral-theoretical basis for an independent American Left redefining itself away from scientific Marxism and its association with the Stalinist USSR from the 1930s through the Cold War period. But when she clarifies that her spiritual Socialists "did not mean formal religion or its theology and observances" but rather "religion reduced to basic human values," it becomes clear that her spiritual Socialists and my Christian leftists constitute two parallel, overlapping, and often-allied traditions of religious radicals (9). Dorothy Day and the Catholic Worker movement play a major role in Cook's narrative, but the Workers' full-throated, traditional, medievalist Catholicism doesn't fit Cook's frame of religion as a source of easily translated moral principles. I address the difficulty of reconciling the Workers' religious particularism with their pluralistic context in chapter 3.

20. See P. Murphy.

21. On Scudder's papers, see findingaids.smith.edu/repositories/2/resources/447.

22. Principally Martin Luther King Jr., whose writings evidence his commitment to Christian Socialism (see Thomas F. Jackson, *From Civil Rights to Human Rights* [Philadelphia: University of Pennsylvania Press, 2007]).

23. The quotation is from Day, "The Final Word Is Love," *Catholic Worker*, May 1980, 4, www.catholicworker.org/dorothyday/articles/867.pdf. This piece is printed as a postscript in recent editions of her autobiography *The Long Loneliness*.

24. Joanna Brooks has recently offered the Methodist "love-feasts"—evenings of testimony capped by a simple meal of bread and water—enjoyed by Olaudah Equiano in his *Interesting Narrative* (1789) as a model for religion-and-literature scholarship. "Religious narratives like Equiano's aim to draw readers into that ensemble [of the love-feast], testing out experience the way one might at a soul feast and expecting readers to join in the breaking of bread and the passing round of mugs of water," she observes ("Soul Matters" 950). She concludes with a series of questions, including, "Is professional literary criticism, or the classroom, a variety of soul feast?" (951). This book represents one possible way of answering in the affirmative.

CHAPTER ONE

1. The quoted phrase is taken from the title of a collect in the *Book of Common Prayer*.

2. See also Markwell 276–77n106.

3. In *Gold, Frankincense, and Myrrh*, as in the contemporaneous *Walled Towns*, treated below, Cram attempts to extend to the bourgeois family the principles undergirding the monastic vows of poverty, chastity, and obedience. In effect, this was an effort to reconcile his 1890s enthusiasm for same-sex monastic community with his post-1900 life as a well-to-do husband, father, and prominent architect. As *Walled Towns* demonstrates, however, that hoped-for reconciliation remained incomplete.

4. In *Tomorrow's Parties* (2013), Peter Coviello notes the paradoxical relationship of Mormonism to Christian (and Jewish) traditions: on the one hand, Joseph Smith inaugurated a "fundamentalist return to Old Testament origins" (106). On the other, Smith rejected outright two thousand years of "Christian tradition" as a canon "of growing estrangement, of mistranslation, misapprehension, and finally apostasy" (116). It is precisely in that two-thousand-year record that Cram and Scudder sought models for their own forms of life.

5. McGarry, Coviello, and Freeman are united in their determination to contest the secularization story of sexuality, derived from Foucault, that makes the Catholic confessional the genealogical ancestor of the psychoanalyst's couch and/or the closet. See also Freeman, "Sacramentality and the Lesbian Premodern."

6. Though Anglican Socialists were not invariably Anglo-Catholic, there was a strong overlap between the two groups (on this, see Markwell). Scudder's father was a Congregationalist missionary, while Cram's was a Unitarian minister in rural New Hampshire.

7. Scudder's and Cram's careers present American Anglo-Catholic parallels to British and French Roman Catholic contemporaries including writers G. K. Chesterton (1874–1936) and Hillaire Belloc (1870–1953), the poet Charles Péguy (1873–1914), and the philosopher Jacques Maritain (1882–1973), each of whom, partially inspired by the papal social teaching inaugurated by *Rerum novarum,* also sought a medieval antidote to modern social poisons.

8. See Markwell 203–5.

9. Stein refers to the turn-of-the twentieth-century British sexologist Havelock Ellis (1859–1939) and the "British homophile writers" with whom he was in contact, whose circa 1890 discovery of Herman Melville's *Moby-Dick* (1851) was prescient by comparison with American literary historians.

10. In other words, I'm connecting the medievalist form of Scudder's political imagination took to her dissent from the American chronobiopolitics that aligns national and economic progress with sexual development toward the telos of heterosexual marriage with children. On chronobiopolitics, see Dana Luciano, *Arranging Grief: Sacred Time and the Body in Nineteenth-Century America* (New York: New York University Press, 2007).

11. The intellectual historian Eugene McCarraher opens his book *Christian Critics* (2000) by quoting this neo-Benedictine prophecy (1). But McCarraher doesn't note the publishing context—or the implicit queerness—of Cram's prediction.

12. Cram also wrote horror; his *Black Spirits and White* (Chicago: Stone and Kimball, 1895) is a minor classic of the weird fiction canon.

13. Aelred of Rievaulx has become a contested icon in contemporary religion-and-sexuality debates. Integrity USA, an organization that is "working for the full equality of LGBT persons in every part of The Episcopal Church"—Cram and Scudder's church—claims Aelred as its "Patron Saint" (Integrity USA, "Welcome"; and "Resources"). Meanwhile, the group blog *Spiritual Friendship,* named for Aelred's treatise, hosts "discussion of celibacy, friendship, [and] the value of the single life," largely by celibate queer Christians who "embrace the traditional understanding that God created us male and female, and that His plan for sexual intimacy is only properly fulfilled in the union of husband and wife in marriage" but remain frustrated by "prevailing narratives about homosexuality from those who embrace this traditionally Christian sexual ethic: an excessive focus on political issues, and the ubiquity of reparative therapy in one form or another" (Belgau and Hill).

14. Since this work chronicles Dante's love for Beatrice, the name of the estate seems to reinscribe the queer community of the estate within heteronormativity. But it's interesting to note that, like the male-male desires intimated in *The Decadent,* Dante's desire for Beatrice remains unconsummated, and is indeed dramatically transformed, as through monastic discipline, into love for God.

15. Cram dedicated the book to "MEO CARO BGG": "My Dear Bertram Grosvenor Good-hue." Cram's Boston bohemian circle—including Day (1864–1933), a pioneering photographer as well as Cram's publisher, and the Catholic poet Louise Guiney (1861–1920)—knew exactly who wrote the anonymous novella and exactly to whom it was dedicated (Shand-Tucci, *Boston Bohemia* 35–46). With Day, Guiney, and Goodhue, Cram played at Jacobite monarchism and published a little magazine of neomedievalist verse and essays called the *Knight Errant* while he worked up *The Decadent* for publication (Cram, *My Life* 20). The *Knight Errant* ran for two issues in 1892. Cram contributed the publication's manifesto-like material and a pair of lyrics to the Virgin Mary.

16. The icon depicts the scene from Genesis 18 where Abraham entertains three angels at the Oak of Mamre. Since Abraham addresses the angels by the personal name of God, the tetragrammaton "YHWH," early Christian interpreters took the scene to be hinting at the doctrine of the Trinity. The icon is a particularly interesting intertext for Cram's novella be-cause in Genesis 18 Abraham pleads with the angels not to destroy the city of Sodom. Without delving into the long and vexed interpretation history of this section of Genesis, I will point out that Sodom's destruction turns on hospitality. In chapter 19, two angels are met with vio-lence rather than Abrahamic welcome in Sodom, leading to the city's destruction despite Abra-ham's intercession.

17. "Being towards reform" is the "content" of modern celibacy, according to Kahan (17).

18. See also Freeman, "Sacra/mentality" 744, 758–60.

19. This lecture (and, indirectly, *Walled Towns*) drew on Cram's experiences as the first chairman of Boston's City Planning Commission during the years of World War I. He consid-ered his improvements to immigrant workers' housing in Boston's North End his greatest ac-complishment in city planning. In the lecture, Cram invokes the Dark Ages to prophesy the fate of a civilization that refuses to democratize beauty. This illustrates the historical texture of his medieval imagination. The Middle Ages were not, for Cram, a static Golden Age but a richly various span of cultural heights and depths.

20. Francis of Assisi continues to serve as a powerful social icon for contemporary writers and thinkers. For example, in *Empire* (Cambridge, MA: Harvard University Press, 2000), Mi-chael Hardt and Antonio Negri present Francis as the model for a newly joyful Communist militant. The journalist Paul Moses finds in Francis a precedent for peaceful Christian-Muslim dialogue in *The Saint and the Sultan: The Crusades, Islam, and Francis of Assisi's Mission of Peace* (New York: Doubleday Religion, 2009). Most recently, Pope Francis has taken the Poor Man of Assisi for his namesake and for a type of Christian environmentalist in his 2015 encycli-cal *Laudato si*, available at w2.vatican.va/content/francesco/en/encyclicals/documents/papa-francesco_20150524_enciclica-laudato-si.html.

21. "Fellowship," styled in medieval spelling as "felowschipe," is also the word Scudder chose to name her relationship to Florence Converse, as seen below.

22. *Socialism and Character*'s particular melding of modern and medieval—political So-cialism and Catholic Christianity—was greeted as revelation by some, as heresy by others (Corcoran 8). Often it wasn't greeted at all. Scudder later called *Socialism and Character* her "favorite though forgotten book" (*On Journey* 168).

23. Here Genette relies implicitly on J. L. Austin. When Austin defined "performatives" as

statements for which "the issuing of the utterance is the performing of the action" in *How to Do Things with Words* (1962), his chief example was the matrimonial "I do" (6).

24. For more on Converse and *Diana Victrix*, see Kate McCullough, "The Boston Marriage as the Future of the Nation: Queerly Regional Sexuality in *Diana Victrix*," *American Literature* 69, no. 1 (1997): 67–103. The novel is briefly mentioned in Kahan's *Celibacies* as well.

25. Scudder strongly implies—not least by dedicating this late book again to her "Comrade and Companion," as she had *Socialism and Character*—that this most intimate friend is Converse without actually naming her.

26. I borrow the phrase "empty secret" from Kahan 3.

27. Qtd. in Corcoran 109–10. It is signed "F.C. to V.D.S., V.D.S. to F.C., S.C.H.C.," indicating the women's initials and the Society of the Companions of the Holy Cross. Though apparently written by Scudder to Converse in this context, the signature begins "F.C. to V.D.S."—Converse to Scudder—and indeed the poem first appears in print as the anonymous dedication ("To. . . . .") in Converse's novel *Long Will: A Romance*. "Lo, here is felowschipe" was printed one last time by Converse as the dedicatory poem ("To Vida D. Scudder") in her *Collected Poems* (New York: Dutton, 1937). The same year, Scudder published her autobiography *On Journey*, with its repetition of *Socialism and Character*'s dedication to Converse as "Comrade and Companion."

28. See Bray 13–41.

29. To take two examples whose terms of analysis overlap most pertinently with my own: The trope of Benedictine monastic community is crucial to John McClure's *Partial Faiths: Postsecular Fictions in the Age of Pynchon and Morrison* (2007). Unlike Christian monasteries, however, McClure's postmodern collectives practice "open dwelling" (192–96). Open dwelling is "a form of communion no longer dependent on absolute conviction and doctrinal conformity" but rather on "weak religion" (5, 12). McClure sees this weakened faith as a necessary rejoinder to a dangerous Christian fundamentalism. On this account, monasticism only becomes postsecular when it is detached from specific creedal and ecclesiastical commitments. Joanna Brooks argues that "creative heterodoxies" offer welcome historiographical alternatives to "the old teleological, developmental narrative that runs from orthodoxy to secularization" ("From Edwards to Baldwin" 449). One of my aims here is to show that there might be such a thing as a creative orthodoxy, too, that could offer a revelatory new religious-literary narrative.

30. See chapter 4 and Maurin, "Back to Christ!—Back to the Land!"

CHAPTER TWO

1. Shand-Tucci makes the case for Cram's relevance vis-à-vis Eliot in his biography of the architect.

2. Scudder's subtler use of the language of orthodoxy is important, though: she contrasts reactionary "surface orthodoxies" with the deeper, more radical "orthodoxy" of Christian Socialism (*Franciscan Adventure* 320). Heresy is not as important a category for her analysis as for Eliot and Ransom.

3. Eliot allowed this text to fall out of print, mortified at the offense he caused Jewish friends like Harold Loeb in his remarks.

4. Nevertheless, Pericles Lewis exempts Lawrence from his study of religious experience

and the modernist novel because Lawrence doesn't "share the bemused detachment character-istic of the other modernists in their treatment of the church" (18).

5. This group was convened by the Scottish Protestant missionary J. H. Oldham (1874–1969), frequented by intellectuals such as the Roman Catholic historian Christopher Dawson (1889–1970) and the Hungarian-born Jewish sociologist Karl Mannheim (1893–1947), and vis-ited by Reinhold Niebuhr, among others. Mannheim's death led to the cessation of its regular meetings. For more on Eliot's involvement in The Moot and related groups, see Kojecky 156–97. Kojecky's study is a sympathetic general overview of Eliot's social thought with valuable bi-ographical insight.

6. Jed Esty gives one of the only recent critical treatments of The Rock in his very good book A Shrinking Island: Modernism and National Culture in England (2004). For Esty, The Rock, along with other modernist pageant-plays of the 1930s, demonstrated the shrinking of late-modernist consciousness from the international to the national, regional, and particular (70–76). This modernist emphasis gives birth eventually (through Eliot's Notes Towards a Theory of Culture, among other texts, and passing on from there to the academic Left) to the emerging Marxist discipline of cultural studies in the 1950s. But The Rock is just as paradoxically con-sumed by Eliot's international Catholicity as his insular Englishness. Salvation for the island nation must come from outside: the play's heroic figure of the Rock embodies the decidedly non-English Peter the Hermit, Saint Peter, and the biblical Nehemiah.

7. See sourcebooks.fordham.edu/source/peterhermit.asp.

8. For a probing examination of the theology of state violence, see William T. Cavanaugh, "Killing for the Telephone Company: Why the Nation-State Is Not the Keeper of the Com-mon Good," Modern Theology 20, no. 2 (April 2004): 243–74.

9. See www.catholicworker.org/dorothyday/articles/566.html.

10. See Sherill Tippins, February House: The Story of W. H. Auden, Carson McCullers, Jane and Paul Bowles, Benjamin Britten, and Gypsy Rose Lee, under One Roof in Brooklyn (New York: Houghton Mifflin Harcourt, 2005).

11. Elizabeth Freeman defines chrononormativity as "the use of time to organize individual human bodies toward maximum productivity"; it "is a mode of implantation, a technique by which institutional forces come to seem like somatic facts" (Time Binds 3).

12. Dix's book is dedicated to the Cowley Fathers, who were important mentors for Ralph Adams Cram. Auden briefly mentions the monastic origin of the offices in The Dyer's Hand (1962) (140).

13. Auden's 1949 poem "Memorial for the City" performs a similar action (Selected Poems 196–201).

14. It should be noted that this is intellectual history; Cochrane is relating the monastic ideal.

15. The later Auden often cloaks religious seriousness in light humor; "The Love Feast," for example, also makes a Eucharist out of a dinner party, or perhaps vice versa (Collected Poems 614–15; cf. Mendelson, Later Auden 279).

16. The historian Thomas F. Jackson has also shown recently, in From Civil Rights to Human Rights (Philadelphia: University of Pennsylvania Press, 2007), that Martin Luther King Jr., as a Baptist minister, is an important inheritor of Scudder's Christian Socialist tradition within liberal Protestantism.

CHAPTER THREE

1. Chappel dubs the ideological outlook of this network "fraternal Catholic modernism," in contradistinction to mainstream "paternal Catholic modernism." (While Chappel focuses on European history, he acknowledges the American Catholic Worker movement as an exemplary incarnation of fraternal Catholic thinking.) Both camps were modern in accepting the legitimacy of secular states and religious pluralism, but the former sought widely distributed sovereignty and cooperation between different religious and nonreligious groups, whereas the latter sought a strong central authority that would protect the prerogatives of the nuclear family. The Spanish Civil War marks the clearest dividing line between the two groups: fraternal Catholic modernists like Jacques Maritain and the Catholic Workers supported the Spanish Republic (though they decried the brutalities of Republican forces, especially against clerics and churches), whereas paternal Catholic modernists supported General Franco's Nationalists. Chappel's thesis that the Catholic modernism that arose in the 1930s, in both fraternal and paternal forms, represented the curtailing of the antimodernist medievalism that dominated Catholic social thought in the 1920s may seem to cut against my argument's emphasis on medievalism. But Chappel contends, "Ironically, fraternal Catholicism was in some ways more faithful to the antimodernism of the social Catholic tradition" than paternal Catholicism (110). Catholic antifascists, including Maritain, "stemmed from the Catholic medievalism of the 1920s and tried to update its antistatist and anticapitalist elements in the 1930s . . . in a progressive way" (114). Medievalism, like antimodernism more generally, was a politically fungible idiom, a tradition of social thought that could point to multiple futures. Claude McKay and the Catholic Workers, like Maritain, "urged a form of Catholic modernism that would salvage the revolutionary, antistatist elements of the [medievalist] tradition for a new age, rather than its hierarchical and racist ones" (Chappel 139). McKay's reckoning, in medievalist terms, with the peculiarly modern problems of white supremacy and religious pluralism is a focus of my reading of "The Middle Ages" below. For a counterpoint to the transnational framing I've adopted here—one that emphasizes the particularly American qualities of the Catholic Workers and their ideology, see Fisher, chaps. 1-3, esp. 43-47.

2. While much has been written about Day and the Catholic Worker movement in the history of social and religious activism and in American Catholic culture, only Paul Elie has sought to accord Day her place in literary history, deftly weaving her story in with those of Walker Percy, Thomas Merton, and Flannery O'Connor in his literary group biography, *The Life You Save May Be Your Own: An American Pilgrimage* (2004). Work on the *Catholic Worker*'s aesthetics has focused on its illustrations, rather than its literature; analyses of Day's writings interpret her in theological and ethical contexts rather than literary-historical ones. For an example of the former, see Rachel Norton's master's thesis on Ade Bethune's *Catholic Worker* illustrations, the "hieratic" style of which combined modernist abstraction, medievalism, and representationalism. For the latter, see Maureen O'Connell's essay on the "harsh and dreadful beauty" of Day's ethics—in practices of mothering and social care and in writing, which Day refused to separate—in *She Who Imagines: Feminist Theological Aesthetics*. (The latter essay contains some errors of typography and detail.)

3. Day hated the title, picked out by her publishers, with its implication of opposition between radicalism and Catholicism (Elie 114).

4. These lines most resemble the style of cofounder Peter Maurin's "Easy Essays," treated below.

5. The "Left Agrarian" Fellowship of Southern Churchmen also started farm cooperatives in the South in the 1930s, as I discuss in chapter 4. Some Catholic Worker farms still operate today.

6. Day and Maurin borrowed the term "personalism" from the French philosopher Emmanuel Mounier (see Hellman, *Emmanuel Mounier and the New Catholic Left, 1930–1950*).

7. This revision to the original masthead was actually suggested to Day by a Black Chicago doctor, Arthur Falls (Karen Johnson 55). In later versions, the white male worker is replaced by a mother holding a child.

8. There are three biographies of Maurin: his disciple Arthur Sheehan's testament, *Peter Maurin: Gay Believer* (1959); Marc Ellis's *Peter Maurin: Prophet in the Twentieth Century* (1981); and Francis J. Sicius's arrangement and expansion of Dorothy Day's notes toward a biography, *Peter Maurin: Apostle to the World* (2004). In her Maurin-inspired ethical study, *The Fear of Beggars: Poverty and Stewardship in Christian Ethics* (2007), Kelly S. Johnson claims that Ellis's biography is "the most complete" (191); I agree with her assessment and largely rely on Ellis for details. Ellis's approach might be termed intelligent hagiography. For a nonhagiographical take on Maurin, the first three chapters of James T. Fisher's *The Catholic Counterculture in America, 1933–1962* (1989) are invaluable. My own method in this chapter, it will become clear, proceeds from the position that it is within the purview of the literary critic and historian to look for signs of saintliness—that the perception of (or desire to perceive) the holy is compatible with critical attention to texts and their contexts. While there is some scholarship that liberally quotes Maurin's poetry, there is none, to my knowledge, that closely analyzes it as I do here. This aim constrains me not to quote extensively but rather to choose a few examples and read them in depth against a thick background. Maurin's poems are collected in various Catholic Worker books, of which the most recent is *The Green Revolution* (1961). A selection of his work can be found on the Web here: www.catholicworker.org/petermaurin/easy-essays.html.

9. See Hyde, esp. 56–73, for a helpful digest of this aspect of gift theory in a literary context.

10. Maurin adopted this term from the French thinker Emmanuel Mounier. Maurin quoted Mounier in his poetry and arranged for the English translation of his *Personalist Manifesto* in 1938 (Fisher 45). On Mounier's personalism, see Hellman, esp. 5–11.

11. Not that the paper didn't also print cartoons. Maurin suggested portraying the saints in this manner to illustrator Ade Bethune (Day, "On Peter Maurin" 19).

12. The internal quote here, though the wording isn't exact, appears to be from Hellman 22. I expand on Péguy below. For brief background on these fascinating figures, see Hellman 21–35. Fisher offers an enlightening comparative study of Maurin and Mounier (43–47). He concludes that the personalism of the Catholic Workers "had less in common with the European philosophy of that name than with the pressing need to define a new American Catholic vision of selfhood" (43).

13. Péguy wrote two different long plays about St. Joan: *Joan of Arc* (1897) and *The Mystery of the Charity of Joan of Arc* (1910).

14. Raymond Moley was a Columbia law professor and advisor to FDR who first championed, and then turned against, the New Deal (Rosen).

15. Maurin's poetic campaign against usury recalls Ezra Pound's similar political ani-

mus. But Maurin was philo-Semitic rather than anti-Semitic (Ellis 146–54). This positive, if fraught, stance was common in French Social Catholicism: Péguy was an ardent Dreyfusard, and Maritain and Bloy each cultivated a Catholic mystique of the Jews.

16. In a similar way, Day (and many others since) saw Maurin himself in his humble poverty as a proper vessel of Christian holiness. The analogy between his person and his poetry is all but irresistible.

17. It seems that Maritain and Maurin spoke in English. Maritain's letter is in English, and in it he laments his lack of fluency that hampered their conversation.

18. This essay appeared in *New Literary History* in 2015, with translation and introduction by Tim Howles. Howles notes a recent resurgence in Péguy studies.

19. This was actually Latour's first published piece of scholarship. I take his final cryptic reference to the "purposes" of "the world of representation" to mean that the repetitions are philosophically, and not only stylistically, significant.

20. "Cracks" here is itself a pun, meaning jokes, fragmented sentences, and off-kilter perceptions. "Background for Peter Maurin" is the best thing Day ever wrote about him; it's one of the best things she ever wrote, period. She interviews him over lunch at a Bowery dive, and the atmospherics are amazing. It's a sort of Dostoyevskeyan vignette replete with imagery of fragmentation and infestation. Peter talks about the sources of his thought in Benedictine, Franciscan, and Jesuit monasticism, French, English, and American literature, contemporary clerics and labor-leaders, and emerging postcolonial activists. In the final sentences, faithfully recorded by Day, he becomes incomprehensible. What comes through to me in this interview, and in poems like "Big Shots and Little Shots," is Maurin's poetic modernism: the proximity of his linguistic experiments to the deceptively plainspoken iterative weirdness of Gertrude Stein, the singsong grammatical distortions of e.e. cummings, and the linguistic *destruktion* of the ending of Wallace Stevens's "The Man on the Dump."

21. This particular text was first published in 1933 and reprinted in many issues, but it just so happens to appear in same the number as Claude McKay's "The Middle Ages," discussed below.

22. See also Moore.

23. See Claude McKay, *My Green Hills of Jamaica* (New York: Heinemann, 1979).

24. Deshmukh may overstate critical hostility to McKay's Catholicism when she alleges that critics have demystified McKay's conversion "by looking for the psychological or material 'reality' *behind* his conversion, or worse, by impugning his motives" (150). Wayne Cooper connects McKay's Catholicism to his desire for patronage from the Church and his rebellion against his fundamentalist Protestant father, while distancing himself those "who have questioned the authenticity and sincerity of McKay's conversion" (*Rebel Sojourner* 368). Barbara Griffin emphasizes the importance of the medical and emotional care McKay received from Catholic friends, but not in order to cast doubt on his sincerity (41–43). Of McKay's major interpreters, the biographer Tyrone Tillery follows most closely the trail blazed by the skeptical Eastman, dismissing the poet's "religious convictions" as "suspect" (180).

25. Writing in *Commonweal*, Griffin Oleynick has recently shown how McKay fulfilled an office of social prophecy even before his conversion in his previously unpublished and recently discovered novel manuscript from 1941, *Amiable with Big Teeth*. Here I focus on what I find to be a richer document of McKay's religious-social prophecies, the poems he wrote after his conversion, many of which were published in the *Catholic Worker*.

26. As such, we might understand McKay's lateness in the more critically valuable sense ar-

ticulated by Edward Said in his posthumously published book *On Late Style* (New York: Pantheon, 2006). However, the religiosity of McKay's poetry makes for an uneasy fit with Said's notion of late style, because Said's critical recuperation of the category of lateness depends on a rigid distinction between the religious and the secular.

27. Hughes's phrase is "dark like me," modulated later in the poem to "black like me" (see Hughes, *Collected Poems* 40). The journalist John Howard Griffin took the title of his famous book from this same poem.

28. According to Chappel, it is the acceptance, and even the celebration, of religious pluralism and the secular state that sets the Catholic modernism of the 1930s, whether of the paternal or fraternal variety, apart from the Catholic antimodernism of the 1920s (and before). The Catholic Workers are in this sense fraternal Catholic modernists, with the proviso that their anarchist bent means that they accept and celebrate religious pluralism but reject the qualified admiration of the secular democratic state expressed by other fraternal Catholics like Maritain.

29. I intend no epistemological slight by the word "myth." I conceive of myths as ubiquitous and in no way opposed to scientific understanding, along the lines proposed by the philosopher Mary Midgley.

30. Jacobs clarifies that the neo-Thomist account of modernity "is not, in my judgment, a very good historical thesis, but it has been almost the only one to offer significant resistance to the emancipatory narrative of the Enlightenment that casts the schoolmen [medieval thinkers like Aquinas] as dull, benighted, superstitious logic-choppers" (*The Year of Our Lord* 41–42).

31. McKay gives the lie to the tongue-in-cheek title of this document in its final paragraph, when he writes that "some modernists may say that my joining the Catholic Church is a backward step. But to me it is the progressive step, which should have been taken long ago" (25).

32. It's illuminating to compare McKay's take on Spain here, based on pre–Civil War travels and memories, to Richard Wright's reflections on Francoist Spain in *Pagan Spain* (1957; New York: Harper Perennial, 2008), which is laced with pity for the plight of Spanish Protestants in a Catholic country—he even calls them *"white Negroes,"* observing a kinship with "American Negroes, Jews, and other oppressed minorities" (162, emphasis in original). Wright's Spain is too Catholic for Wright's lapsed Protestant comfort but also somehow *"not yet even Christian!"* (229, emphasis in original). Spain's status as bridge between past and present, Europe and Africa, Christianity and Islam, makes it a territory seething with danger for Wright, rather than instinct with possibility, as for McKay.

33. See Acts 8:26–40.

34. The theologian Willie James Jennings's 2011 book *The Christian Imagination* is particularly clear on this point.

35. For example, look at the way the contemporary Alt-Right has embraced "medieval memes," as *The Economist* put it recently in "The Far Right's New Fascination."

36. See Schultz, *Tri-Faith America*. Schultz's argument centers on the sociologist Will Herberg's landmark midcentury study of American religion *Protestant, Catholic, Jew: An Essay in American Religious Sociology* (New York: Doubleday, 1955).

CHAPTER FOUR

1. In the 1930s, Maurin and Cram both visited and supported the National Catholic Rural Life Conference, an organization representing a midwestern Catholic Benedictine agrarian-

ism centered on St. John's University in Minnesota, and which still exists today. At St. John's, Fr. Virgil Michel, OSB, helped to unite Roman Catholic movements for liturgical revival and rural life. The Benedictines of St. John's translated Emmanuel Mounier's *Personalist Manifesto* into English at Peter Maurin's behest, and Fr. Michel wrote the foreword. Cram spoke at the National Catholic Rural Life Conference's 1937 meeting and published in its magazine (see Michael J. Woods, SJ, *Cultivating Soil and Soul: Twentieth-Century Catholic Agrarians Embrace the Liturgical Movement* [Collegeville, MN: Liturgical Press, 2009]).

2. Gordon objected to the novel's reception as coded autobiography, but it sticks undeniably close to fact (see Makowsky 206–10).

3. Gordon planned to dedicate the novel to Dorothy Day, but when Day read the manuscript, the actions of the character Gordon based on her (she participates in alchemical and occult experiments) caused Day to ask Gordon to remove the dedication—and change some of the actions (Makowsky 209). One more aspect of this fascinating novel deserves comment: a major milestone in Claiborne/Tate's spiritual development is overcoming, to at least some degree, his internalized homophobia, which is linked to trauma he suffers over the suicide of his gay poet friend Horne Watts—an avatar of Tate's real-life friend Hart Crane. Claiborne/ Tate must come to see Watts/Crane not as an unfortunately deviant genius, but as a burning icon of human thirst for love, which finds satisfaction only in the divine. In the novel, Watts's poetic masterwork is called "Pontifex"—not only a Latin title for the pope but, literally translated, "bridge-builder"; the historical Crane's mystical modernist epic is of course "The Bridge," named for the Brooklyn Bridge that is its central metaphor. In the novel, the memory of Watts becomes Claiborne's bridge to conversion. Gordon, Tate, Crane, and Day (along with Malcolm and Peggy Cowley and others) were all companions in the Greenwich Village literary bohemia of the 1920s, and all were haunted in later years by Crane's suicide. Gordon also hints that Claiborne's homophobia stems from his difficulty in reconciling himself to what he calls at one point "the bugger in me" (90). Even more interesting, what Claiborne names "the bugger in [him]" is his wish to live as a hermit; Claiborne reads his own desire for an eremitic/monastic vocation as queer. On the homoerotics of the Southern Agrarians, see John Jeremiah Sullivan's essay "Mr. Lytle" in *Pulphead* (New York: Farrar, Straus and Giroux, 2011).

4. See P. Murphy.

5. Denis Donoghue claims that "by orthodoxy Ransom evidently meant the Eastern church from which the Western churches had lapsed" (14). While Ransom does hold up Eastern Orthodoxy as exemplary to Western Christendom for its reluctance to tame God, in the end he suggests, "We had better work within the religious institutions that we have, and do what we can to recover the excellencies of the ancient faith," for to "go into the Greek communion" would be "not in the least practicable" (*God without Thunder* 325).

6. On this score, Kieran Quinlan's book *John Crowe Ransom's Secular Faith* (1989) too often reads Ransom's late secularism back into his early career. Quinlan naturalizes Ransom's late secularism as the maturation of his philosophical outlook, but the ideological assumption of Quinlan's argument—that religiosity is a kind of intellectual adolescence—is just the sort of thing I wish to challenge. In the 1930s, it was far from clear that Ransom's development would take a secular turn, and his earlier, more religious work may be a richer legacy than his later, quasi-scientific approach to criticism.

7. But perhaps criticism is essentially an ulterior genre, rather than a form-in-itself or a

form-for-itself. Criticism, it seems to me, is almost always something "by other means"—whether political theory or poetry, science or theology.

8. In this simultaneous othering and valorizing of the God and religion of Israel, Ransom echoes the dicey philo-Semitism of French Social Catholics like Léon Bloy and Jacques Maritain.

9. Despite the controversy around the term "neo-orthodoxy"—Reinhold Niebuhr preferred the moniker of "Christian Realism"—I use it here because I think it's noteworthy that readers of Barth and the Niebuhrs saw them as up to similar projects, and that that project appeared to observers as an "unorthodox defense of orthodoxy" like Ransom's.

10. Niebuhr's talk was later published in the magazine the *Student World* and then printed in Niebuhr's essay collection *Christianity and Power Politics* (1940). This quote is taken from the latter version, anthologized in *The Essential Reinhold Niebuhr* (1986).

11. A historical rage at having been born *now*, into modernity, with its diminished moral prospects, where even sins are meaner than before: this is the dark, roiling heart of Ransom's "Southern Renascence." Out of that rage come the Renascence's most powerful protest and its most childish petulance.

12. The exact number of attendees is unclear. John Salmond (1999) and Robert F. Martin (1983) both report approximately 80 attendees (Salmond 115; Martin 67). In *The Encyclopedia of Religion in the South* (2005), Anthony Dunbar reports 180, but in his earlier book-length treatment *Against the Grain: Southern Radicals and Prophets 1929–1959* (1981), he clarifies that while 180 people responded to James Dombrowski's invitation to the Conference with interest, "only about 40" attended the meeting (60). Fellowship member and Conference attendee David Burgess, reflecting on the event nearly twenty years after, refers to the Churchmen in attendance as "the little band," which seems to make 40 the most probable number (Burgess 1).

13. Koinonia Farm remains in operation today: www.koinoniafarm.org.

14. Dombrowski is perhaps best known as the defendant in the landmark Supreme Court civil rights/civil liberties case *Dombrowski v. Pfister* (1965), which produced the "chilling effect" on First Amendment rights as a civil liberties doctrine (Adams 3).

15. It seems to me that Scudder deserves a much larger role in this work; certainly she merited a chapter of her own. Her relative obscurity in the book is probably attributable to the fact that she was still a living and somewhat actively writing scholar at the time. Dombrowski's book takes Scudder as an established academic peer rather than a subject of historical-philosophical inquiry. Scudder's major statement of social theory, *Socialism and Character,* did not appear until 1910, after the endpoint of Dombrowski's study.

16. David Burgess, distancing the relation a bit, calls Niebuhr "the spiritual godfather of the Fellowship" (1). Niebuhr was also on the advisory board of Highlander Folk School (Adams 306), and he was active in the founding of Delta and Providence Cooperative Farms (Smith).

17. Scudder titled an essay collection *The Church and the Hour: Reflections of a Socialist Churchwoman* (1917), and she often referred to herself as a churchwoman in her other writings.

18. Robert F. Martin reports that by 1949, 20 percent of the Fellowship's four hundred members were Black, and 41 percent were women (67). The theologian Nelle Morton, a white woman, was one of the FSC's three executive secretaries during its existence; she served from 1945 to 1950 (Martin 68). As the story I've told here indicates, however, the organization's leadership at the time of the Monteagle Conference was overwhelmingly white and male.

19. The "Statement" is unsigned, but its style is recognizably Campbell's.

20. On this note, *Katallagete* was the most important early American reception point for the writings of the French Christian anarchist theologian Jacques Ellul; one special issue was devoted to Ellul's writings. The journal published other Christians with anarchist sympathies, too, such as the New York attorney William Stringfellow. "While he did not use the term 'Christian anarchy,' Campbell's reflections on the 1960s activism of the churches nevertheless reveals an anarchist perspective" (Hawkins 80). On Campbell and Christian anarchism, see Hawkins, 75–86.

CHAPTER FIVE

1. Ironically, Campbell envisions these secular northerners as "crusaders," reversing Eliot's imagery from *The Rock*.

2. The essay was vintage Percy and one of the strongest ever published by the Churchmen—a fact Campbell and his editor acknowledged by making it the lead and title piece in an edited collection culled from the pages of their magazine. Its title, "The Failure and the Hope," adumbrated the Committee's shift from tragedy to comedy.

3. The Churchmen were not *all* white and male; a 1971 list of Committee members includes, for example, the leading civil rights activist Fannie Lou Hamer (1917–1977) (Holloway/Katallagete papers). *Katallagete* published writing by Baptist SNCC founder (and, later, Georgia congressman) John Lewis (1940–2020) and Mennonite historian Vincent Harding (1931–2014), for example—both of these in the same summer 1967 issue. Publishing white and Black Southern Christian intellectuals side by side was one of *Katallagete*'s strongest equalitarian statements.

4. The failure of the Stoic philosophy of white southern elites is dramatically adumbrated by Quentin Compson's suicide, following his sister's loss of "virtue," in Faulkner's *The Sound and the Fury* (1929). Percy inveighed against southern Stoicism at length in his essay "Stoicism in the South," originally published in *Commonweal* in 1956 and collected in *Signposts in a Strange Land*, ed. Patrick Samway, SJ, 83–88 (New York: Picador, 1991).

5. I've specified that the Churchmen rejected the *early* Faulkner because they greatly admired the later "humanist" Faulkner, epitomized in his Nobel acceptance speech (1950), and they tended, like many midcentury American literary types, to read back into the Faulkner of the 1930s the novelist's more optimistic, and more Christian, postwar philosophy. The Churchmen appended an excerpt from Faulkner's *The Town* (1957) to the spring 1968 issue of *Katallagete*, and they introduced the summer 1967 issue with an excerpt from *Light in August* (1932). On the two Faulkners, see Greif 116–21.

6. Dabbs wrote his English dissertation on "The Poetic Experience" at Columbia University in the 1920s, although he was never awarded the Ph.D., and worked as an English professor from 1921 to 1942, first at the University of South Carolina and later at Coker College, a women's college not far from his native Mayesville.

7. One way to think about Dabbs's works as a whole is to see them, along with books such as W. J. Cash's *The Mind of the South* (New York: Knopf, 1941) and Lillian Smith's *Killers of the Dream* (New York: Norton, 1949), as among the first quasi-scholarly entries of southern cultural studies.

8. Dabbs was acutely conscious of the global context of decolonialization in which the civil rights movement was carried out; he has in mind here race relations in the South as an exemplar for relations between the developed and the newly decolonial developing world.

9. Dabbs leaned on the exiled Russian Christian existentialist philosopher Nicholas Berdyaev (1874–1948) to make this point: "It is through tragedy that man makes his way to Christianity in which tragedy is finally resolved" (qtd. in Dabbs, "Beyond Tragedy" 454).

10. One of Dabbs's favorite phrases, this derives from the Spanish liberal philosopher Ortega y Gasset's *Revolt of the Masses*. The metaphor is of a shipwrecked man looking for flotsam to grasp and save his life.

11. There is an interesting overlap between Dabbs's thinking on development and the contextualist theories of the Vienna-born architect Christopher Alexander (1936–) and his Center for Environmental Structure, "a non-profit organization dedicated to the shaping of our built environment so that it becomes deeply comfortable, beautiful and supportive for all human beings" (Center for Environmental Structure). Alexander's most well-known book is *A Pattern Language: Towns, Buildings, Construction* (New York: Oxford University Press, 1977). The same overlap obtains for many of the writers in this dissertation when they turn their thoughts to architecture and design, not least Cram.

12. This chapter's argument owes much to Wood's two chapters on Percy in *The Comedy of Redemption: Christian Faith and Comic Vision in Four American Novelists* (1988). In limpid, witty prose Wood argues, following Karl Barth and contra Reinhold Niebuhr, that the Christian faith's response to post-Enlightenment Western culture is best presented as comedy rather than tragedy, and that the novelists Percy, Flannery O'Connor, John Updike, and Peter De Vries point the way in comedic evangelization. Wood's analysis highlights the important overlap between Niebuhr's theology and that of southern tragic modernists like John Crowe Ransom (a connection I explore in the previous chapter) and William Alexander Percy. Wood is especially good on the biographical circumstances that led Walker Percy to embrace a Christian comedic outlook over the Stoic tragic outlook of his "Uncle Will." Wood's literary analysis focuses on Percy's novel *The Moviegoer* (1960), whereas mine takes up *The Last Gentleman* (1966). Where I depart from Wood in my analysis is in taking the conflict of tragic vs. comic outlook as primarily a political or political-theological issue; for Wood this conflict is a "religious" issue which is "deeper" than problems of politics or ethics, though it inflects one's politics (143). The primary historical context shaping Percy's embrace of comedy is, for my purposes, the civil rights movement. The larger aim of Wood's book, "to sketch a new theology of culture that would open a way beyond both conservatism and liberalism," has some affinity with my own (280).

13. Phin found a better treatment for his terrors when Uncle Will sent him up to Johns Hopkins to be analyzed by the eminent American neo-Freudian psychiatrist Harry Stack Sullivan (Tolson 138).

14. There's a running joke at the Homeric underpinnings of James Joyce's *Ulysses* in *The Last Gentleman*. One character nicknames Barrett's Trav-l-Aire trailer "Ulysses," and the journey to Ithaca is a false homecoming for Will. But *The Odyssey*, too, ends not with a homecoming but with another journey, and the Homeric tale's episodic nature is a fit analogue for Percy's rather plotless structure. Will Barrett, like Joyce's Leopold Bloom, is both a send-up and an antitype of Odysseus the wily wanderer.

15. Aiken may be a reference to John Howard Griffin and *Black Like Me* (1961). But Griffin was a fellow Catholic and colleague in the Committee of Southern Churchmen. Griffin was a Texan, not a northerner like the fictional Aiken (though not a southerner, either, at least in Percy's estimation; Percy's writerly animus against Texans is rivaled only by his grievance toward Ohioans—though one suspects neither is wholly serious). If Griffin is being sent up here, the criticism is being leveled by a friendly cobelligerent.

16. A related sentence closes the main text of *The Moviegoer*, before that novel's epilogue, as well: "It is impossible to say" (235).

17. As early as 1960 (or earlier, because he wrote the book earlier, though that's when it was published), Dabbs had expressed grave doubts about the possibility of a divinely comic approach to history: "When one passes beyond tragedy what else is there? *The Divine Comedy* perhaps? I read it once, but it told me very little. Perhaps I should read it again. Perhaps not. Perhaps I've never become really a Christian, nor has the drama of life become for me a divine comedy. I don't know" (Dabbs, *The Road Home* 117).

18. See the contributions of Kareem U. Crayton, Brenton Mock, and Barbara Combs to "Does the Confederate Flag Breed Racism?," *New York Times*, June 19, 2015, www.nytimes.com/roomfordebate/2015/06/19/does-the-confederate-flag-breed-racism.

19. See Tim Tyson, "Can Honest History Allow for Hope?," *Atlantic*, December 18, 2015, www.theatlantic.com/politics/archive/2015/12/can-hope-and-history-coexist/420651/.

20. In 1983, James Y. Holloway, the editor of the Churchmen's magazine *Katallagete*, invited Berry to give the commencement address at Berea College, the tuition-free liberal arts school founded by the Kentucky abolitionist Cassius Marcellus Clay where Holloway was a professor of philosophy and religion. Berry's address was subsequently published in the summer/fall 1983 issue of *Katallagete*—one of the last issues before the Committee and the magazine parted ways (both dissolved soon after). Like the Churchmen, Berry has also written penetratingly on racism in American life, especially in his book-length essay *The Hidden Wound* (2010; first published 1970).

21. In *The Achievement of Wendell Berry*, Fritz Oehlschlaeger has suggested that the Mad Farmer's rage against consumerism and his foxy opacity can "contribute to the salvation of political life in America" by embodying virtues of thrift and privacy desperately needed by an indebted and overly image-conscious culture (43–44). I have a similar estimation of the Mad Farmer but for a somewhat different reason: his anarchistic refusal to abide invidious distinctions between sacred and secular, living and dead, rebellion and restfulness. The Mad Farmer rejects life-destroying boundaries of a human-created industrial capitalism in favor of the life-giving—and death-dealing, for life and death aren't opposites on the farm or in the natural world—limits of nature. In a 2012 interview with radical magazine *Dissent*, in response to the question of whether he is a Socialist, Berry said, "From what I've read and heard, socialism and communism have been just as committed to industrial principles as capitalism. My own inclination is not to start with a political idea or theory and think downward to the land and the people, but instead to start with the land and the people, the *necessity* for harmony between local ecosystems and local economies, and think upward to conserving policies" (Leonard). This literally grassroots style of political thought resonates most with the Christian anarchisms of Will Campbell and Dorothy Day among the radical streams I enumerate here.

22. While his rejection of the Churchmen's Southern exceptionalism is welcome, it seems to me that the relentless particularity of Berry's perspective misses something supplied by the

large-scale structural imagination of Socialist thinkers such as Scudder. On this, see George Scialabba, "Back to the Land: Wendell Berry in the Path of Modernity," *Baffler Salvos*, no. 49, January 2020, thebaffler.com/salvos/back-to-the-land-scialabba.

CHAPTER SIX

1. Since New Directions published Wheelwright's *Collected Poems* in 1972, only Alan Wald, literary historian of the American Left, and the venerable poet John Ashbery have given Wheelwright sustained consideration. Massachusetts-based lit mag *spoKe* devoted a special section to Wheelwright in 2015, including an essay by Wald.

2. Austin Warren, reviewing *Lord Weary's Castle* for *Poetry* magazine in 1946, likewise noted the poets' similar styles.

3. Lowell's Notebook poems were famously subject to revision; the Matthiessen elegy appears in *Notebook 1967–68* (1969), *Notebook* (1970), and *History* (1973) in three different forms. I quote from the *Notebook* version, which is in my estimation the best, throughout this chapter.

4. Matthiessen's letters reveal recurrent bouts of depression, but not mania—though it's impossible to know precisely how he would have been diagnosed twenty years after his death, let alone today.

5. As in my reading of Cram and Scudder in chapter 1, I'm drawing here on Benjamin Kahan's resistance to paranoid interpretations of celibacy in his book *Celibacies: American Modernism and Sexual Life* (2013). Kahan argues for the productiveness of leaving "the knottedness of coding and difficulty intact, reading the blockage [of celibacy] not as an impediment obstructing a flow elsewhere but an elegant formation in and of itself" (5).

6. See Chappel.

7. See Damon R. Young, "Public Thinker: Jack Halberstam on Wildness, Anarchy, and Growing Up Punk," *Public Books*, March 26, 2019, www.publicbooks.org/public-thinker-jack-halberstam-on-wildness-anarchy-and-growing-up-punk/.

8. In a particularly vociferous essay in *Partisan Review*, Irving Howe characterized *From the Heart of Europe* as the work of "a political thinker . . . sentimental and befuddled," "a usually sober sensibility . . . victimized by dubious politics" (1126, 1125).

9. Though the Soviet Union would not acquire nuclear weapons until 1949, the United States' deployment of the atom bomb haunts the pages of *From the Heart of Europe*, as here: "Ever since that summer day of Hiroshima it has been almost impossible to feel that anything we do is permanent" (66).

10. In a keen reading of Matthiessen's *American Renaissance*, which turns on Ahab's three different roles as the book's antagonist, George Blaustein argues: "The first, and likely the boldest, is Ahab the monomaniacal proto-industrialist. Matthiessen read Ahab forward in time, as a prophecy of the Gilded Age" (176).

CONCLUSION

1. See Jia Tolentino, "What Will Become of the Dirtbag Left?," *New Yorker*, November 18, 2016, www.newyorker.com/culture/persons-of-interest/what-will-become-of-the-dirtbag-left?verso=true.

2. The podcast's website is themagnificast.com.

3. Antiliberalism of a particularly conservative Roman Catholic stripe associated with *First Things* magazine has recently attracted some attention from observers of the academy (see Jon Baskin, "Academia's Holy Warriors," *Chronicle of Higher Education*, September 12, 2019, www .chronicle.com/interactives/20190912-academias-holy-warriors).

4. The Tradinista! archive can be found at tradinista.tumblr.com. At some point since 2016, they seem to have lost the exclamation point; compare web.archive.org/web/20161002185621/ http://tradinista.com/.

The Tradinistas might well have Nicaragua on their minds, given the prominence of the poet-priest-revolutionary Ernesto Cardenal, the first Sandinista minister of culture, in the movement. Cardenal studied with Thomas Merton at Gethsemani Monastery in Kentucky; later, he was disciplined by Pope John Paul II for taking a government post in Nicaragua's Marxist regime. In the 1990s, he distanced himself from the Sandinista party, alleging corruption; in 2015, Pope Francis—the first Latin American pope—reinstated Cardenal fully as a priest (see Jonathan Cohen, "Introduction: *Songs of Heaven and Earth*," in *Pluriverse: Selected Poems* [New York: New Directions, 2009]).

5. See Rev. Robert A. Sirico, "Free Economies and the Common Good," *Acton Commentary*, May 1, 2007, www.acton.org/pub/commentary/2007/05/01/free-economies-and-common-good; and Paul Ryan, "Free Enterprise, Faith, and the Common Good," Benedictine College commencement address, May 11, 2013, www.thegregorian.org/2013/free-enterprise-faith-and-the-common-good.

6. See Matthew Schmitz, "I Think I'm Not a Contra," *First Things*, September 29, 2016, www.firstthings.com/blogs/firstthoughts/2016/09/i-think-im-not-a-contra; and R. R. Reno, "What's at Stake in the French-Ahmari Debate?," *First Things*, September 19, 2019, www .firstthings.com/web-exclusives/2019/09/whats-at-stake-in-the-french-ahmari-debate). See also Reno, "Common Good Conservatism," *First Things*, November 2018, www.firstthings .com/article/2018/11/common-good-conservatism. Reno and fellow *First Things* editor Mark Bauerlein were among the signees of the pro-Trump "Scholars and Writers for America" petition in 2016 (see amgreatness.com/2016/09/28/writes-scholars-for-trump/).

7. There's perhaps an echo here of the Bhagavad Gita, in which the divine Lord Krishna is Arjuna's military lieutenant and carriage driver—a reference that acknowledges Thomas's traditional link to Indian Christianity.

8. Wheelwright's Thomas poems traffic in some of the gender and sexuality essentialism their gnostic source texts seem to display (see Logion 114 of the Gospel of Thomas: www. earlychristianwritings.com/thomas/gospelthomas114.html). But as with the gnostic writings, Wheelwright's poems contain entwined and perhaps contradictory stances on sex and gender (in the Gospel of Thomas, compare Logion 22: www.earlychristianwritings.com/thomas/ gospelthomas22.html). Just before his praise of Teckla's fertility, Wheelwright's Thomas petitions the Holy Spirit: "Consummate Dove / weave your androgynous nest / for sex of sexless trees and rocks and stars." According to Alan Wald, Wheelwright's "sexuality remains suggestively elusive," though there is anecdotal and textual evidence of his "bisexual longings and at least some activities with both sexes" ("Wheelwright and His Kind" 203–4).

9. I should acknowledge again what a huge debt I owe Alan Wald. Without his 1983 book *The Revolutionary Imagination*, there would be no sustained critical consideration of Wheelwright in print. I should also say that I don't have access to all the biographical resources that

Wald does—he worked on his book in the late 1970s, did interviews with and received personal letters from many people who knew Wheelwright personally and were still alive. However, it seems to me that if Wheelwright died intending to publish "Evening" and "Morning" in his next collection (though it's true they had appeared earlier in magazines) and with "The Other" nearing completion, then he wasn't done with the myth of Doubting Thomas—or with Christianity. He hadn't grown beyond his faith and its narratives to find more appropriate symbols first in Socialism and then in Trotskyist Communism. Where Wald seems to frame Wheelwright's move from Christianity to Marxism as a progressive climb of self-development, the journey Wheelwright sketched in the manuscripts left at his death seems more recursive. In his last months—though he couldn't have known they were his last—Wheelwright returned to the myth of Thomas, and to Christianity, holding his faith in suspension with his commitment to Marxism. Wheelwright's return to the myth of Saint Thomas in *Dusk to Dusk* and "The Other" raises the possibility that we view the Thomas poems as an incomplete masterwork, cut short by his death, and not a regrettable poetic byway en route to a more plainspoken secular Trotskyist poetics. Had Wheelwright lived, perhaps his Thomas "verse novel" would stand as a theopoetic late modernist monument, akin to H.D.'s *Trilogy* or Eliot's *Four Quartets*. In any case, I don't believe Wheelwright's poetry is really any more obscure than these. Wheelwright's poetry does not support a narrative of the poet's career as an ascent from Christianity to Marxism if we question one of crucial background assumptions Wald seems to make: that religious understanding inevitably gives way to secular knowledge when confronting social reality. The history of modern Christian radicalism I've presented throughout this book gives many reasons for disputing this assumption.

10. Wheelwright dedicated one of the poems in *Political Self-Portrait* to Day (*Collected Poems* 169).

WORKS CITED

Abelove, Henry. *Deep Gossip*. Minneapolis: University of Minnesota Press, 2003.

Adams, Frank T. *James A. Dombrowski: An American Heretic, 1897–1983*. Knoxville: University of Tennessee Press, 1992.

Aelred of Rievaulx. *The Mirror of Charity*. Translated by Geoffrey Webb and Adrian Walker. London: A. R. Mowbray, 1962.

Alexander, Laura E. "'Christian Left' Is Reviving in America, Appalled by Treatment of Immigrants." *Religion News Service*, August 16, 2019. religionnews.com/2019/08/16/christian-left-is-reviving-in-america-appalled-by-treatment-of-migrants.

Alexander, Michelle. *The New Jim Crow: Mass Incarceration in the Age of Colorblindness*. New York: New Press, 2010.

Allaire, James, and Rosemary Broughton. "An Introduction to the Life and Spirituality of Dorothy Day." www.catholicworker.org/dorothyday/ddbiographytext.cfm?number=3.

Asad, Talal. "On Ritual and Discipline in Medieval Christian Monasticism." *Economy and Society* 16, no. 2 (1987): 159–203.

Auden, W. H. *Collected Poems*. Edited by Edward Mendelson. London: Faber and Faber, 1994.

———. "Criticism in a Mass Society." In *The Intent of the Critic*, edited by Donald A. Stauffer. Princeton, NJ: Princeton University Press, 1941.

———. *The Dyer's Hand*. New York: Random House, 1962.

———. "The Fall of Rome." In *The Complete Works of W. H. Auden: Prose*. Volume 5: *1963–1968*, edited by Edward Mendelson, 214–28. Princeton, NJ: Princeton University Press, 2015.

———. *Forewords and Afterwords*. 1973. New York: Vintage, 1989.

———. *Nones*. New York: Random House, 1950.

———. *Selected Poems*. Edited and with an introduction by Edward Mendelson. 2nd ed. New York: Vintage, 2007.

Auerbach, Erich. *Mimesis*. Translated by Willard R. Trask. Princeton, NJ: Princeton University Press, 1953.

Austin, J. L. *How to Do Things with Words.* 2nd ed. Cambridge, MA: Harvard University Press, 1975.

Badiou, Alain. *The Century.* Translated by Alberto Toscano. Cambridge, UK: Polity, 2007.

Belgau, Ron, and Wesley Hill. "About." In Spiritual Friendship. spiritualfriendship. org/about.

Berry, Wendell. *New Collected Poems.* Berkeley, CA: Counterpoint, 2012.

————. *This Day: Collected & New Sabbath Poems.* Berkeley, CA: Counterpoint, 2014.

Bilbro, Jeffrey. *Virtues of Renewal: Wendell Berry's Sustainable Forms.* Lexington: University Press of Kentucky, 2018.

Blaustein, George. *Nightmare Envy & Other Stories: American Culture and European Reconstruction.* New York: Oxford University Press, 2018.

Boswell, John. *Christianity, Social Tolerance, and Homosexuality: Gay People in Western Europe from the Beginning of the Christian Era to the Fourteenth Century.* Chicago: University of Chicago Press, 1980.

————. *Same-Sex Unions in Premodern Europe.* New York: Villard, 1994.

Bourne, Randolph. "An Hour in Chartres." *Atlantic Monthly,* August 1914, 214–17.

Bozorth, Richard R. *Auden's Games of Knowledge: Poetry and the Meanings of Homosexuality.* New York: Columbia University Press, 2001.

Brackney, William H. "Neo-Orthodoxy." In *Historical Dictionary of Radical Christianity,* 214–15. Lanham, MD: Scarecrow, 2012.

Bray, Alan. *The Friend.* Chicago: University of Chicago Press, 2003.

Brooks, David. "The Conservative Future." *New York Times,* November 19, 2012. www. nytimes.com/2012/11/20/opinion/brooks-the-conservative-future.html?_ r=0.

Brooks, Joanna. "From Edwards to Baldwin: Heterodoxy, Discontinuity, and New Narratives of American Religious-Literary History." *American Literary History* 22, no. 2 (2010): 439–53.

————. "Soul Matters." *PMLA* 128, no. 4 (2013): 947–52.

Brooks, Van Wyck. "On Creating a Usable Past." *Dial,* April 11, 1918, 337–41.

Brown, Peter. "Alms, Work, and the Holy Poor: Early Christian Monasticism Between Syria and Egypt." The James M. and Margaret H. Costan Lecture in Early Christianity, Georgetown University. December 4, 2014. theology.georgetown.edu/inaugural-costan-lecture-2014-peter-brown.

Bruenig, Elizabeth. "Talk of a Rising Religious Left Is Unfounded: It Already Exists." *Washington Post,* April 11, 2019. www.washingtonpost.com/opinions/the-religious-left-is-always-just-about-to-happen-will-it-ever-arrive/2019/04/11/f4500bc6–5c83–11e9–9625–01d48d50ef75_story.html.

Burgess, David. *The Fellowship of Southern Churchmen: Its History and Promise.* Pamphlet. N.d. Katallagete/James Y. Holloway Collection, J. D. Williams Library, Department of Archives and Special Collections, University of Mississippi.

Burke, Kenneth. "Literature as Equipment for Living." In *The Critical Tradition: Clas-*

sic Texts and Contemporary Trends, 2nd ed., edited by David H. Richter, 593–98. Boston: Bedford, 1998.

Burton, Tara Isabella. "Christianity Gets Weird." *New York Times*, May 8, 2020. www .nytimes.com/2020/05/08/opinion/sunday/weird-christians.html.

Bustion, Olivia F. "Queering the City of God: W. H. Auden's Later Poetry and the Ethics of Friendship." Ph.D. diss., University of Michigan, 2012. deepblue.lib. umich.edu/handle/2027.42/96141.

Campbell, Will D. "The Day of Our Birth." *Katallagete* 1, no. 1 (1965): 3–5.

———. Letter to Walker Percy. September 2, 1965. Civil Rights in Mississippi Collection, University of Southern Mississippi. digilib.usm.edu/cdm/compoundobject/collection/manu/id/2665/rec/1.

———. "Statement Adopted by Committee of Southern Churchmen, Nashville, Tennessee, February 6, 1964." *Katallagete* 1, no. 1 (1965), n.p. (inside front cover).

Cartwright, Michael G. "Stanley Hauerwas's Essays in Theological Ethics: A Reader's Guide." In *The Hauerwas Reader*, edited by John Berkman and Michael Cartwright, 623–71. Durham, NC: Duke University Press, 2001.

Cep, Casey. "Is There a Religious Left?" *New Yorker*, June 11, 2020. www.newyorker. com/books/under-review/is-there-a-religious-left.

Chappel, James. *Catholic Modern: The Challenge of Totalitarianism and the Remaking of the Church*. Cambridge, MA: Harvard University Press, 2018.

Christians for Socialism. "The Wind Blows Where It Chooses!" christiansforsocialism.org/manifesto.

Clancy, Walter B. "Jesus in the Brush Arbor: An Interview with Will Campbell." *New Orleans Review* 4, no. 3 (1974): 228–31.

Coates, Ta-Nehisi. "Hope and the Historian." *Atlantic*, December 10, 2015. www .theatlantic.com/politics/archive/2015/12/hope-and-the-historian/419961.

———. "Letter to My Son." *Atlantic*, July 4, 2015. www.theatlantic.com/politics/ archive/2015/07/tanehisi-coates-between-the-world-and-me/397619.

Cochrane, Charles. *Christianity and Classical Culture: A Study of Thought and Action from Augustus to Augustine*. Oxford: Oxford University Press, 1940.

Conference of Younger Churchmen of the South. "Findings." 1934. Katallagete/ James Y. Holloway Collection, J. D. Williams Library, Department of Archives and Special Collections, University of Mississippi.

Conn, Peter. *The American 1930s: A Literary History*. New York: Cambridge University Press, 2009.

Converse, Francis. *Collected Poems*. New York: Dutton, 1937.

———. *Diana Victrix*. Boston: Houghton Mifflin, 1897.

———. *Long Will: A Romance*. Everyman's Library Edition. London: J. M. Dent, 1908.

Cook, Vaneesa. *Spiritual Socialists: Religion and the American Left*. Philadelphia: University of Pennsylvania Press, 2019.

Cooper, Wayne. *Claude McKay: Rebel Sojourner in the Harlem Renaissance*. Baton Rouge: LSU Press, 1987.

———, ed. *The Passion of Claude McKay: Selected Poetry and Prose*. New York: Schocken, 1973.

Corcoran, Teresa, S.C. *Vida Dutton Scudder*. Boston: Twayne, 1982.

Coviello, Peter. *Tomorrow's Parties: Sex and the Untimely in Nineteenth-Century America*. New York: New York University Press, 2013.

Coviello, Peter, and Jared Hickman. "Introduction: After the Postsecular." *American Literature* 86, no. 4 (2014): 645–54.

Cowan, Thomas B. "Excerpts from 'History of The Fellowship of Southern Churchmen.'" Ca. 1938. Katallagete/James Y. Holloway Collection, J. D. Williams Library, Department of Archives and Special Collections, University of Mississippi.

Cowley, Malcolm. *Exile's Return: A Literary Odyssey of the 1920s*. New York: Penguin, 1994.

Cram, Ralph Adams. *The Decadent: Being the Gospel of Inaction: Wherein Are Set Forth in Romance Form Certain Reflections Touching the Curious Characteristics of These Ultimate Years, and the Divers Causes Thereof*. Copeland and Day: Boston, 1893. Project Gutenberg eBook. www.gutenberg.org/files/41490/41490-h/41490-h.htm.

———. *Gold, Frankincense, and Myrrh*. Boston: Marshall Jones, 1919.

———. *The Great Thousand Years*. Chicago: Brothers of the Book, 1918.

———. *My Life in Architecture*. Boston: Little, Brown, 1935.

———. Preface to *Mont-Saint-Michel and Chartres*, by Henry Adams. Boston: Harper and Row, 1913.

———. "Scrapping the Slums." *American Architect*, December 25, 1918, 761.

———. *Walled Towns*. Boston: Marshall Jones, 1919.

Dabbs, James McBride. "Beyond Tragedy." *Christendom* 1, no. 3 (1936): 453–63.

———. *Haunted by God*. Richmond, VA: John Knox, 1972.

———. Interview by Mike Wallace. *The Mike Wallace Interview*. August 31, 1958. Mike Wallace Interview Collection, Harry Ransom Center at the University of Texas at Austin. www.hrc.utexas.edu/multimedia/video/2008/wallace/dabbs_james_mcbride_t.html.

———. Letter to Will Campbell. May 17, 1970. Katallagete/James Y. Holloway Collection, J. D. Williams Library, Department of Archives and Special Collections, University of Mississippi

———. *The Road Home*. Philadelphia: Christian Education Press, 1960.

———. "Southern Churchmen: Fellowship to Committee." *Katallagete* 1, no. 1 (1965): 7–11.

———. *The Southern Heritage*. New York: Knopf, 1958.

———. "Southern Indirection/The Southerner and Time." *Katallagete* 1, no. 2 (1965): 22–23.

———. *Who Speaks for the South?* New York: Funk and Wagnalls, 1964.

Davidson, James. "Mr and Mr and Mrs and Mrs." *London Review of Books* 27, no.

11 (2005). www.lrb.co.uk/v27/n11/james-davidson/mr-and-mr-and-mrs-and-mrs.

Day, Dorothy. "Background for Peter Maurin." *Catholic Worker,* February 1945, 3, 7.

———. "Catholic Worker Celebrates 3rd Birthday: A Restatement of C. W. Aims and Ideals." *Catholic Worker,* May 1936, 1, 6.

———. "Chapter 1: Why." *From Union Square to Rome.* 1938. Online edition at Dorothy Day Collection. dorothyday.catholicworker.org/articles/201.pdf.

———. "Day after Day." *Catholic Worker,* February 1943, 1, 4. Online edition at Dorothy Day Collection. dorothyday.catholicworker.org/articles/148.html.

———. Foreword to *House of Hospitality* (1939). Online edition. www.catholicworker.org/dorothyday/articles/435.html.

———. "Letter to Our Readers at the Beginning of our Fifteenth Year." *Catholic Worker,* May 1947, 1.

———. "Liturgy and Sociology." *Catholic Worker,* January 1936, 5. Online edition at Dorothy Day Collection. dorothyday.catholicworker.org/articles/296.html.

———. *The Long Loneliness.* 1952. Reprint. New York: HarperCollins, 1997.

———. "Maurin's Program." *Catholic Worker,* June–July 1933, 4. Online edition at Dorothy Day Collection. dorothyday.catholicworker.org/articles/266.html.

———. "The Mystical Body and Spain." *Catholic Worker,* August 1936, 4. Online edition at Dorothy Day Collection. dorothyday.catholicworker.org/articles/303.html.

———. "On Peter Maurin." Collection of *Catholic Worker* articles, 1943–77. The Catholic Worker Movement. www.catholicworker.org/dorothyday/themes/peter-maurin.html.

———. "On Pilgrimage—January 1970." *Catholic Worker,* January 1970, 1–2, 8. Online edition at Dorothy Day Collection. dorothyday.catholicworker.org/articles/498.html.

———. *Peter Maurin: Apostle to the World.* With Francis J. Sicius. Maryknoll, NY: Orbis, 2004.

———. "The Story of Three Deaths—Peter Maurin, Lawrence Heaney, Willie Lurey." *Catholic Worker,* June 1949, 1–2. Online edition at the Dorothy Day Collection. dorothyday.catholicworker.org/articles/495.html.

———. "To Our Readers." *Catholic Worker,* May 1933. 4. Online edition at Dorothy Day Collection. dorothyday.catholicworker.org/articles/12.html.

Deer, Patrick. "Two Cities: Berlin and New York." In *W. H. Auden in Context,* edited by Tony Sharpe. New York: Cambridge University Press, 2013.

Deshmukh, Madhuri. "Claude McKay's Road to Catholicism." *Callaloo* 37, no. 1 (2014): 148–68.

Dix, Dom Gregory. *The Shape of the Liturgy.* London: Dacre, 1945.

Dombrowski, James. *The Early Days of Christian Socialism in America.* New York: Columbia University Press, 1936.

Donoghue, Denis. *Adam's Curse: Reflections on Religion and Literature.* Notre Dame, IN: University of Notre Dame Press, 2000.

Douglas, Christopher. *If God Meant to Interfere: American Literature and the Rise of the Christian Right*. Ithaca, NY: Cornell University Press, 2016.

Duke, David. *In the Trenches with Jesus and Marx: Harry F. Ward and the Struggle for Social Justice*. Tuscaloosa: University of Alabama Press, 2006.

Dunbar, Anthony P. *Against the Grain: Southern Radicals and Prophets, 1929–1959*. Charlottesville: University of Virginia Press, 1981.

———. "Fellowship of Southern Churchmen." In *Encyclopedia of Religion in the South*, edited by Samuel S. Hill et al. Macon, GA: Mercer University Press, 2005.

Edelman, Lee. *No Future: Queer Theory and the Death Drive*. Durham, NC: Duke University Press, 2004.

Edwards, Mark Thomas. *The Right of the Protestant Left: God's Totalitarianism*. New York: Palgrave Macmillan, 2012.

Elie, Paul. *The Life You Save May Be Your Own: An American Pilgrimage*. New York: Farrar, Straus and Giroux, 2003.

Eliot, T.S. *After Strange Gods: A Primer of Modern Heresy*. London: Faber and Faber, 1934.

———. *Christianity and Culture*. 1977. San Diego: Harvest Harcourt, n.d.

———. *The Complete Poems & Plays*. Paperback ed. London: Faber and Faber, 2004.

———. *Essays Ancient and Modern*. London: Faber and Faber, 1936.

———. *The Poems of T. S. Eliot, Volume I*. Edited by Christopher Ricks and Jim McCue. New York: Farrar, Straus and Giroux, 2018.

———. *Selected Essays*. New York: Harcourt, Brace, 1950.

Ellis, Marc. *Peter Maurin: Prophet in the Twentieth Century*. New York: Paulist Press, 1981.

Emerson, Ralph Waldo. "New England Reformers." In *Essays: Second Series [1844]*. Transcendentalism Web. archive.vcu.edu/english/engweb/transcendentalism/authors/emerson/essays/nereformers.html.

Empson, William. *Some Versions of Pastoral*. New York: New Directions, 1974.

Esty, Jed. *A Shrinking Island: Modernism and National Culture in England*. Princeton, NJ: Princeton University Press, 2004.

"The Far Right's New Fascination with the Middle Ages." *Economist*, January 2, 2017. www.economist.com/democracy-in-america/2017/01/02/the-far-rights-new-fascination-with-the-middle-ages.

Fessenden, Tracy. "The Problem of the Postsecular." *American Literary History* 26, no. 1 (2014): 154–67.

Fisher, James Terence. *The Catholic Counterculture in America, 1933–1962*. Chapel Hill: University of North Carolina Press, 1989.

Foote, Shelby, and Walker Percy. *The Correspondence of Shelby Foote and Walker Percy*. Edited by Jay Tolson. New York: Center for Documentary Studies, 1996.

Freeman, Elizabeth. "Packing History, Count(er)ing Generations." *New Literary History* 31, no. 4 (2000): 727–44.

———. "Sacramentality and the Lesbian Premodern." In *The Lesbian Premodern*, edited by Noreen Giffney, Michelle M. Sauer, and Diane Watts, 179–86. New York: Palgrave Macmillan, 2011.

———. "Sacra/mentality in Djuna Barnes' *Nightwood*." *American Literature* 86, no. 4 (2014): 737–65.

———. *Time Binds: Queer Temporalities, Queer Histories*. Durham, NC: Duke University Press, 2010.

The Fundamentals: A Testimony to the Truth. 7 vols. Chicago: Testimony, 1910–15.

Genette, Gérard. *Paratexts: Thresholds of Interpretation*. Translated by Jane E. Lewin. New York: Cambridge University Press, 1997.

Gordon, Caroline. *The Malefactors: A Novel*. 1956. Providence, RI: Cluny Classics, 2019.

Griffin, Barbara. "The Last Word: Claude McKay's Unpublished 'Cycle Manuscript.'" *MELUS* 21, no. 1 (1996): 41–57.

Grocholski, Krystyna. "Orestes Brownson, 1803–1876." Transcendentalism Web. archive.vcu.edu/english/engweb/transcendentalism/authors/brownson.

Grossman, Jay. "'Autobiography Even in the Loose Sense': F. O. Matthiessen and Melville." *Leviathan* 13, no. 1 (2011): 45–57.

———. "The Canon in the Closet: Matthiessen's Whitman, Whitman's Matthiessen." *American Literature* 70, no. 4 (1998): 799–832.

Hamilton, Ian. *Robert Lowell: A Biography*. New York: Random House, 1982.

Hawkins, Merrill M. *Will Campbell: Radical Prophet of the South*. Macon, GA: Mercer University Press, 1997.

Hellman, John. *Emmanuel Mounier and the New Catholic Left, 1930–1950*. Toronto: University of Toronto Press, 1981.

Hesiod. *Theogony*. Translated by Hugh G. Evelyn-White. Perseus Digital Library, Tufts University. 1914. data.perseus.org/texts/urn:cts:greekLit:tlg0020.tlg001.perseus-eng1.

Highlander Research and Education Center. "Timeline." highlandercenter.org/media/timeline.

Hilliard, David. "Unenglish and Unmanly: Anglo-Catholicism and Homosexuality." *Victorian Studies* 25, no. 2 (1982): 181–210.

Hillier, H. Chad. "Ibn Rushd (Averroes)." In *Internet Encyclopedia of Philosophy*. www.iep.utm.edu/ibnrushd.

Hinson-Hasty, Elizabeth. *Beyond the Social Maze: Exploring Vida Dutton Scudder's Theological Ethics*. New York: T & T Clark, 2006.

Hobson, Fred. "James McBride Dabbs: Isaac McCaslin in South Carolina." In *The Silencing of Emily Mullen and Other Essays*, 80–96. Baton Rouge: Louisiana State University Press, 2005.

Holsinger, Bruce. *The Premodern Condition: Medievalism and the Making of Theory*. Chicago: University of Chicago Press, 2005.

Houston, Benjamin. "'The Aquinas of the Rednecks': Reconciliation, the Southern Character, and the Bootleg Ministry of Will D. Campbell." *The Sixties: A Journal of History, Politics, and Culture* 4, no. 2 (2011): 135–50.

Howe, Irving. "The Sentimental Fellow-Traveling of F. O. Matthiessen." *Partisan Review* 15, no. 10 (October 1948): 1125–29.

Hughes, Langston. *The Collected Poems of Langston Hughes*. Edited by Arnold Rampersad and David Roessel. New York: Vintage Classics, 1995.

Hungerford, Amy. *Postmodern Belief: American Literature and Religion since 1960*. Princeton, NJ: Princeton University Press, 2010.

Hyde, Lewis. *The Gift: Imagination and the Erotic Life of Property*. Paperback ed. New York: Vintage, 1983.

Integrity USA. "Resources for St. Aelred's Day." www.integrityusa.org/aelred.

———. "Welcome." www.integrityusa.org/welcome.

Jacklin, Thomas M. "Mission to the Sharecroppers: Neo-Orthodox Radicalism and the Delta Farm Venture, 1936–1940." *South Atlantic Quarterly* 78 (1979): 302–16.

Jacobs, Alan. "Auden's Theology." In *W. H. Auden in Context*, edited by Tony Sharpe. New York: Cambridge University Press, 2013.

———. *What Became of Wystan: Change and Continuity in Auden's Poetry*. Fayetteville: University of Arkansas Press, 1998.

———. *The Year of Our Lord 1943: Christian Humanism in an Age of Crisis*. New York: Oxford University Press, 2018.

Jagose, Annamarie. "Feminism's Queer Theory." *Feminism and Psychology* 19, no. 2 (2009): 157–74.

James, William. *The Varieties of Religious Experience: A Study in Human Nature*. 2nd. ed. 1902. Reprint, Mineola, NY: Dover, 2002.

Jamison, Kay Redfield. *Robert Lowell: Setting the River on Fire: A Study of Genius, Mania, and Character*. New York: Vintage, 2017.

Jarrell, Randall. *Poetry and the Age*. New York: Vintage, 1953.

Jarrett-Kerr, Martin, C. R. "Twenty Years of the Christendom Trust." The M. B. Reckitt Trust. www.mbreckitttrust.org/jarrettkerr.html.

Jennings, Willie James. *The Christian Imagination: Theology and the Origins of Race*. New Haven, CT: Yale University Press, 2011.

Johnson, Karen Joy. "Healing the Mystical Body: Catholic Attempts to Overcome the Racial Divide in Chicago, 1930–1948." In *Christianity and the Color Line: Race and Religion after "Divided by Faith,"* edited by J. Russell Hawkins and Phillip Luke Sinitiere. New York: Oxford University Press, 2014.

Johnson, Kelly S. *The Fear of Beggars: Stewardship and Poverty in Christian Ethics*. Grand Rapids, MI: Eerdmans, 2007.

Jones, Ben. "The Confederate Flag Is a Matter of Pride and Heritage, Not Hatred." *New York Times*, December 22, 2015. www.nytimes.com/roomfordebate /2015/06/19/does-the-confederate-flag-breed-racism/the-confederate-flag-is-a-matter-of-pride-and-heritage-not-hatred.

Kahan, Benjamin. *Celibacies: American Modernism and Sexual Life*. Durham, NC: Duke University Press, 2013.

Kaufmann, Michael. "The Religious, the Secular, and Literary Studies: Rethinking the Secularization Narrative in Histories of the Profession." *New Literary History* 38, no. 4 (2007): 607–28.

Kazin, Michael. *American Dreamers: How the Left Changed a Nation.* New York: Knopf, 2001.

King, Martin Luther, Jr. "Letter from a Birmingham Jail." 1963. www.africa.upenn .edu/Articles_Gen/Letter_Birmingham.html.

———. "Our God Is Marching On." The Martin Luther King, Jr. Research and Education Institute. mlk-kpp01.stanford.edu/index.php/kingpapers/article/our _god_is_marching_on.

Kirk, Rudolf, and Clara Kirk. "Howells and the Church of the Carpenter." *New England Quarterly* 32, no. 2 (1959): 185–206.

Kirk, Russell. *The Conservative Mind: From Burke to Santayana.* Chicago: Henry Regnery, 1953.

Kojecky, Roger. *T. S. Eliot's Social Criticism.* London: Faber and Faber, 1971.

Larkin, Philip. "What's Become of Wystan?" *Spectator,* July 15, 1960, 19–29.

Lasch, Christopher. *The True and Only Heaven: Progress and Its Critics.* New York: Norton, 1991.

Latour, Bruno. "Charles Péguy: Time, Space, and le Monde Moderne." Translated by Tim Howles. *New Literary History* 46, no. 1 (2015): 41–62.

———. "Pourquoi Péguy se répète-t-Ii? Péguy est-il illisible?" (Why does Péguy repeat himself? Is Péguy unreadable?). www.bruno-latour.fr/sites/default/files /o1-PEGUY- FR.pdf. Published as "Les raisons profondes du style répétitif de Péguy" in *Péguy Ecrivain, Colloque du Centenaire,* 78–102. Klinsieck: Paris, 1973.

Lawler, Peter Augustine, and Brian A. Smith, eds. *A Political Companion to Walker Percy.* Lexington: University Press of Kentucky, 2013.

Lears, T. J. Jackson. *No Place of Grace: Antimodernism and the Transformation of American Culture 1880–1920.* 1981. Reprint, Chicago: University of Chicago Press, 1994.

Leonard, Sarah. "Nature as an Ally: An Interview with Wendell Berry." *Dissent,* Spring 2012. https://www.dissentmagazine.org/article/nature-as-an-ally-an-interview-with-wendell-berry

Lewis, Pericles. *Religious Experience and the Modernist Novel.* New York: Cambridge University Press, 2010.

Lissner, Will. "Slum Fine Levied on Dorothy Day." *New York Times,* March 1, 1956, 25.

Lowell, Robert. *Collected Poems.* Edited by Frank Bidart et al. New York: Farrar, Straus and Giroux, 2003.

———. *The Letters of Robert Lowell,* Edited by Saskia Hamilton. New York: Farrar, Straus and Giroux, 2007.

———. *Notebook.* New York: Farrar, Straus and Giroux, 1970.

MacIntyre, Alasdair. *Whose Justice? Which Rationality?* Notre Dame, IN: University of Notre Dame Press, 1989.

Maglin, Nan Bauer. "Vida to Florence: 'Comrade and Companion.'" *Frontiers: A Journal of Women Studies* 4, no. 3 (1979): 13–20.

Makowsky, Veronica A. *Caroline Gordon: A Biography.* New York: Oxford University Press, 1989.

Markwell, Bernard. *The Anglican Left.* Brooklyn, NY: Carlson, 1991.

Martin, Robert F. "Critique of Southern Society and Vision of a New Order: The Fellowship of Southern Churchmen, 1934–1957." *Church History* 52, no. 1 (1983): 66–80.

Matthiessen, F. O. *American Renaissance: Art and Expression in the Age of Emerson and Whitman.* 1941. New York: Oxford University Press, 1968.

———. *From the Heart of Europe.* New York: Oxford University Press, 1948.

Matthiessen, F. O., and Russell Cheney. *Rat and the Devil: Journal Letters of F. O. Matthiessen and Russell Cheney.* Edited by Louis Hyde. Hamden, CT: Archon, 1978.

Maurin, Peter. "Back to Christ!—Back to the Land!" *Catholic Worker* 3, no. 6 (November 1935): 1, 8.

———. *The Green Revolution: Easy Essays on Catholic Radicalism.* Fresno, CA: Academy Guild Press, 1961.

———. "Legalized Usury." *Catholic Worker* 1, no. 7 (December 15, 1933), 7.

———. "Wealth-Producing Maniacs." *Catholic Worker* 1, no. 1 (May 1, 1933): 8.

McCarraher, Eugene. *Christian Critics: Religion and the Impasse in Modern American Social Thought.* Ithaca, NY: Cornell University Press, 2000.

McClure, John. *Partial Faiths: Postsecular Fiction in the Age of Pynchon and Morrison.* Athens: University of Georgia Press, 2007.

McGarry, Molly. *Ghosts of Futures Past: Spiritualism and the Cultural Politics of Nineteenth-Century America.* Berkeley: University of California Press, 2008.

McKay, Claude. *Banjo: A Story without a Plot.* New York: Harper and Brothers, 1929.

———. *Complete Poems.* Edited and with an introduction by William J. Maxwell. Urbana: University of Illinois Press, 2004.

———. *Harlem Shadows.* New York: Harcourt, Brace, 1922.

———. *Home to Harlem.* 1928. Boston: Northeastern University Press, 1987.

———. "The Middle Ages." *Catholic Worker,* May 1946, 5.

———. "[Oh, One Was Black of the Wise Men of the East]." *Catholic Worker,* October 1945, 4–5.

———. "On Becoming a Roman Catholic." In *"Stamped with the Image of God": African Americans as God's Image in Black,* edited by Cyprian Davis, O.S.B., and Jamie Phelps, 105–7. O.P. American Catholic Identities: A Documentary History. Maryknoll, NY: Orbis, 2003.

———. "Right Turn to Catholicism." MSS 27, Box 9, Folder 298. James Weldon Johnson Collection, Yale Beinecke Library.

———. "Russian Cathedral." *Survey Graphic* 53, no. 11 (March 1925): 662.

———. "St. Isaac's Church Petrograd." *Catholic Worker,* October 1947, 8.

———. "Why I Became a Catholic." *Ebony* 1, no. 5 (March 1946): 32.

Melville, Herman. "Hawthorne and His Mosses." In *Nathaniel Hawthorne's Tales,* edited by James McIntosh, 370–84. Second Norton Critical Edition. New York: Norton, 2012.

———. *Moby-Dick.* 1851. New York: Barnes and Noble Classics, 2003.

Mendelson, Edward. *Later Auden.* New York: Farrar, Straus and Giroux, 1999.

———. "The Secret Auden." *New York Review of Books,* March 20, 2014. www .nybooks.com/articles/2014/03/20/secret-auden.

Miller, Steven P. "From Politics to Reconciliation: *Katallagete*, Biblicism, and Southern Liberalism." *Journal of Southern Religion* 7 (2004).

Milton, John. *Paradise Lost.* 1674. www.dartmouth.edu/~milton/reading_room/pl/book_12/text.shtml.

Moore, Cecelia. "The Sources and Meaning of the Conversion of Claude McKay." *Journal of the Black Catholic Theological Symposium* 2 (2008): 59–80.

Muñoz, José Esteban. *Cruising Utopia: The Then and There of Queer Futurity.* New York: New York University Press, 2009.

Murphy, Francesca Aran. *Christ the Form of Beauty: A Study in Theology and Literature.* Edinburgh: T&T Clark, 1995.

Murphy, Paul V. *The Rebuke of History: The Southern Agrarians and American Conservative Thought.* Chapel Hill: University of North Carolina Press, 2001.

"Museum History." *The Museum Complex—The State Museum, St. Isaac's Cathedral.* eng.cathedral.ru/istoriya.

Niebuhr, H. Richard. *Christ and Culture.* 1937. New York: Harper and Row, 1951.

———. *The Kingdom of God in America.* Middletown, CT: Wesleyan University Press, 1988.

Niebuhr, Reinhold. *The Essential Reinhold Niebuhr.* Edited by Robert McAfee Brown. New Haven, CT: Yale University Press, 1986.

———. *Moral Man and Immoral Society: A Study in Ethics and Politics.* 1932, Louisville, KY: Westminster John Knox, 2013.

Niebuhr, Ursula. "Memories of the 1940s." In *W. H. Auden: A Tribute,* edited by Stephen Spender. New York: Macmillan, 1975.

Norton, Rachel E. "'Useful to the Mind': Ade Bethune's Illustrations for *The Catholic Worker,* 1934–1945." Master's thesis, University of Maryland College Park. 2006.

Novitsky, Anthony. "Peter Maurin's Green Revolution: The Radical Implications of Reactionary Social Catholicism." *Review of Politics* 37, no. 1 (1975): 83–103.

N. M. "Dorothy Day and W. H. Auden: On Poetry, Piety, and the Pope." Prospero: Books, Arts, and Culture. *Economist,* September 29, 2015. www.economist .com/node/21669064.

O'Connell, Maureen. "A Harsh and Dreadful Beauty: The Aesthetic Dimension of Dorothy Day's Ethics." In *She Who Imagines: Feminist Theological Aesthetics,* edited by Laurie Cassidy and O'Connell, 161–80. Collegeville, MN: Liturgical Press, 2012.

Oehlschlaeger, Fritz. *The Achievement of Wendell Berry: The Hard History of Love.* Lexington: University Press of Kentucky, 2011.

Oleynick, Griffin. "Prophet of Harlem: The Conversion of Claude McKay." *Common-weal*, July 7, 2017. www.commonwealmagazine.org/prophet-harlem.

Ortega y Gasset, José. *The Revolt of the Masses.* Translated by Anonymous. New York: Norton, 1932.

Percy, Walker. "The Failure and the Hope." In *The Failure and the Hope: Essays of Southern Churchmen,* edited by Will D. Campbell and James Y. Holloway, 13–28. Reprint, n.d. Grand Rapids, MI: Eerdmans, 1972.

———. "The Fire This Time." *New York Review of Books.* July 1, 1965. www.nybooks .com/articles/archives/1965/jul/01/the-fire-this-time/?pagination=false&printpage =true.

———. *The Last Gentleman.* New York: Farrar, Straus and Giroux, 1966.

———. *The Moviegoer.* New York: Knopf, 1961.

———. "Notes for a Novel about the End of the World." *Katallagete* 1, no. 5 (1967): 7–14.

Perloff, Marjorie. "Response to Ronald Schuchard." *Modernism/Modernity* 10, no. 1 (2003): 51–56. marjorieperloff.com/stein-duchamp-picasso/ronald-schuchard.

Pope Leo XIII. *Rerum novarum.* May 15, 1891. w2.vatican.va/content/leo-xiii/enencyclicals/ documents/hf_l-xiii_enc_15051891_rerum-novarum.html.

Puchner, Martin. *Poetry of the Revolution: Marx, Manifestos, and the Avant-Gardes.* Princeton, NJ: Princeton University Press, 2006.

Protestant Episcopal Church. *The Book of Common Prayer.* 1892 Standard Edition. New York: 1892.

Quinlan, Kieran. *John Crowe Ransom's Secular Faith.* Baton Rouge: Louisiana State University Press, 1989.

Ransom, John Crowe. "Criticism, Inc." *Virginia Quarterly Review* 13, no. 4 (1937). www .vqronline.org/articles/1937/autumn/ransom-criticism-inc.

———. *God without Thunder: An Unorthodox Defense of Orthodoxy.* New York: Harcourt, Brace, 1930.

———. *Land! The Case for an Agrarian Economy.* Edited by Jason Peters. Notre Dame, IN: University of Notre Dame Press, 2017.

———. "What Does the South Want?" In *Who Owns America? A New Declaration of Independence,* edited by Herbert Agar and Allen Tate, 178–93. Boston: Houghton Mifflin, 1936.

Rauschenbusch, Walter. *Christianity and the Social Crisis in the 21st Century: The Classic That Woke up the Church.* 1907. Edited by Paul B. Rauschenbusch. New York: HarperCollins, 2007.

———. *A Theology for the Social Gospel.* New York: Abingdon, 1917.

Reid, George. "Biblical Criticism (Higher)." In *The Catholic Encyclopedia,* vol. 4. New York: Appleton, 1908. www.newadvent.org/cathen/04491c.htm.

Rice, Daniel F. *Reinhold Niebuhr and His Circle of Influence.* New York: Cambridge University Press, 2013.

Ricoeur, Paul. "Emmanuel Mounier: Personalist Philosopher." In *History and Truth,* by Ricoeur, translated with an introduction by Charles A. Kelbley, 133–61. Evanston, IL: Northwestern University Press, 1965.

Rivett, Sarah. "Early American Religion in a Postsecular Age." *PMLA* 128, no. 4 (2013): 989–96.

Robinson, Paschal. "St. Francis of Assisi." In *The Catholic Encyclopedia*, vol. 6. New York: Robert Appleton Co., 1909. www.newadvent.org/cathen/06221a.htm.

Rorty, Richard. *Achieving Our Country: Leftist Thought in Twentieth-Century America*. Cambridge, MA: Harvard University Press, 1998.

Rosen, Elliot A. "Raymond Moley." *American National Biography*. www.anb.org/articles/07/07-00456.html?a=1&n=raymond%20moley&d=10&ss=0&q=1.

Rossinow, Doug. *Visions of Progress: The Left-Liberal Tradition in America*. Philadelphia: University of Pennsylvania Press, 2009.

Salmond, John A. "The South in the Depression Decades." In *Debating Southern History: Ideas and Action in the Twentieth Century*, edited by Bruce Clayton and Salmond. Lanham, MD: Rowman and Littlefield, 1999.

Schmidt, Leigh Eric. *Restless Souls: The Making of American Spirituality*. 2nd ed. Berkeley: University of California Press, 2012.

Schuchard, Ronald. *Eliot's Dark Angel: Intersections of Life and Art*. New York: Oxford University Press, 1999.

Schultz, Kevin M. *Tri-Faith America: How Catholics and Jews Held America to Its Protestant Promise*. New York: Oxford University Press, 2011.

Scudder, Vida Dutton. *Brother John: A Tale of the First Franciscans*. Boston: Little, Brown, 1926.

———. *The Franciscan Adventure*. London: J. M. Dent and Sons, 1931.

———. *A Listener in Babel*. Boston: Houghton Mifflin, 1903.

———. *On Journey*. New York: Dutton, 1937.

———. *Social Ideals in English Letters*. 2nd ed. Boston: Houghton Mifflin, 1923.

———. *Social Teachings of the Christian Year*. New York: Dutton, 1921.

———. *Socialism and Character*. Boston: Houghton Mifflin, 1912.

———. *St. Catherine of Siena: As Seen in Her Letters*. Translated and edited with an introduction by Scudder. New York: Dutton, 1905.

Seeskin, Kenneth, "Maimonides." *The Stanford Encyclopedia of Philosophy*. Spring 2014 Edition. Edited by Edward N. Zalta. plato.stanford.edu/archives/spr2014/entries/maimonides.

Shand-Tucci, Douglass. *Ralph Adams Cram, Life and Architecture I: Boston Bohemia, 1881–1900*. Amherst: University of Massachusetts Press, 1995.

———. *Ralph Adams Cram, Life and Architecture II: An Architect's Four Quests: Medieval, Modernist, American, Ecumenical*. Amherst: University of Massachusetts Press, 2005.

Sheehan, Arthur. *Peter Maurin: Gay Believer*. Garden City, NY: Hanover House, 1959.

Sitman, Matthew. "Against Moral Austerity: On the Need for a Christian Left." *Dis-*

sent, Summer 2017. www.dissentmagazine.org/article/moral-austerity-need-christian-left.

Stein, Jordan Alexander. "American Literary History and Queer Temporalities." *American Literary History* 25, no. 4 (2013): 855–69.

———. "History's Dick Jokes: On Melville and Hawthorne." *Los Angeles Review of Books*, December 15, 2015. lareviewofbooks.org/article/historys-dick-jokes-on-melville-and-hawthorne.

Sullivan, John Jeremiah. *Pulphead: Essays*. New York: Farrar, Straus and Giroux, 2011.

Sweezy, Paul M., and Leo Huberman, eds. *F. O. Matthiessen (1902–1950): A Collective Portrait*. New York: Henry Schuman, 1950.

Taylor, Charles. *A Secular Age*. Cambridge, MA: Belknap Press of Harvard University Press, 2007.

Thoreau, Henry David. *Walden and Civil Disobedience*. 1854. New York: Penguin, 1983.

———. "Walking." *Atlantic*, June 1862. www.theatlantic.com/magazine/archive/1862/06/walking/304674.

Tillery, Tyrone. *Claude McKay: A Black Poet's Struggle for Identity*. Amherst: University of Massachusetts Press, 1992.

Tolson, Jay. *Pilgrim in the Ruins: A Life of Walker Percy*. New York: Simon and Schuster, 1992.

"Tradinista Manifesto." *Combat Liberalism: A Tumblr of the Tradinista Collective*. tradinista.tumblr.com/manifesto.

Twelve Southerners. *I'll Take My Stand: The South and the Agrarian Tradition*. Louisiana paperback ed. Baton Rouge: Louisiana State University Press, 1977.

Waggoner, Walter H. "Herbert W. Schneider, A Professor." *New York Times*, October 24, 1984. www.nytimes.com/1984/10/24/obituaries/herbert-w-schneider-a-professor.html.

Wald, Alan. *American Night*. Chapel Hill: University of North Carolina Press, 2012.

———. *Exiles from a Future Time*. Chapel Hill: University of North Carolina Press, 2002.

———. *The Revolutionary Imagination: The Poetry and Politics of John Wheelwright and Sherry Mangan*. Chapel Hill: University of North Carolina Press, 1983.

———. *Trinity of Passion*. Chapel Hill: University of North Carolina Press, 2007.

———. "Wheelwright and His Kind." *Spoke* 3 (2015): 194–208.

Wasley, Aidan. *The Age of Auden: Postwar Poetry and the American Scene*. Princeton, NJ: Princeton University Press, 2010.

Wheelwright, John. *John Wheelwright*. Boston: Prince Society, 1876.

Wheelwright, John Brooks. *Collected Poems*. New York: New Directions, 1971.

Williamson, Alan. *Pity the Monsters: The Political Vision of Robert Lowell*. New Haven, CT: Yale University Press, 1974.

Wilson, Edmund. *The Shores of Light: A Literary Chronicle of the Twenties and Thirties*. New York: Farrar, Straus and Young, 1952.

Wood, Ralph C. *The Comedy of Redemption: Christian Faith and Comic Vision in Four American Novelists*. Notre Dame, IN: University of Notre Dame Press, 1988.

Wordsworth, William. "The Solitary Reaper." In *The Oxford Book of English Verse, 1250–1900*, edited by Arthur Quiller-Couch. 1919. www.bartleby.com/101/528.html.

Yeames, James. "The Church." *Dawn* 2, no. 1 (1890): 40–43.

INDEX